THE
SECRET LORE
OF
EGYPT

THE SECRET LORE OF EGYPT

ITS IMPACT ON THE WEST

ERIK HORNUNG

Translated from the German by David Lorton

CORNELL UNIVERSITY PRESS

ITHACA AND LONDON

English translation first published 2001 by Cornell University Press

Printed in the United States of America

Library of Congress Cataloging-in-Publication Data

Hornung, Erik.
  [Esoterische Agypten. English]
  The secret lore of Egypt : its impact on the West / by Erik Hornung;
translated from the German by David Lorton.
      p.   cm.
  Originally published: Das esoterische Aegypten. Mèunchen : Beck,
c1999.
  Includes bibliographical references and index.
  ISBN 0-8014-3847-0 (cloth)
  1. Occultism—Egypt.   2. Occultism—History.   I. Title.
BF1434.E3 H6713 2001
135'.4—dc21   2001004361

Cloth printing   10 9 8 7 6 5 4 3 2 1

CONTENTS

TRANSLATOR'S NOTE

The texts known as the Rosicrucian Classics are available in English translation in the *Rosicrucian Manual* (New York, 1920), pp. 67–131; the citations from these documents in chapter 13 are drawn from this edition. The lines from Rilke are cited from *New Poems: The Other Part*, trans. E. Snow (San Francisco, 1987), p. 61.

In chapter 15, the citations from Herder are taken from *Reflections on the Philosophy of the History of Mankind*, trans. F. E. Manuel (Chicago, 1968), pp. 153 and 155–56. The quotation from Kant is taken from *The Critique of Judgement*, trans. J. C. Meredith (Oxford, 1952), p. 179, n. 1. The passage from Hölderlin's "The Archipelago" is from *Selected Poems of Friedrich Hölderlin*, 2d ed. (London, 1954), p. 137.

In chapter 18, the passage from Lucian of Samosata is drawn from *The True History and Lucius the Ass*, trans. P. Turner (London, 1957), pp. 10–11. The citation from Herder is taken from *Reflections on the Philosophy of the History of Mankind*, trans. F. E. Manuel (Chicago, 1968), p. 158.

In chapter 19, the citations from Hesse are from *The Journey to the East*, trans. Hilda Rosner (London, 1956), pp. 12–13 and 27. The passages from Rilke are taken from *Duino Elegies*, trans. David Young (New York, 1978), pp. 68, 67, 91, and 23, respectively; these are followed by a brief passage from another poem, and then a citation from *Duino Elegies*, p. 33. The brief quotation from Thomas Mann's novel is taken from *Joseph and His Broth-*

ers, trans. H. T. Lowe-Porter (New York, 1948), p. 3. The citation from Karl Jaspers is from *The Origin and Goal of History* (London, 1953), p. 50.

Except as indicated above, the translations are my own.

There are texts from ancient Egypt assuring us that priests were required to maintain secrecy regarding certain information they possessed. But the idea that western-style metaphysical concepts are derived from a secret lore guarded by these priests is a western myth whose origins can be traced back to classical antiquity. For the very first time, Erik Hornung has traced the history of this influential notion—this "Egyptosophy," as he calls it—from antiquity down to our own times. I wish to express my appreciation to Cornell University Press for asking me to assist with this project, and to the author and Dr. Eckhard Eichler for their help along the way. Also, a special note of thanks to Mr. Don Rosa (see p. 186) for the information he graciously provided.

D.L.

THE
SECRET LORE
OF
EGYPT

INTRODUCTION

Already in antiquity, there was an opinion that the land of the Nile was the fount of all wisdom and the stronghold of hermetic lore. Thus began a tradition that is still alive today, and which I venture to designate "Egyptosophy." It was only after the decipherment of the hieroglyphs by Jean-François Champollion in 1822 that its younger sister, the discipline of Egyptology, made its appearance. As is well known, the relationship between the two sisters has often been a problematic one, and there has clearly been a reluctance to treat this topic. Egyptosophy often imagines itself to be far superior to any discipline that is blind to its true wisdom, and we constantly witness the astonishing phenomenon of people who belong to its circle making highly "scientific" demonstrations that the scientific discipline of Egyptology is wrong.

For its part, Egyptology is often all too hastily inclined to ignore anything having to do with Egyptosophy, forgetting in the process that it is a part of our own western cultural and intellectual heritage and that it represents a hunger for hidden truths and deep, underlying relationships that is not satisfied by the scientific discipline and is in this respect entirely legitimate. And while we in Egyptology take the picture of Egypt in classical antiquity quite seriously, we have trouble taking its continuation down into modern esoteric movements and its unbelievably widespread influence equally seriously. The adoption of Egyptian forms and motifs stands in the foreground of work on Western encounters with Egypt, which is enjoying a growing popularity. For Siegfried Morenz, in his groundbreaking *Die Begegnung Europas mit Ägypten* [Europe's encounter with Egypt] (1968/69), the ideology of a specifically Egyptian "wisdom" that decisively characterized this adoption is merely a smoke screen that obscures the essence of the spirit of ancient Egypt. The esoteric undercurrent is therefore only occasionally to be glimpsed in his book. Here, we shall follow its course down through the last two millennia, emphasizing points rather different from those stressed by Morenz.

Scholarly concern with the esoteric tradition is still in its infancy and stands in inverse proportion to the immense importance of the esoteric among the general public. Even today, there is only one professorship of esoteric lore in all the world, at the Sorbonne in Paris. This professorship was established in 1965, and its first incumbent was François Secret, a specialist in Christian cabala; in 1979, he was succeeded by Antoine Faivre, a Germanist, and the exact description of his research specialty at that time read, "history of esoteric and mystical currents in modern and contemporary Europe." Meanwhile, in 1999, a professorship in the History of Hermetic Philosophy was created in Amsterdam, where the helpful Bibliotheca Philosophica Hermetica is also located. The first occupant of the chair is Wouter J. Hanegraaff. In Basel, which has its own esoteric tradition thanks to Paracelsus, Cagliostro, and others, and where many important works on the esoteric have been published, efforts are being made to establish an independent Institute for the History and Hermeneutics of Mysticism, and in Carlos Gilly, the teaching staff of Basel University has a recognized specialist in the history of the Rosicrucians. Efforts are also being made to found an Institute for Hermetic Philosophy in Bamberg, and we can observe that recently there has been a marked increase in scholarly interest in and serious publications on the topic of the esoteric.

Nevertheless, it would be productive for both sides if there were more bridges and less reluctance between the scholarly disciplines and esoteric pursuits. We need think only of the psychological insights won by Carl Gustav Jung from his study of alchemy, and I regret only that he did not have better sources on ancient Egypt at his disposal. In esoteric circles, people are too dependent on the old, outdated works of Budge and ought to take into account more recent literature, which has much to offer of esoteric interest.

The theme I shall treat here falls within the larger framework of uses

made of ancient Egypt, which for some time has been the object of growing interest in Egyptology. These uses include, of course, the adoption of
Egyptian forms, motifs, and themes in art, literature, and music, as well as
the use of Egypt in advertising. Such topics will be dealt with at best only
marginally here. Instead, I shall concentrate on what I take to be Egyptosophy: the study of an imaginary Egypt viewed as the profound source of
all esoteric lore. This Egypt is a timeless *idea* bearing only a loose relationship to the historical reality.

We shall deal here with a religion whose founder and prophet was Hermes Trismegistus, who uniquely incorporated a god and the founder of
his own religion in a single person. Our theme thus also belongs to the
history of religion, and in the spirit of this discipline, we shall confine ourselves to investigating phenomena and intellectual connections, ignoring
entirely the issue of their truth. We shall thus be concerned not with the
truth of, for example, theosophical or astrological doctrines but only with
their relationship to Egypt and to other, related movements. We shall
make exceptions only in cases that obviously contradict what is securely
known. In any event, it is futile to try to prove or disprove esoteric truths
that are nourished solely by revelation, faith, and displays of intuition, for
we are moving here on two entirely different levels of argumentation.

It is possible to make an academic study of esoteric matters, which is
what I intend to do here. It is also possible for adherents of esoteric doctrines to adduce knowledge from the academic discipline of Egyptology
with profit and incorporate it into their systems. But one must at all costs
avoid hopelessly mixing the two areas of interest, as unfortunately continues to happen—especially when esoteric doctrines are covered with some
academic veneer and thus purportedly "proven."

My intent is to treat esoterica relating to Egypt. To be sure, even in antiquity, India also served as a model of the esoteric: Apollonius of Tyana
was comfortable dealing with both areas, and we shall often encounter the
combination of Egypt and India. In our day, the Far East and the Celtic
and Indian worlds have grown more important, not to mention the "extraterrestrial," all of which have been making major strides forward; so
long as they do not overlap with Egypt, as in the case of theosophy, such
matters necessarily fall outside our area of concern.

Esoteric matters have to do with hidden, often deliberately concealed
truths that can be grasped only through intuition or revelation and that

elude any and all experimental verification. The esoteric is a way of thinking unto itself, irrational and intuitive, aimed at the overarching unity of nature and the correspondences within it and at the possibility of unbounded transubstantiation. It lives on the magic of the mysterious, believing itself to be in possession of a higher state of consciousness that remains closed to those who are not yet "initiated" into these mysteries. In our own time, the loosening of religious ties has led to an ever-increasing role of the esoteric as an ersatz religion, to the point where it has become a source of assistance in practical affairs and has in the process lost its secret character.

THE ANCIENT ROOTS OF THE "OTHER" EGYPT

Amenhotpe son of Hapu, a favorite of Amenophis III, directed such projects as the erection of the Colossi of Memnon; later, he was worshiped as a deified sage and a healing god. On one of his statues from the temple of Karnak (c. 1360 B.C.E.), he states, "I was introduced to the book of the god, I saw the transfigurations of Thoth and was equipped with their mysteries."

These formulations already sound quite hermetic, with their initiation into the wisdom of the Egyptian god Thoth, the later Hermes Trismegistus, and into a "divine book" that the god wrote and revealed. But the roots of Hermetism might reach deeper, back to the beginning of the second millennium B.C.E.

According to Edmund Hermsen, it was the priests of the temple of Thoth in Hermopolis of Dynasty 12 (c. 1938–1759 B.C.E.) who conceived of the Book of Two Ways, which can be called the first hermetic work; as the earliest description of the hereafter, it is an important precursor of the Books of the Netherworld of the New Kingdom. Nearly all our copies of this book stem from el-Bersha, the burial place of the nomarchs of the fifteenth nome of Upper Egypt, and thus the rulers of Hermopolis, the city of Thoth. In their inscriptions, they call themselves "genuine son of Thoth." Thoth was viewed as the embodiment of wisdom even earlier, in Dynasty 11: the leader of an expedition to the Wadi Hammamat calls himself "more intelligent than Thoth," and otherwise in the early Middle

Kingdom, we often encounter the claim that someone was instructed by Thoth.

In the Old Kingdom, the god's violent traits still predominated. As "lord of foreign countries" and "lord of slaughter, who overthrows Asia" (thus in Wadi Kharig in the Sinai), he was credited with trampling foes underfoot and assisting the king in "smiting the enemies." In the Pyramid Texts (§§ 962–63), he lops off heads and cuts out hearts; his oft-mentioned "knife" is surely the crescent moon, which also served Khons, the other moon god, as a weapon. But he is already also a judge and messenger of the gods, as well as the guardian of the Eye of Horus, and his wings assist the deceased in ascending to the sky. His origin was as shady as his nature: according to the Contendings of Horus and Seth, Thoth originated from the seed of Horus, but he was borne by Seth, and thus he united in himself the contradictory essences of these eternally combating brothers, between whom he constantly mediated.

The preferred representations of Thoth were as an ibis or a baboon, and as a composite figure with the body of a man and the head of an ibis. Though it seldom happened, he could also be pictured as purely human in form, as in the Khons chapel in the small Tuthmosid temple at Luxor, which is important in that later Hermes Trismegistus was often viewed not as a god but as a human sage.

It is in the Coffin Texts—religious spells written on the coffins of officials of the Middle Kingdom—that we first hear of a "divine book of Thoth" (III 240b, and see also VII 118); this historical period thus inaugurated the important tradition that viewed the god as the author of sacred writings. At the same time, as already mentioned, he became lord of wisdom (V 305–6 as all-knowing) and lord of rituals and offerings; he was connected with magic (V 315), while in the tale of the Eloquent Peasant, his judicial function makes him the protector of the legal system.

His nature developed still further in the New Kingdom, when he was regarded as the deity responsible for all culture and invention. Pharaoh could thus be called "Thoth in every respect," for the god's qualities were united in him. Sacred writings were ascribed to the god or said to be found at the feet of his statue. He plays an important role in a number of spells from the Book of the Dead, especially in the first spell, in which the deceased, identified with Thoth, turns to Osiris as "bull of the West" and legitimates himself through his knowledge. He functioned as scribe whenever divine documents—letters, decrees, testaments—had to be written, and as "lord of the divine words," he was responsible for the Egyptian writing system. He also oversaw the calendar and the measurement of time. In the representations in the temple of Deir el-Bahari depicting Queen Hatshepsut's expedition to Punt, he personally records the products brought from that distant land; and in many scenes to be found in temples, he writes the name of the king on the leaves of the sacred *ished*-tree. In depictions of the Judgment of the Dead, he records the results, and he sometimes also tends to the scale. He is often depicted in the sun barque, especially as a baboon, and he functions as the sun god's "deputy." In the colophon of spell 100 of the Book of the Dead, he is accorded the task of registering the passengers in the sun barque as they "disembark and embark."

Even Akhenaten can be viewed as a "Hermetist," for he founded his new capital of Akhetaten in the fifteenth nome of Upper Egypt, the Hermopolitan nome, where Hadrian later founded his new city of Antinoopolis. And it is precisely from Akhetaten (Tell el-Amarna) that we have an especially beautiful example (Cairo J. 59291, Figure 1) of a type of group statue in the New Kingdom depicting a scribe seated at the feet of Thoth, the baboon, writing down with inspiration, as it were, what the wisdom of Thoth reveals to him. The viceroy of Nubia who functioned under Akhenaten, as well as one of the king's leading sculptors, to whom we owe the bust of Nefertiti now in Berlin, both had the name Tuthmosis, written with the determinative of the ibis-headed god. In other cases as well, it appears that Thoth enjoyed a certain toleration under Akhenaten and did not fall victim to his radical persecution of the old gods.

From immediately after Akhenaten's reign, we have Haremhab's hymn to Thoth. In it, the god is again the all-knowing one "who knows the mysteries" and comprehends the nature of humans and deities, who informs the sun god of all that happens. Ramesses IV boasted that he was steeped in all the writings of Thoth that were stored in the "House of Life" (the temple archives), and that he had learned from them the essence of Osiris.

In the New Kingdom, Thoth also acquired a female companion in the form of Nehemet-awai, "she who acquires what has been stolen." In the Graeco-Roman Period, she had a son, Harnefer; in that period, deities were usually grouped into triads, groups of three consisting of a divine couple and their son. More important and more ancient was the associa-

1. Scribe seated at the feet of the god Thoth, who is depicted as a baboon with the symbol of the moon on his head. From Tell el-Amarna. Cairo J 59291. From Edward L. B. Terrace and Henry G. Fischer, *Treasures of Egyptian Art from the Cairo Museum* (Boston, 1970), p. 130.

tion of Thoth with the goddess Maat, embodiment of the order of the cosmos. Thoth brings and "examines" (*ip*) Maat, according to a hymn to the goddess in the tomb of Ramesses VI, and her responsibility for harmony and order is closely connected to the all-encompassing symbol of the *udjat*-eye, especially in the motif of an ape holding an *udjat*. Already in spell 167 of the Book of the Dead, where Thoth is said to "pacify" the eye, we have a reference to his bringing home the Distant Goddess. In the myth of the Distant Goddess, he displays his skill at communication and persuades the goddess, who has fled in anger, to return to the Nile valley; in the barren desert of Nubia, he lures her with the prospect of the verdant fields of the land of the Nile. The return of the pacified goddess ends with universal rejoicing, order is restored to the world, and Thoth stands once again helpfully at the side of humanity and the gods. Millions of carefully wrapped ibis mummies testify to the worship of this animal sacred to Thoth.

In the Late Period, Thoth became the authoritative god in the area of magic, and magical spells written by him were considered especially effective. The Egyptians were therefore—as Cicero was aware (*De natura deorum* III.56)—reluctant to speak his name. He wrote letters of introduction for the deceased to smooth their way through the netherworld, and he and Isis were supposed to have composed the Books of Breathing, which came in part to replace the Book of the Dead.

But above all, it was in the later periods that the Egyptian Thoth was transformed into the universal Hermes Trismegistus, the "thrice great." A first step was his designation as "twice great" (Egyptian *aa aa*, Figure 2), which he already bears on a stela, now in Lausanne, which is dated to year 20 of King Apries, that is, 570 B.C.E., and records a grant of land by Pharaoh to Thoth, the "twice great," lord of Hermopolis (in the delta). From the same reign comes the title "overseer of the prophets of Thoth, the twice great, lord of Hermopolis," born by Ankhhor, an official of Nitocris, God's Wife of Amun in Thebes. The epithet "twice great" appears written in Demotic beginning with the reign of Darius I, and from the third century B.C.E. on, it is intensified by means of the adverb *wer*, "exceedingly," leading to the development of "thrice great" beginning with the late second century B.C.E. We even find a "five times great" in the First Story of Setne and other texts. From the Egyptian form "thrice great, exceedingly" (the language had no grammatical form for the superlative),

2. King Apries (right) dedicating fields in his 20th regnal year to "Thoth, the Twice-great" and his consort Nehemet-awai. Stela in Lausanne, Musée Cantonal des Beaux-Arts, Eg. 24. Photo by Yves Siza.

there developed the classical epithet Trismegistus, which after some delay first appears in the third century C.E.; it is first attested in an inscription from Akhmim dating to c. 240 C.E. With that, the founder of hermetic religion was born, and he would soon stand in the company of Moses and Zarathustra. We shall turn to the parallel rise of Imhotep in the divine realm, in which he was eventually revered as Asclepius, in our treatment of hermetic doctrine in chapter 6.

Because the hieroglyphic writing system, which was invented by Thoth, played an all-powerful role in the later esoteric tradition, we must cast our gaze on this root of the esoteric as well. The writing system was invented around 3000 B.C.E., basically to represent sounds, thus making it possible to indicate in writing what could not be expressed through pictures: in particular, personal names. Although it was not originally "picture writing," from the very beginning, it contained pictorial elements that became more numerous in the course of further developments. Along with determinatives, which serve to classify words according to categories of meaning, there were some ancient, basic signs that owed their reading to a symbolic meaning. Examples are the billowing sail as a sign for "breath, air"; the mast for "to stand"; the cultic flag for "god"; the flamingo for "red"; the taut bowstring for "strong"; and the egg for "within." In the Pyramid Texts, there was even an empty space for "hidden."

"Enigmatic writing" or "cryptography" made use of this possibility of investing signs with symbolic content. Isolated examples of it are to be found already in the Middle Kingdom, but it came into its own in the New Kingdom; later, it had a powerful effect on the writing system of the Ptolemaic and Roman Periods. For example, various animals associated with royalty could serve as a hieroglyph for the word *neb*, "lord": sphinx, lion, bull, crocodile, and mongoose. Unlike the "normal" writing system, which always aimed at clarity in its writings, enigmatic writing cultivated polyvalence; this is particularly evident in the fact that any hieroglyph depicting a bird could be substituted for any other, in the omission of weak consonants, and in the sparse use of helpful determinatives. Often, the same sign was repeated, but with a different reading; for example, two stars could be written to indicate *dua netjer*, "praise god"; at Esna, we find this phenomenon taken to an extreme with two hymns, one of which is written entirely with crocodile signs, the other with rams, honoring the ram god Khnum, who was the chief deity worshiped in this temple. The scribe could choose among seven different readings for the crocodile sign.

From the New Kingdom on, entire pictures could be used to represent phonetic values. Thus, in the tomb of Ramesses IX, we find the pharaoh smiting foreign enemies for the verb *der*, "to vanquish," and jackals towing the sun barque for the verb *setja*, "to drag." In the Ptolemaic Period, a representation of the sky goddess arched over the earth could be used to write the verb *pesedj*, "to shine," while the divine name Ptah could be written with a depiction of the god separating sky and earth, referring to his activity as a creator. The name of the goddess Menhyt could be written with signs that could also be read "she who came into being at the beginning." In the face of such examples and such possibilities for transformation, Serge Sauneron has aptly spoken of "graphic alchemy" in the writing system at Esna. In this temple, there are 143 different writings for the name of Khnum, the chief god of the temple; for the name of Osiris, the priests made do with "only" seventy-three writings!

In his *Hieroglyphika*, which dates to the fifth century C.E., Horapollo—like Chaeromon before him in the first century C.E.—gives entirely correct readings for individual signs, such as the hare as the hieroglyph for "to open" and the vulture as the sign for "mother." But he tries consistently (as Chaeremon did not do) to explain these readings symbolically and as profoundly as possible. In the case of the hare, he indicates, "for this animal always has its eyes open." As Erich and Ute Winter have noted, a keen observation of nature stands behind his explanation of the vulture, "for there is no distinct male in this sort of animal"; in the case of vultures, it is extremely difficult to distinguish between male and female young.

Horapollo offers many valid insights with which Egyptologists should reacquaint themselves. For instance, he indicates that the word "soul" is written with a falcon. It is indeed striking, and not yet satisfactorily explained, how it is that when the *ba*-bird has a human head, the bird no longer has the appearance of a stork, but rather, that of a falcon. As Heinz-Joseph Thissen has noted, many interpretations rest on a misunderstanding of the cursive writing system. But there prevail the (to our taste) fantastic and artificial explanations in which there is doubtless reflected something of the thought processes of the priesthoods in the temples of the Roman Period. Similar explanations characterize the *Physiologus*, which so strongly influenced the Middle Ages and the Renaissance; here, for instance, we encounter the motif of the serpent that rejuvenates itself by shedding its skin.

These late explanations dissolve the boundaries, originally clearly drawn, between hieroglyph and symbol. Thus arose the misunderstanding, not to be resolved until Champollion, that all hieroglyphs were to be "read" in a purely symbolic manner. For a time, the understanding of the Egyptian writing system was entirely lost. But the fact that they could not be read served only to increase the prestige of the hieroglyphs, for they were believed to embody the secret knowledge ascribed to the Egyptians.

Among the purely symbolic signs, the symbol of the ouroboros, the serpent biting its own tail (called in Egyptian simply "Tail-in-mouth"), was not used as a hieroglyph, but it would have a tremendously rich career. An important predecessor of the symbol was the serpent "Many-faced," which in the Amduat, the oldest Book of the Afterlife, coils itself protectively around the corpse of the sun god and displays five heads that touch its tail. The "true" ouroboros first occurs on the gilded shrines of Tutankhamun, and later, especially in the evidence for magic. In alchemy, the serpent became a dragon, and the well-known image in the Codex Marcianus of the eleventh century, now in Venice, was a constantly reproduced example. Rich use was also made of this symbol in Graeco-Roman magic, in Gnosticism, and in Hermetism.

We come to the problem of initiation in ancient Egypt, which many esoteric movements assume as self-evident. The so-called "Osiris mysteries" of Abydos are often explained as initiation "mysteries" in the Hellenic sense, but the sources clearly point to a public festival drama centered on a strictly ordered procession and not to secret "mysteries." Only in this manner can we explain the festival route, with its innumerable stelae and shrines, and the general rejoicing and dance at its end. In the Graeco-Roman Period, the Christian author Minucius Felix (c. 200 C.E.) still displayed knowledge of these "mysteries" as a public ritual when he wrote, somewhat ironically, "The poor worshipers of Isis beat their breasts and imitate the grief of the unfortunate mother. Immediately afterward, the little one is found; Isis rejoices, the priests cheer, and Dog-head (i.e., Anubis) is celebrated as the discoverer. This is repeated year after year, yet they do not cease to lose what they find and to find what they lose."

Behind the description is a festival reenactment of the myth, first recorded in continuous form by Plutarch around 100 C.E., of good King

Osiris, who was murdered and dismembered by his brother Seth. Their sister Isis, who embodied a redemptive female element, collected the scattered members and woke Osiris to new life. From this new life sprang his heir, Horus, who would be protected by Isis from all the usurper's attacks and ultimately receive the royal heritage of Osiris.

A mystical initiation ritual is assured for the Isis mysteries of the Hellenistic era, and there were even three degrees of initiation. Apuleius is our most important source for these matters (though as an initiate, he was actually not supposed to reveal anything!), and his account in Book 11 of the *Metamorphoses* had a profound effect on lore regarding mysteries in all succeeding periods. After experiencing a symbolic death, initiates would confront the gods and pass through all the elements. The decisive mystery was that of the sun at midnight, which they had to behold, and which conveyed the certainty of overcoming death. Related concepts occur in Greek magical texts from Egypt, which aim at achieving an encounter with the divine and the overcoming of fate.

In this initiation, we find ourselves reminded of the nightly journey of the sun in the Egyptian Books of the Netherworld (Figure 3), wherein, at midnight, the sun completes its renewal, the rekindling of the light that will be borne "on the arms of darkness." In scene 73 of the Book of Gates, one can gaze, without perishing, directly at the face of the sun, which is being conveyed in a barque of its own; by way of contrast, according to Exodus 33, Moses may not look upon the face of God and must content himself with a view of His back. After the Amarna Period (c. 1350 B.C.E.), every individual could share in this hope—or certainty—even outside the royal sphere of the Books of the Netherworld, for there were numerous scenes on tomb walls, coffins, and papyri in which the daily course of the sun was condensed into a single representation, usually a pair of woman's arms holding the sun. But there was an important distinction, in that in ancient Egypt, this was a matter of a constantly renewed regeneration; in Hellenism, however, it was a release from the forces of fate and mortality, freedom from imprisonment in this world.

Nevertheless, there are astonishing formal correspondences, as in the examination in the netherworld (by the ferryman, attested already at the end of the Old Kingdom, or by the guardians of gateways), or in the stress on *secret* knowledge that one must carry with oneself. But as Jan Assmann

3. The sun god traveling by night through the netherworld in his barque. Book of Gates in the tomb of Sethos I (c. 1290 B.C.E.). Photo by E. Hornung.

has pointed out, this secrecy pertained to the desired efficacy of magical texts. The corpse of the sun was treated as a great, inexpressible mystery that in itself remained invisible to the blessed dead, while it was seen by, of all people, the damned who burned in the "Place of Annihilation." But in particular, we can see the *cista* (chest) of the later mysteries in the mysterious chest in the Hidden Room, which contained the body of Osiris.

In the Hellenistic mysteries, initiates entered into the solar course and gazed upon the "sun at midnight," the deepest of mysteries. In ancient Egypt, this glimpse was available to everyone, immediately upon crossing the threshold of death, for participation in the course of the sun meant ongoing regeneration for themselves as well as for the heavenly body; and they encountered the gods "face to face," as a harper's song in the tomb of Neferhotep puts it. We can certainly interpret the nightly course of the sun as an initiatory route leading to human renewal; but it is characteristic that it is not traveled by the living. In the ancient Egyptian view, no one, not even Pharaoh himself, could become an Osiris during life; only death opened this possibility.

But Egyptians could already share, during their lifetimes, in the "mysterious" knowledge of the afterlife by studying the pertinent writings, which in the New Kingdom developed into an ever-richer literature. No initiation was needed to do this, and in the social structure of ancient Egypt, whose religion was a state cult, there was nowhere a circle of initiates to be glimpsed—the priests had *ex officio* access to the writings, and Pharaoh, who appointed the priests as he did the civil officials, certainly needed no initiation; this was prohibited by royal ideology, of which we have precise knowledge. A number of kings boasted that they had acquired the requisite knowledge through their own efforts by studying the age-old writings.

It seems indicative to me that Egyptian wisdom literature extols the position of scribe but never makes reference to priests. The scribe, who was also a civil official, was the one with knowledge, the one to whom all lay open through his knowledge of writing. And the priest who celebrated the divine cult in the holy of holies of the temple beheld there all the secrets of the celestial realm where the gods dwelled.

The lack of clear references to initiation has often been "explained" by asserting that this was a matter of secret knowledge that was kept hidden from the public (for Theosophists, it remained a problem whether secret knowledge should be spread or not). But classical authors showed little hesitation in making such knowledge public, so it is striking that, except for the unequivocally Hellenistic Isis mysteries, they have nothing of this sort to report. Yet it seems to be an unalterable credo that all initiation rituals have their archetype in ancient Egypt.

Since many esoteric movements presuppose a "fall" of humankind from an original, paradisiacal condition, a fall that must be offset by a redemption, we should point in this connection to the Book of the Heavenly Cow. Originating in the milieu of the Amarna Period (c. 1350 B.C.E.), it represents a precedent for later gnostic teachings about redemption. The text accounts for the present, imperfect condition of the world, which resulted from an unavoidable process of alteration. Humankind, which was not yet separated from the gods in the original paradise, rose up against the aged sun god. Humanity was punished; part of it perished through the action of the fiery solar eye (the goddess Hathor as uraeus); in Egypt, divine wrath took the form of fire, not a flood. The remainder of humankind was saved, but it was punished by the withdrawal of the sun god, who rose to the distant sky on the back of the heavenly cow.

The original paradise was thus lost; the work of the creator god was damaged and rendered imperfect. Strife and death came into the world, and the eternal light of day yielded to the alternation of day and night. All aspirations were directed back on the original unity, which Egyptians wished to regain so as to overcome the former "fall." Many of the myth's motifs reappear in the text of the naos from el-Arish, which probably belongs to the fourth century B.C.E., while from the Roman Period, the Book of the Faiyum and texts in the temple of Esna preserve recollections of the myth, which was thus still known at the time when gnostic and hermetic writings began to appear.

There was certainly no Hermetism per se in ancient Egypt, but from at least the New Kingdom on, there prevailed an intellectual climate that was favorable to the rise of hermetic lore. In its positivistic phase, which was characterized by names like Adolph Erman, Kurt Sethe, and Alan H. Gardiner, Egyptology had no feel for this climate, and to an Erman, Egyptian religion seemed rather ludicrous and abstruse. There has been a fundamental change of attitude in more recent Egyptology, and circumstances are currently more auspicious for uncovering possible Egyptian roots of hermetic lore.

Jan Assmann has done just that with regard to hermetic belief, finding its roots in the concept of the divine of the Ramesside Period. At that time, as a reaction to Akhenaten's monotheism, there developed a concept of the unity of the cosmos, of a single god who was hidden in the multiplicity of things and whose name remained secret from both deities and humans. But essentially, the old creator god Atum was already the single one who was "the All." Hymns of the Ramesside Period impressively invoke the sublime nature of this god, as in chapter 200 of Papyrus Leiden I 350:

One is Amun, who hides himself from them,
who hides himself from the gods, no one knows his essence.
He is more distant than the sky,
and deeper than the netherworld.
No god knows his true form,

his image is not unfolded in the papyrus rolls.
He is too mysterious to be disclosed,
too great to be investigated,
too mighty to be known. . . .
No god can call him by his name.

A new formula was coined for this all-god, "the one who made himself into millions," which Assmann views as a precursor of the hermetic formulas *hen kai pan*, "one and all," or *una quae es omnia*, "you who are all," an expression used to designate Isis. The Ramesside theologians thus "laid the foundations for hermetic thought" (*Moses*, p. 267), and their new concept of the divine lived on in hymns and magical texts of the Late Period and down into the Greek magical texts from Egypt.

FOREIGN WONDERLAND ON THE NILE

The Greek Writers

Herodotus of Halicarnassus (Figure 4), who visited Egypt in the middle of the fifth century B.C.E., when the land was under Persian rule, acquired information from priests and scribes in the sanctuaries of Sais, Memphis, and Thebes. But while the delta and the temple of Ptah at Memphis are often mentioned in his *Histories*, Middle and Upper Egypt remain relatively shadowy. Evidently, Herodotus (unlike Diodorus, with his detailed descriptions), did not know these parts of the land from first-hand observation, notwithstanding his claim that he traveled all the way to Elephantine. Some have gone so far as to deny that Herodotus even went to Egypt, but it seems unlikely to me that his highly detailed information regarding the delta and the pyramid region came entirely from hearsay and other sources.

Herodotus was overwhelmingly impressed by the alterity of the Egyptian culture and lifestyle, by its bizarre animal cults, and by the incredible antiquity of this land, whose historical memory stretched back over 300 generations. On a superficial level, he was quite impressed by the pyramids (he surely never saw the temples of Thebes), but they remained free of anything esoteric. He seems not to have known that famous Greeks had been nourished by the wisdom of Egypt. He notes only that Solon, "who visited many lands for the pleasure of knowledge," sojourned at the court of King Amasis, the noted Hellenophile, and at that of Croesus of Lydia—though this information leads to chronological problems.

4. Herodotus of Halicarnassus (c. 484–425 B.C.E.). Copperplate by Johann Georg Mansfeld (1764–1817), color added later. Photo courtesy of Archiv für Kunst und Geschichte, Berlin.

In Herodotus' work, we first encounter the phenomenon of syncretism, the identification of deities with one another, which would characterize the Hellenistic Period. Ptah is Hephaestus, Horus is Apollo, Isis is Demeter (but later also Hecate and Aphrodite), Neith is Athena, and so forth. It is indicative that Thoth-Hermes makes no special appearance, but is mentioned only indirectly, through a connection of the sacred ibis with the city he calls Hermopolis (II 67). Though Herodotus lived too early to be placed in the hermetic-esoteric tradition, he had a tremendous influence on all the later travelers to Egypt.

The dialogues of Plato, who was probably (if at all) in Egypt in 393 B.C.E., already testify to a lively exchange with the land of the Nile. In the *Timaeus* and the *Critias*, he writes of Solon's visit to Egypt and of his confrontation with the priestly tradition of 9000 years of history, in the face of which the Greeks seemed like children. In this connection, he included the tale of Atlantis, which continues to stimulate esoteric thinkers to this very day. The name of the sunken continent in the west, which has been identified with such places as Crete and Helgoland, might be of Egyptian origin; Wolfgang Schenkel has attempted to explain it as "Nameless" (*iuty renes*), while J. Gwyn Griffiths prefers "Great is its name" (*aat renes*), though he refers to such interpretations with the German term "Glasperlenspiel" (intellectual games). Griffiths also points to the striking parallel of the "island of *ka*" in the Tale of the Shipwrecked Sailor, which was supposed to have sunk after its serpent-god uttered a prophecy; the genuinely Egyptian concept of a "primeval mound" that appeared at the time of creation has also been adduced to account for the Atlantis tradition.

Plato has an important account of "Theuth," as he calls him, as the inventor of writing in the *Phaedrus* and the *Philebus*; in the latter, he writes that it was "some god or some divine man" who first made the "unlimited variety of sound" into an object of reflection. This was the artful Thoth, who invented "numbers and calculation, mathematics and astronomy, drafts and dice, and even the alphabet," as he states in the *Phaedrus*. Here, we catch an unexpected glimpse of the early stages of the legend of Hermes Trismegistus!

In the *Euthydemus*, Plato calls the sea spirit Proteus, son of Poseidon, an "Egyptian sophist." In true Egyptian fashion, Proteus could assume any form whatsoever to slip away from irksome inquirers, and he was connected with Egypt as early as book 4 of the *Odyssey* (and invoked by Goethe in the classic Walpurgisnacht of his *Faust*). Herodotus makes Proteus an Egyptian king, while for Euripides, he was the guardian of the "true" Helen, who remained safe in Egypt during the Trojan War. In the *Gorgias*, Socrates swears "by the dog, the god of the Egyptians," that is, by the dog-headed Anubis. Plato also knew of mummification, animal cults, and the Judgment of the Dead, and he has important things to say in the *Politicus* (290de) about the esteem enjoyed by the Egyptian priests. The frequent contacts between Egyptians and Phoenicians mentioned by Plato point to an even older cultural encounter: Egyptian objects and religious concepts were spread throughout the Mediterranean world by Phoenician traders and colonists.

Contemporary with Plato, c. 385 B.C.E., was the work *Busiris*, by the orator Isocrates, an idealization of Egyptian "philosophy," which was the origin of all philosophy. For Isocrates, Busiris was king, legislator, and culture hero, just as Menes would be for Diodorus. The work also mentions Pythagoras' stay in Egypt. According to information handed down later by Iamblichus, he was supposed to have spent twenty-two years in Egypt, where he was initiated into all the divine mysteries, after which the Persian conquest (525 B.C.E.) took him to the magi of Babylon.

The next important figure is Diodorus of Sicily (c. 80–20 B.C.E.); he was in Egypt shortly after 60 B.C.E., and in his account, he draws in part on an otherwise lost work of Hecataeus of Abdera (c. 300 B.C.E.). As Herodotus had done, he derived much of his information from Egyptian priests, such as when he furnishes a whole list of famous Greeks (I 96) who were supposed to have visited Egypt in olden times. His enumeration begins with Orpheus and Musaeus and reaches the historical period with Homer and Lycurgus; there follow Solon, Plato, Pythagoras, Eudoxus, Democritus, and Oenopides of Chios. In certain cases, he was evidently shown the houses in which these Greek sages had dwelled, as Strabo (17, 1, 29) also reports for Plato and Eudoxus in the city of Heliopolis. In other cases, he was shown statues of these men, and it is stressed that everything for which the Greeks admired them was derived from Egypt, as Diodorus demonstrates in detail in the case of Orpheus. Pythagoras obtained the idea of the transmigration of souls in Egypt, and Diodorus connects Democritus and Eudoxus with astrology.

In late antiquity, certain writers went so far as to name the Egyptian priests with whom Solon and Plato were supposed to have associated. In a number of traditions, Homer, whom many lands and cities claimed as their native son, was viewed as an Egyptian. More than a century after Diodorus, Plutarch enumerated visitors to Egypt: Solon, Thales, Plato, Eudoxus, Pythagoras, and Lycurgus. Eudoxus was supposed to have translated works from Egyptian, and even to have died in Egypt (356 B.C.E.); in any case, he prepared the way in Greece for the Egyptian calendar and its solar year.

For our theme, it is irrelevant whether Pythagoras and others were actually in Egypt. What is important is the nimbus with which they could be surrounded through their supposed contact with Egypt and the wisdom of its priests. Iamblichus affirms that Thales sent Pythagoras to Egypt, for Thales himself had derived everything for which he was considered a sage from association with the priests of Memphis and Thebes. The theme that all wisdom sprang originally from Egypt became ever more tightly woven into the legends. In his *The Age of Constantine the Great*, Jacob Burckhardt refers to "the age-old reverence of the Greek before the priestly wisdom of the Egyptian," which had taken form from Diodorus on.

We also find a clear tendency to extend the tradition by bringing ever more names into play. One of the most beautiful pieces of information is from the romance writer Heliodorus, who lived in the middle of the third century C.E. According to his *Aethiopica* (III 14), Homer was a son of Hermes Trismegistus and was conceived by the wife of a priest while she slept in a temple at Thebes—the poet thus had a highly personal connection to Thebes, a city whose praises he sings in the *Iliad*! According to another anecdote, Homer supposedly received the manuscript of the *Iliad* in Memphis. Such stories were prevalent in late antiquity and were apparently taken seriously, and they are also to be found in the writings of Byzantine authors.

According to Diodorus (I 9, 6), the gods and goddesses originated in Egypt. Osiris and Isis stood in the foreground of his account of Egyptian religion, a fact that had an extraordinary influence on succeeding periods down to the eighteenth century of our own era. Hermes also appears in a number of places in his work; he is the illustrious inventor of, among other things, writing, and he is the creator of all the arts and the first lawgiver. In one place (I 94, 1) Zarathustra and Moses appear parallel to Hermes: a triad of luminaries that we later encounter again and again, and an expression of the syncretism of the culture of the Hellenistic world.

The Ionic natural philosophers do not yet make their appearance in Diodorus. Plutarch was the first to relate that Thales learned from Egyptian priests that water was to be viewed as the substance underlying everything, and we have already noted Iamblichus' testimony that Thales sent Pythagoras to the priests of Egypt. In the case of Anaximander, Cyril of Alexandria (d. 444, C.E.) was the first to credit him with a visit to Egypt. According to this Christian author, Solon and Plato became acquainted with the wisdom of Moses in Egypt. Thales' connection with Egypt was stressed again by Josephus and Clement of Alexandria, and yet again by Cyril. There is an isolated reference in Diodorus (V 37) to a visit to Egypt by Archimedes.

The philosopher Democritus, whom tradition also viewed as a magus and astrologer, apparently wrote a satire *Peri tôn en Hadou* (On those in

Hades), which has not been preserved. From the title, we may suspect that it borrowed from Egyptian concepts of the afterlife, and the tradition of such compositions as the Books of the Netherworld did in fact extend down into the early Ptolemaic Period. Democritus fits in with hermetic tradition, because he viewed man as a microcosm.

It is only in our own time, in afrocentric ideology (see chapter 18), that Aristotle, the great opponent of hermetic thought, has been included in the company of those who traveled to Egypt. None of the ancient writers displays any knowledge of such a journey, so this new assertion must be supported by clues in the philosopher's writings. This claim is impressive proof that the formation of legends still flourishes today.

Strabo (c. 64 B.C.E.–21 C.E.), the last of the major authorities on the picture of Egypt in classical antiquity, came from Amasia in Asia Minor. Shortly after the Roman conquest of Egypt, he traveled extensively to collect material for his *Geography*, whose seventeenth book is devoted to Egypt. According to his portrayal, he journeyed up the Nile valley as far as Philae, and he adds a great deal of information about "Ethiopia" (i.e., Nubia), such as the ritual murder of the king by the priests, which was common in Nubia (XVII, 2, 3). He gives an especially detailed account of the animal cults, and he must have scoured the pyramid field at Giza, where he was struck by the distinctive stone casing of the pyramid of Mycerinus, though he has nothing to say about the Great Sphinx.

The architectural form of the pyramid had already made an impression on Hellenistic rulers and inspired imitations. Among Alexander the Great's final, excessive plans that were never carried out was a "pyramid equal to the tallest in Egypt" for his father Philip (Diodorus XVIII 4, 5). Beginning in the middle of the second century B.C.E., the Maccabees employed the pyramid form for their tombs.

The form of the sphinx did not attract attention until relatively late. In his *Natural History* (36, § 77), Pliny (23–79 C.E.) mentions it as the supposed burial monument of King Harmais. It is in the works of Plutarch and Clement of Alexandria that it evidently made its first appearance as an image embodying the mysterious wisdom of Egypt, as it would again in the works of Pico della Mirandola in the Renaissance. Both these writers refer to the sphinx-lined routes (also mentioned by Strabo) in front of temples, and not to the Great Sphinx that lies before the pyramids of Giza, whose body was covered by sand in classical antiquity, so that its lion's form was not recognizable. The prefect Titus Claudius Balbillus, who served under Nero in 55–59 C.E., finally cleared the body from the sands, and after that, a few Greek dedicatory inscriptions were left by pilgrims. Pliny was even able to supply the exact dimensions of the monument. He had only contempt for the pyramids: they were "useless and stupid (*otiosa ac stulta*)" displays of the wealth of the pharaohs (§ 75). He enumerates all the authors who wrote about the pyramids, beginning with Herodotus, but he does not know the names of the kings who had them built, or does not want to know, so as not to extol their vanity; thus, he merely peddles the old dragomen's tale about how many radishes, heads of garlic, and onions were consumed during their construction. He was far more interested in the obelisks, some of which already stood in Rome; so far as I know, he was the first to assert that they bore inscriptions "that contain a description of the nature of things (*rerum naturae*) *according to the philosophy of the Egyptians*" (§ 71). This would be the opinion of Athanasius Kircher and other scholars 1600 years later, but in Pliny's day, obelisks were being correctly and intelligibly inscribed in Italy itself.

In any case, we find a clear resistance to the esoteric-mystical view of Egypt in Pliny and his contemporaries, and Pliny has nothing to say about magic. Heraclitus (fragments 14–15) had already turned against magicians and mystics, for "the mysteries common among people" were "celebrated in an unholy manner." In particular, the Egyptian animal-headed deities and the animal cults continually evoked annoyance, and even scorn and mockery, in the classical authors, and they were even the object of comic poetry (e.g., Anaxandrides). Juvenal (c. 60–140 C.E.), who according to a dubious tradition was banished to Egypt by Domitian because of his criticism of an actor and served as commandant of the garrison at Aswan, says in his fifteenth satire, "Who does not know . . . what monstrosities Egypt worships in its delusions?" He goes on to mention crocodiles, ibises, baboons, cats, fish, and dogs. He also makes an outraged report of an incidence of cannibalism that was supposed to have occurred in upper Egypt in the year 127, when an inhabitant of Dendara was captured and consumed by hostile individuals from Ombos (Nagada). This was the other side that Egypt displayed to visitors in antiquity. But on the whole, there prevailed a reverence for the evidence of its ancient culture and for the age-old wisdom of its priests, and interest in the mystical Egypt increased from the first century C.E. on.

THREE

POWER AND INFLUENCE OF THE STARS

"**A**strology was foreign to the ancient Egyptians, and even among the Greeks, it only reached its prime in the later Hellenistic Period. Then, however, it was claimed to be an Egyptian invention by two eminent writers: in the book by Nechepso-Petosiris, and by the Alexandrian *hierogrammateus* Chaeremon, who was both an Egyptian priest and a Stoic philosopher and was even called to Rome to serve as tutor to Prince Nero. After Chaeremon, there was a universal certainty that astrology was an Egyptian science"—so writes Reinhold Merkelbach in the third volume of his *Abrasax* (p. 78). László Kákosy has expressed himself rather more positively; according to him, "an independent and original form of astrology already existed in ancient Egypt in pre-Hellenistic times," and in particular, astromagy was a special branch of magic in pharaonic Egypt. In the Greek magical papyri from Egypt, there are indeed constant references to constellations.

In the Pyramid Texts of the third millennium B.C.E., the orientation toward a celestial afterlife led to intense concern with stars; in these texts, the king is a star in the sky among the gods (§ 1583). But in this oldest corpus of texts the solar afterlife is fundamentally more important than the stellar, and soon thereafter, emphasis shifted to the netherworld, where the sun was the only heavenly body to play a predominant role, assisting the dead in acquiring renewed life by means of its nightly journey.

Nevertheless, the sky is often included in the tombs and mortuary temples of the New Kingdom (Figure 5). The earliest example is the astro-

5. Constellations of the northern sky on the "astronomical ceiling" in the tomb of Sethos I (c. 1290 B.C.E.). Photo by E. Hornung.

nomical ceiling in the tomb of Senenmut, the close confidant of Queen Hatshepsut, with its depiction of the months and of the most important stars. There is a comparable ceiling in the Ramesseum; at its center, the baboon of Thoth is seated on a *djed*-pillar (the hieroglyph for "endurance"), indicating that Thoth was also lord of the calendar and the reckoning of time.

In the Book of the Dead, the vignette to spell 135, which is concerned with the rejuvenation of the moon, depicts the deceased in prayer before a dark blue night sky filled with stars; there is a beautiful example in the well-known tomb of Sennedjem at Deir el-Medina. From about the same time, we have a stela, now in Hanover, with an unusual depiction of the adoration of stars. Here, the ibis-headed Thoth as moon god (who is also called "bull among the stars") is flanked by two goddesses, each of whom bears a star on her head; they are anonymous, but they might stand for the entire host of stars, or perhaps for the decans, for in the text, the deceased prays to Thoth as the moon and to the "stars in the sky."

What is plainly lacking in the pharaonic period is belief in the influence of the planets and their alignments. The planets were designated with divine names, which were formulated with that of Horus, but they occur almost entirely in lists and play no role in religious concepts, quite unlike Mesopotamia. We may, however, see a certain prelude to astrology in the decans and their importance; in this regard, we are especially indebted to the ground-breaking contributions of László Kákosy and Joachim Friedrich Quack.

Decans were stars or constellations in the proximity of the ecliptic whose rising or culmination determined the hours of the night; every ten days (hence their designation), a different decan rose at a given hour. They are already mentioned in the Pyramid Texts, but the system of thirty-six decans with which we are familiar was not developed until the First Intermediate Period and the Middle Kingdom; our chief source of information regarding them is a series of coffins from Asyut. Because of the regular invisibility and return of these stars, the Egyptians viewed them as one of the many evidences of the regeneration to which they aspired after death. In the New Kingdom, lists of decans appear in the royal mortuary temples, beginning with Deir el-Bahari, and on the ceilings of the royal tombs of the Ramesside Period; the material has been drawn together by Otto Neugebauer and Richard A. Parker in their exemplary *Egyptian Astronomical Texts* (*EAT*). A representation at the far end of the tomb of Ramesses VI depicts two rows of decans turned reverently toward the concluding representation of the Book of Gates, which is concerned with the rebirth of the sun; in the upper pillared hall of the tomb, the same king prays to the planet Venus as the *benu*-phoenix (*EAT* III, pl. 12). The decans make their first appearance as dangerous beings in texts from amulets containing divine decrees from Dynasty 21. Those wearing such amulets were supposed to be protected "from the seven stars of the Great Bear, from a star that falls from the sky, and from the decan stars."

The decans appear in an entirely new form for the first time around 850 B.C.E., in the tomb of Osorkon II at Tanis (*EAT* III, pl. 17) and on two armbands of Prince Harnakhte from the same tomb. They are now depicted with serpents' bodies and lions' heads, and they have evidently become deities whose function is to protect the deceased; on one armband, they appear along with Osiris, Horus, Thoth, Isis, and Nephthys. It is significant for later astrology that here, they are already connected with the concept of *shai*, "fate." Now, or a little later, they appear on amulets, which suits their function as protective deities. In particular, these amulets depict lion-headed goddesses seated on a throne that is decorated with decans; according to finds at Meroe, this type might stem from the seventh and sixth centuries B.C.E. On one amulet in Baltimore depicting the goddess Bastet, she appears along with wishes for the New Year, which we encounter rather often on amulets that served as seals. The mistress of the decans was probably Sakhmet, the dangerous goddess who sent all illnesses and also had the power to cure them, and thus had a special connection with fate (Kákosy, p. 176). Also related to the decans was the hippopotamus goddess, who appears in connection with the sky under the names Taweret and Opet, or as a striking constellation: a hippopotamus with a crocodile on its back. A neckband in Budapest depicting thirty-six figures (Kákosy, p. 186, fig. 15) clearly refers to the totality of decans, under whose protection the wearer of the neckband placed himself. Quack (p. 100) cites a text from Esna testifying to their dangerousness:

> who announce what happens, who keep people alive and kill sinners as they please, . . . who bombard the lands with fire, at whose approach everyone trembles. . . . They rove around as the Eye of Re, as messengers in the cities and nomes, who shoot arrows from their mouths at those who see them from afar.

The representation on amulets and *menit*s (the designation of a part of a necklace) was followed by depictions of the decans on temple walls, beginning with the temple of Hibis in el-Kharga Oasis, from the reign of Darius I. Next, we have the decan naos of Nectanebo I (380–362 B.C.E.) and a chapel of Ptolemy VIII at Deir el-Bahari, where the decans are depicted only schematically as thirty-six stars in an oval, though they receive offerings and are thus divine beings. The texts on the naos speak of the influence of the decans on water and wind; they bring fertility to the fields, but they also cause illness and sudden death. The decans also influence certain parts of the body, a belief that would later be systematically elaborated. Their protective function was also conjured up by statues of decans in temples, as attested especially at Dendara.

The gnostic *Apocryphon of John* retains the much older concept of the influence of the decans on the parts of the human body, which perhaps goes back to the New Kingdom, though it appeals to a "Book of Zor(o)aster" (Nag Hammadi Codex II 19, 10). Quack has been able to show that a number of the names in this work can be interpreted as Egyptian, though there are also Semitic and Greek names. The connection between parts of the body and constellations long remained influential, and it forms part of the correspondence between the microcosm and the macrocosm that played so great a role in Hermetism. For this same reason, minerals and metals were also brought into a relationship with the decans, creating a bridge between astrology and alchemy. In another Coptic text, which relates the death of Joseph, demonic, "many-faced" decans, enveloped in smoke and brimstone, appear in the following of Death and the Devil.

A sort of astral religion was thus gradually taking shape, one that was foreign to the earlier period. At its center stood the Greek notion of *heimarmene*, "fate" (or *ananke*, "destiny"), along with the question of how one could overcome one's preassigned fate, which was reflected in the constellations. In Greek magical texts that designate themselves the Eighth Book of Moses, there is a full-blown ritual for "wiping out" an unlucky birth constellation with a new one—with the help of Sarapis, "for this god makes everything possible." The god is called upon: "Protect me from every compulsion from the stars that pertains to me, dissolve my adverse fate." Using special breathing techniques, the suppliant ascends beyond the planetary spheres to the celestial realm of the fixed stars and penetrates it, for it is in the otherworldly region of the eternal that new birth constellations were possible. Even the early Christians hoped that Jesus and baptism could free them from the bonds of fate.

There must have been astrologers active in the court of the Ptolemies at Alexandria, creatively developing their "imported" art. On a statue found in the delta, Harchebis informs us of his observations of the heavens, which in particular concerned the planet Venus. He avers that he knows the mysteries of the stars, and those of the serpents, for he was an astrologer and a snake charmer rolled into one; he was evidently active in the time of Ptolemy VI and Ptolemy VIII. At about the same time, the priest Petosiris was asserted to be the author of an astrological handbook that also laid claim to the authority of "King Nechepso" (perhaps Necho II of Dynasty 26).

The zodiac was adopted early in the Ptolemaic Period; the earliest, still rectangular example stems from an older temple at Esna and belongs to the time of Ptolemy III and Ptolemy IV. The form of some of the signs—especially the "goat-fish" for Capricorn, Sagittarius (two-headed, riding a winged horse with a scorpion's tail), the maiden with the ears of wheat, and Cancer (the crab was often reinterpreted as a scarab)—point to its Babylonian origin, but some signs were Egyptianized (e.g., Aquarius as a Nile god), and the zodiac was completely integrated into the Egyptian sky. In a number of studies, Christiane Desroches Noblecourt has argued for an Egyptian origin of the signs of the zodiac, connecting them with the cycle of the sun and Osiris; she would even like to see Egyptian prototypes for the signs of the zodiac and other figures in the cathedral of Vézelay. The best-known example of the integration of the zodiac into a traditional Egyptian representation of the sky is the round zodiac on the ceiling of the Osiris chapel at Dendara (Figure 6), whose original is now in the Louvre; it belongs to the end of the Ptolemaic Period (i.e., the middle of the first century B.C.E.), but it has constantly been taken to be more ancient still. In any event, the heyday of Egyptian astrology did not really begin until the Roman conquest.

A decree of Augustus, promulgated in 11 C.E., forbade the private consultation of astrologers, while the emperor himself had coins struck with his zodiacal sign, and he conceived of his gigantic Solarium on the Campus Martius as a huge horoscope filled with cosmic symbolism. His successor Tiberius had a great fondness for astrology, and he ordered the execution of persons whose horoscopes indicated they might become emperor. With the passage of time, Egyptian astrologers played a role at the imperial court, in particular Balbillus, whom Nero appointed prefect of Egypt (he served from 55–59 C.E.). Vitellius and Domitian again had astrologers executed, while Hadrian personally practiced astrology.

From Hadrian's reign, we have the coffin of Heter and other coffins from the family tomb of Soter at Thebes. On each of them, there is a traditional representation of Nut (as already in the New Kingdom), but the goddess is surrounded by the signs of the zodiac and the goddesses of the hours; their purpose is to integrate the deceased into the course of the solar year. On some of these coffins, we still find symbols of the sun's daily journey (barques, baboons, scarabs), the four winds, and ancient Egyptian constellations (Orion, Sothis, constellations of the northern sky), while on Heter's coffin, the positions of the planets are also noted in Demotic. His horoscope points to October, 93 C.E., and belongs to a tradition

6. The zodiac of Dendara. From *Mélanges Adolphe Gutbub* (Montpelier, 1984), pl. 3, p. 112.

that can be traced back to shortly before the Roman Period. The oldest known horoscope from Egypt, which is written in the Demotic script, stems from May 4, 38 B.C.E., while in Mesopotamia, we have a horoscope from as early as the year 410 B.C.E.

In the Roman Period, the afterlife once again took on astral traits; netherworld phenomena were transferred to the sky, and even the Judgment of the Dead was now connected with the constellation Libra. In the tomb of Heter, there was found a copy of the Embalming Ritual (Papyrus Boulaq III), which contains the promise that his *ba*-soul would "do what you will in the sky, for you are with the stars, and your *ba* belongs to the thirty-six stars (i.e., the decans)."

Clement of Alexandria writes of four astrological books of Hermes (Trismegistus), and a series of astrological writings circulated under the name of Zoroaster; the *Aprocryphon of John* relies on the latter for its doctrine of the responsibility of the decans for the individual parts of the human body.

Like magic, gnosis, and alchemy, astrology outlasted the victory of Christianity. But the importance of horoscopes declined suddenly at the end of the fourth century C.E., and the last one was drawn up at Oxyrhynchus in the year 478 (P. Ox. XVI 2060), though the philosopher Olympiodorus was still lecturing on astrology at Alexandria in 564. Astrology did not enjoy a new upswing and a wide dissemination in Europe until the translation of Arabic texts into Latin in the twelfth century, after flourishing previously at the Abbassid court in Baghdad—there was no royal court without a court astrologer! To reconcile it with the church, Roger Bacon (1214–1294) and others attempted to derive it from the Bible and thus legitimate it anew. In his *Kultur der Renaissance* (Culture of the Renaissance), Jacob Burckhardt has made an impressive demonstration of the ubiquity of astrology in Renaissance Italy.

Modern astrology, though freed from its earlier connection with initiation and secret lore, nevertheless continues to flourish. It remains committed to the ancient hermetic principle of the correspondence of macrocosm and microcosm, and it retains connections with the world of Egyptian thought: in France, a special "Egyptian astrology" is practiced, which uses Egyptian deities instead of the signs of the zodiac.

FOUR

ALCHEMY

The Art of Transformation

At the heart of alchemy stands an Egyptian, Zosimus of Panopolis (modern Akhmim), who was active around 300 C.E. We know nothing about his life, but some authentic writings of his have survived; posterity would hold him in high regard, and he was being read by Arabs as early as the ninth and tenth centuries. The authorities he drew on were Hermes (Trismegistus, Figure 7) and Zoroaster, as well as Agathodaemon, the Persian Ostanes, and Mary the Jew. There were other ancient alchemists with purely Egyptian names, such as Petasius (= Peteese), Phimenas, and Pebechius, or who were clearly active in Egypt, including the earliest writer, Bolus of Mendes (prior to 200 B.C.E.), and one of the latest, the philosopher Stephanus of Alexandria, who lectured on alchemy in the seventh century, shortly before the Arab conquest.

The standard alchemic work, the *Physika kai Mystika* of Pseudo-Democritus, which probably goes back to Bolus of Mendes, speaks of instruction in an Egyptian temple (presumably that of Ptah at Memphis), and the most recent authority cited is "the great Ostanes," who initiated Democritus and "the Egyptian priests" into alchemy. There is even an endeavor to derive the word "(al)chemy" from Egyptian, for instance, from *kem* "black," and there are other derivations as well.

Did alchemy really originate in Egypt? François Daumas, who has concerned himself with this question, presumes that a Graeco-Egyptian milieu would have been fertile soil for such a development. The earliest

7. Hermes Trismegistus. Paint on wood. Placed (between Hippocrates and Aesculapius) in the Innsbruck Hofapotheke c. 1740, today in the Pharmazie-Historisches Museum, Basel. Photo courtesy of the Pharmazie-Historisches Museum.

sources, which stem from the second century B.C.E., are all in Greek. Corresponding Egyptian texts are as yet unknown, but the Greek texts make frequent mention of Egyptian deities, especially Isis, Osiris, and Horus, while the month names that are used and certain other formulations also point to Egypt. Indicative is the fact that Cheops (who appears as Souphis in Manetho) is the supposed author of one alchemical work; in the Roman Period, his pyramid was connected with alchemy. Egyptian culture indeed had a good deal to do with stone, and we may cite books with such titles as *Staat aus dem Stein* (State from stone, by Hans Gerhard Evers) and *Stein und Zeit* (Stone and time, by Jan Assmann).

Daumas is of the opinion that the roots of alchemy can be traced back to the New Kingdom. He quotes from the decree of the god Ptah for Ramesses II at Abu Simbel:

I cause that the mountains bring forth great, mighty, and tall monuments for you. I cause that the deserts create all the precious stones for you, in order to carve them with documents in your name.

He points to similar statements in texts from the late temples of Dendara and Esna, as well as to the skill of the Egyptians at working with artificial materials that served as substitutes for those that were costly and rare. Daumas is also struck by the "alchemic" tone of the inscription of the expedition leader Harwerre from year six of Amenemhet III (c. 1813 B.C.E.), in which he portrays how he endeavored to quarry "stone" (turquoise) of the right color in the blazing heat of summer in the Sinai, with the advice of savvy miners.

We have important evidence from Amenophis III (1390–1353 B.C.E.), in his dedicatory inscription in the temple of Montu at Karnak. There, he speaks of erecting a "god's house" of sandstone "cleansed in its entire length with *djam*-gold, decorated with all kinds of precious stones, its entire floor of (normal) *nebwy*-gold, its door leaves of cedar (covered) with Asiatic copper"; this statement is followed by a list of the materials used in this construction:

djam-gold	31,485 ⅔ *deben*
nebwy-gold	25,182 ¾ *deben*
black copper	4,620 ⅔ *deben*
lapis-lazuli	6,406 *deben*
turquoise	1,731 ⅔ *deben*
bronze, pieces of copper . . .	
(*Urk.* IV 1668; 1 *deben* = 91 g)	

He included a second list in his building inscription on the Third Pylon of Karnak, calling it the "weight of this monument." Most of the entries are lost; only those for turquoise (4,820 *deben*) and jasper (6,823 *deben*) are still preserved (*Urk.* IV 1729; there is yet another list on p. 1731). Never before and never again did an Egyptian king supply such precise details regarding quantities of the precious materials he used for a construction. We sense a genuinely alchemic zeal for the opus, even though the "stone" here is a temple construction.

On a stela from the vicinity of Heliopolis, Ramesses II (1279–1213 B.C.E.) stresses his concern with the correct stone for statues. He personally carried out the prospecting in the quarries.

From a much later date, the "laboratory" of the temple of Dendara contains texts that Philippe Derchain has connected with the beginnings of alchemy. Designated the "House of Gold," the room served to prepare cultic implements. On the divine level, Thoth (i.e., Hermes, here called "twice great") was responsible for these activities, and the king is called the son or the heir of this god in the offering scene at the doorway. The goddess Hathor says to the king, "Receive the costly materials of the mountains to carry out every work in the House of Gold" (*Dendara* VIII 132, 3–8). Needless to say, the actual technicians were not royalty but rather priests and artisans with special authorization, and a veil of secrecy surrounded their activities. At Dendara, the mysteries of Osiris evidently included a transsubstantiation of grain into gold (Cauville). The levels of outward appearance and underlying reality were still clearly separated (Derchain, p. 223); it was only later, in alchemy, that the boundaries were blurred.

Horus of Edfu was a god "who made mountains and brought precious stones into being." In the treasury of his Ptolemaic Period temple, where valuable materials were stored, the mountains are depicted offering their rich gifts: gold, silver, lapis-lazuli, turquoise, jasper, carnelian, hematite, and other semiprecious stones. The texts of the "laboratory" of this temple, which were carved under Ptolemy VI, include a number of formulas for preparing incense and ointment for the divine statues: "It is a mystery that has been seen and heard by no one." Various mixtures were to be heated and reheated at two-day intervals, as in later alchemic instructions. With regard to a particular ointment, on the seventh day of heating, "when it is hot, add 2 *kite* (1 *kite* = 9 g) of each of all kinds of precious stones, namely, of gold, silver, genuine lapis-lazuli, genuine red jasper, genuine green feldspar, turquoise, genuine faïence, and genuine carnelian, crumbling each of these especially fine." This is genuine alchemy, already in the second century B.C.E.!

For the Egyptians, minerals were living entities; already in the Pyramid Texts (§ 513), lapis-lazuli "grows" like a plant. We also read that the bodies of deities consisted of valuable materials, gold and lapis-lazuli. In the aforementioned decree of Ptah, the god forms the body of the king in the same manner:

I have fashioned your body of gold,
your bones of bronze,
your arms of metal.

For the offering of precious stones and metals to deities, Daumas points to a basalt slab from Dynasty 30 (Cairo J. 45936) on which silver, gold, feldspar, and lapis-lazuli are mentioned in an offering list. An unequivocally non-Egyptian ingredient in alchemy, however, is the connection of certain minerals and metals with the planets; we have already seen that the planets played practically no role in the pharaonic period. Even the assigning of precious metals to specific deities, which was an Assyrian practice, seems not to have been an Egyptian practice. Another non-Egyptian element was Bolus of Mendes' elaborate doctrine of the sympathy and antipathy between objects and substances.

In his treatment of two early Arabic texts, the *Risalat as-Sirr* ("Circular letter of the mystery") and *ar-Risala al-falakiya al-kubra* ("Great circular letter of the spheres"), Ingolf Vereno has elaborated the truly striking parallels between alchemic *opus* and Egyptian cultic practices; in the Arabic tradition, alchemy was the "science of the temples" (*'ilm al-barabi*), and the temples of Egypt were the places where it was practiced and where its secrets were still to be found. According to Zosimus, the sought-after wisdom was inscribed by Hermes and the Egyptian priests in the darkness of the rooms of the temples, where it was carved on the walls using symbolic signs.

The first of these texts itself maintains that it was found at Akhmim under a slab of marble in a crypt where a dead woman lay buried; the text was recorded on a golden tablet under her head (she was Theosebeia, "Blessed of God," behind whom was concealed Isis). This was supposed to have happened at the time that al-Ma'amûn was in Egypt, that is, in the year 832. This caliph, son of a Persian slave woman, was especially open to the sciences, and he supported the translation of Greek manuscripts into Arabic.

The second text was supposed to have been found under a statue of Artemis, thus the Egyptian Isis-Hathor, in a subterranean passageway (probably a crypt) of the temple of Dendara; it purports to be a circular letter from Hermes of Dendara whose contents were taught by the high priest Uwirus (i.e., Osiris). The author of the first text, however, was Hermes *Budaširdi*, which Vereno would like to connect with Busiris; according to al-Mas'udi, though, al-Budašir was an Egyptian priest and king. Indeed, in Arabic tradition, there were as many as three figures named Hermes: the first lived in Upper Egypt before the Flood and built the temple of Akhmim; the second was deposited in Babylon (i.e., Old Cairo) after the flood and was believed to be the teacher of Pythagoras; the third, who was also postdiluvian, lived in the city of Misr and wrote a book on alchemy. The first text also supplies an impressive filiation: "Hermes, the Busirite (son) of Ostanes, son of Hermes"—two Hermes thus already make their appearance in the title of the work. Vereno states (p. 183), "both texts are hermetic revelations whose roots lie in Hellenistic Egypt." There are other alchemic books in the Arabic language that were supposed to have been written by Hermes, but we have so many manuscripts that most have yet to be studied. The *Turba philosophorum*, which is preserved only in Latin translation, depicts a gathering of the pupils of Hermes, presided over by Pythagoras.

Such stories about how texts were discovered are typically Egyptian—spells from the Book of the Dead were found "under the feet of Thoth," that is, under a statue of the god (spells 30B, 64, and 137A). The characters and—how could it be otherwise?—the action itself are derived from the myth of Osiris: after his death, a king, in the process of decaying (the *nigredo*, the "black condition"), engenders the heir in whom he will live again. Even the analogy between the alchemic *aqua vitae*, quicksilver, which unites in itself the colors of gold and silver, and the Nile inundation (which, moreover, is the same as Nun, the primeval water), points to the myth of Osiris, to which the alchemic "Isis the Prophetess to Her Son Horus" alludes more directly still, and the *opus* was brought to a conclusion on the Egyptian New Year's Day (July 19). Zosimus even refers to the alchemic process as "Osirification," and wondrous powers of renewal were ascribed to the discharges of the murdered Osiris already in early mortuary texts. In the Coffin Texts (VII 473), the deceased affirms, "I have come, that I might behold Osiris, that I might live at his side, that I might rot at his side." In the New Kingdom, the nocturnal aspect of the sun god in the netherworld was even designated "Decaying One whose putrefaction is veiled" (Litany of Re, address 60); the figure it names is painted red, and it is followed immediately by an analogous figure called "The Child."

All alchemic work thus boiled down to bringing Osiris back to life through decay and putrefaction. In his *Arcana arcanissima* (1614), Michael Meier refers to the myth of Osiris as representing the alchemic process. This view did not preclude an entirely different interpretation of the pro-

cess as a repetition of the creation of the world, whether as a mystical process or in the sense of Jungian psychiatric theory. However explained, the
issue was transformation and renewal, and of course not simply the making of gold.

The preparation of a statue or a mummy in ancient Egypt was brought
to an end by the "Opening of the Mouth" ritual, which was supposed to
enable full use of all the sense organs. This ritual, with which every Egyptian *opus* concluded, was replaced in alchemy by the drawing together of
the four elements. In the *Tabula smaragdina* (see chapter 6), sun, moon,
wind, and earth embody the four terrestrial elements, and there is also a
fifth, the celestial "quintessence." There is debate over the extent to which
we can find the doctrine of the four elements in ancient Egypt. B. H.
Stricker and others have believed they have found attestations of it, but
there is in fact no clear indication. For example, in the hymn to the creator
god in the Instruction for Merikare, sky, earth, water, and breath are mentioned in succession, but the element of fire is conspicuously absent. Other
supposed attestations are similarly incomplete.

Alchemy had to do with transformation, in particular of base metals
into precious ones. "And all things are woven together, and all things are
dissolved, and all things are mixed with one another, and all things are
combined, and all things are again unmixed," as Zosimus formulates it
(Haage, p. 89). And when grain turns into gold in the temple of Dendara,
for example, or wine into blood at Communion, the same process is at
work. All chemistry is in fact transformation, as is the splitting of the atom
in modern times, from which entirely new elements can arise, though special energies are needed. But alchemy also had an inner side, translating
mystical experiences into chemical language and using this language to
cover over a gnostic redemptive path to the salvation of humankind, as in
the ascent of Theosebeia through the seven heavens to the divine realm of
light. What links alchemy to modern natural science, though, is its effort
to gain mastery over nature, its sense of being capable of transforming
everything.

Arabic writers began to translate alchemic texts in the ninth century,
but relevant tractates in the Arabic language already appeared a century
earlier; some of them were ascribed to the Ommayad prince Khalid. In
1144, Robert of Chester made the first translation of an Arabic work on
alchemy into Latin (he is also the first known translator of the Quran),

thereby introducing this *ars nova* into Europe. Subsequently, alchemy would remain a part of western tradition, and it spread like wildfire in the thirteenth century. From the Renaissance on, we see it closely connected with the Hermetic tradition; characteristic is the *Musaeum hermeticum*, the title of a collection of alchemic treatises published in 1625. Rosicrucians and Freemasons adopted its vivid language, and alchemy was still in full bloom in the last decades of the eighteenth century—so much so that in 1785, Kaiser Joseph II saw fit to forbid it in his Austro-Hungarian realm.

Alchemy, the art of transformation, itself experienced several transformations. It led to the "modern alchemy" of atomic physics, which can even create new elements, and to the psychological explanation of the alchemic process as a route to human purification. The latter appeared as early as 1865 with the American writer Ethan Allen Hitchcock, and it assumed its "classical" form in Carl Gustav Jung's *Psychology and Alchemy* (1944), though Jung's sources for ancient Egypt were not the best. Meanwhile, this psychological point of view has opened new ways of understanding alchemy, especially with respect to the writings of Marie-Luise von Franz. In his 1990 Eranos lecture on "stone," instead of a Christian-spiritual intepretation, James Hillman stated: "I prefer to read alchemy, and its goals, as images of psychic conditions always available." Alchemic gold and the process of "turning the world to gold" thus became the image of a condition that imparts the luster of indestructibility to the decay that adheres to all things.

There have also been modern efforts to connect alchemy ever more strongly with ancient Egypt. In his Eranos lecture of 1970, the Egyptologist Helmuth Jacobsohn of Marburg, who was influenced by Jung, wished to recognize the *benben*-stone of Heliopolis as the archetype of the "philosopher's stone," while others have tried to explain the white and red crowns of the Egyptian king as symbols for silver and gold (Edmund O. von Lippmann), and most recently, there have been attempts to recognize the roots of alchemy in the New Kingdom Books of the Netherworld, whose central theme is the renewal of the sun. In particular, what happens in the "Place of Annihilation," where the damned are to be found, along with the corpse of the sun, offers astonishing parallels to the alchemic process. In this place, the sun regenerated itself daily, its light was held and rejuvenated by "the arms of darkness"; in this place the depths of the cosmos swallowed and dissolved everything but also renewed it, and new life arose from decay and putrefaction. It was also the place of expired time, where all the past was present and returned transformed. What was there belonged to nonbeing but constantly passed into new being. Those in search of the "stone" today must descend into this cosmic abyss.

GNOSIS

Creation as Flaw

Gnosis, one of the chief forms of syncretism in late classical antiquity, drew on every area of culture in its day, including the *Iliad* and the *Odyssey*. For a time, it was considered possible that Gnosticism had its origin in Iran, but its Egyptian components received a fresh boost in 1945 from the find at Nag Hammadi, which contained thirteen codices and a total of fifty-two texts. With its origins at least in part on Egyptian soil—Simon Magus, one of its founding fathers, was supposed to have acquired his learning in Egypt—and with Alexandria as one of its most important centers, it also incorporated concepts from pharaonic Egypt. In particular, there were elements of cosmology and cosmogony, such as the primeval ocean Nun and the "outer darkness," both of which were now equated with the Greek word *chaos*, and there was *Amente* (the "west") for the netherworld and realm of the dead, as well as the system of the Ogdoad, which Iranaeus of Lyon knew as *Aqua* (Nun), *Tenebrae*, *Abyssus*, and *Chaos* (perhaps the Egyptian Heh) in his polemic against the Gnostics (*Adversus haereses* I 30, a). It is questionable whether the designation of the highest god as "Hidden One" (*kalyptos*) in many tractates is connected with the creator god Amun; in any case, his anonymity in other texts stands in a good Egyptian tradition, as is also true of the deliberately paradoxical statements regarding the highest god, who is accorded a "nonexistent existence" in the tractate *Allogenes* (Codex XI).

The listing and description of the eons and the archons (depicted with animal heads, following ancient Egyptian tradition) who rule them also draw on Egyptian sources; here, Typhon (i.e., Seth) becomes an archon with the face of a donkey. Above all, there are also the endless emanations that emerge from the nonexistent, ineffable, nameless light-god of the beginning, just as the primeval god Atum separated the first divine pair, Shu and Tefnut, from himself. Along with the primeval father or androgynous "mother/father," there was also a first hypostasis, a female element called Ennoia, Sophia, or Barbelo. A number of Gnostic groups practiced an actual sex cult that can be connected with rites from the Osiris cult of the later periods of Egyptian history. The serpent cult in the Ophite sect of Gnosticism had its origin in the great importance of serpents in ancient Egypt; for this faction, the first Gnostic was the Serpent of Paradise, who was in possession of original knowledge and attempted to communicate it to Adam and Eve.

Gnosticism also employed magical spells, such as those that had to be recited against the archons in the starry spheres during the dangerous ascent to heaven; additionally, there was a mysticism involving numbers and letters that also touched on the world of Egyptian magical texts. In chapter 136 of the *Pistis Sophia*, there is a "great dragon whose tail is in its mouth"; this is the old, familiar symbol of the *ouroboros*. Along with commonalities of cosmogony, including the legend of the Phoenix and the origin of the soul in the sweat and tears of the archons, there is also a stress on knowledge, through which alone, in good Egyptian tradition, salvation and redemption can be achieved; again and again, it is stressed that this is *secret* knowledge. There is also the role of names, which were often formed by word-plays at the time of creation, as at the origin of Ialdabaoth and his sons.

There are also more direct references to Egypt in the Gnostic texts, and not only in the title of the "Gospel of the Egyptians" contained in Codex III and Codex IV from Nag Hammadi. Hippolytus states expressly that Basilides learned his Gnosis in Egypt. Especially well known, and cited by a number of writers, including Augustine, is the passage in the *Asclepius* in which Egypt is praised as the temple of the world and in which the demise of its religion is prophesied. In the untitled text from Nag Hammadi Codex II, which deals above all with cosmogony, we read (170–71): "These great signs appeared only in Egypt. In no other land is there a sign that it is like the paradise of God."

It seems striking to me that there is nothing to be found of the negative attitude toward Egypt that characterizes the Old Testament, notwithstanding the fact that Old Testament concepts constantly play a role in gnostic texts, while their speculations about Seth and the angels are clearly borrowed from Jewish thought. With respect to this Jewish influence, we must recollect that the proportion of Jews in the population of Alexandria in the Roman Period is estimated to have been forty percent. But Gnosticism thoroughly rejected and scorned all laws, especially those of the Old Testament. This attitude gave rise, not least of all, to the charge of sexually licentious behavior that the representatives of the Church leveled against the Gnostics.

The basic belief of Gnosis that a portion of the divine had fallen, had been caught up in matter and needed to be freed from it, is thoroughly un-Egyptian, as is the idea of a Savior. The same is true of the inimical nature of the world, the negative valuation of the visible world as "filth" into which the precious pearls (or gold) had fallen and now had to await a "call" from the realm of light to free themselves again. The gnostic texts attempt to communicate this call, to remind humanity of its origin in the realm of light, which it has forgotten. "Remember that you are a son of kings," the Hymn of the Pearl from the *Acts of Thomas* admonishes humankind. In contrast to the ancient Egyptian wish to enter into the course of the stars to achieve ever-renewed-coming-into-being, Gnostics longed to be freed from the world, to ascend from the realm of being, "not to come into being again," as Hippolytus formulates it. Put in modern terms, the Gnostics were "dropouts," and their movement sought to preserve the esoteric tradition over against the official Church.

But in Gnostic belief, ultimate release would not come until the end of the cosmos, with the annihilation of matter. Since the cosmos originated "through a flaw" (*Gospel of Philip*) or error, the reversal of the error also meant the dissolution of the cosmos, which would be consumed by fire. Only the pure realm of light would survive this end, Nun and darkness would be destroyed, just as light had already existed before the darkness of the beginning and before chaos—"light will return to its root" (so said the untitled text from Codex II). Every Gnostic was a spark from the kingdom of light who glowed in this world of darkness and absent-mindedness; in Christian Gnosis, Jesus became a messenger and savior from the realm of light. Of the apostles, only Judas, the "traitor," recognized the truth and "carried out the mystery of his treachery" (so said Irenaeus); he betrayed Christ because the latter wished to "pervert the truth" (Pseudo-Tertullian).

To a large extent, gnostic writings draw on Old Testament concepts, with God the creator demoted into a demiurge (with the name Ialdabaoth, whose mother is Nun and whose father is Darkness) who is subordinate to the ineffable god of light of the beginning, of whose existence he is ignorant. He is the first of the archons who emerged from chaos and now rule this world, an evil god who cruelly punishes humankind and cannot recognize his own limitations. In his blindness and his pride, he thinks there is no other god but him, but then a voice calls out to him from the "imperishable," that is, the realm of light, "You err, Samael"—a dig at the corresponding assurance of the Old Testament God, "I am the Lord, and there is no other, there is no God but me" (Isaiah 45.5 and 46.9).

The un-Egyptian concept of the wandering of the soul was connected with the Pythagoreans and the school of Plato, but it was widespread throughout Hellenism, as was also the case with belief in the power of fate (*heimarmene*), on which even the archons were dependent, and with belief in the multiplicity of spheres. The express dualism (light and darkness, good and evil, God and matter/world) is oriented toward Persia; gnostic and Manichaean writings (Mani developed his teachings in Iran) concur on this point, and Zoroaster was one of the authorities cited by the Gnostics. The Egyptian descent into the netherworld was transformed into an ascent through the spheres of the stars, which also embodied the power of fate.

Gnosticism was thus a colorful mixture of various religious elements. Its breakup into innumerable schools of thought and sects prevented it from having a widespread impact like that of Christianity, and the movement was left with no future. But in the second and third centuries, Gnosis enjoyed a flowering that would extend its influence beyond the triumph of Christianity; elements of Gnosticism lived on for several centuries in Coptic magical formulas and other Coptic texts.

Gnosis was also granted continued life in the new universal religion founded by Mani in the Near East around the middle of the third century; for a time, its missionary work extended all the way from Spain to China. Mani himself came from an entirely different cultural milieu and was even familiar with Indian concepts; nevertheless, if we are to believe his opponent, Ephraim the Syrian, Hermes (Trismegistus) was an influence on him, along with Plato and Jesus. Manichaeans made their way into Egypt, probably in the wake of the Palmyrene conquest of 269 C.E.; the Manichaean texts found at Medinet Maadi in the Faiyum in 1929 and at Nag Hammadi in 1945 stem from the fourth century. The Manichaean communities in Egypt did not last for long; even the Gnostics seemed doomed to die out, but their ideas resurfaced in the Middle Ages, in particular among the Bogomils and the Cathari. Later, they would be claimed as precursors by the Freemasons and the Rosicrucians, and they would be discovered anew by the Romantics. Gnostic thought lives on today in theosophy and anthroposophy, and it even assumes concrete form in modern gnostic "churches." For Eric Vogelin, modernity is essentially gnostic antiquity; and with his "thrownness" of existence, Martin Heidegger seized on an ancient gnostic buzzword.

HERMETISM

Thoth as Hermes Trismegistus

As we have seen in chapter 1, Hermes Trismegistus was anticipated in Egyptian sources by the end of the second century B.C.E., though the Greek form of his name first occurred in the third century. From around the turn of the era, or shortly after, we have the *Corpus Hermeticum*, of which eighteen texts are preserved, along with a Latin translation of a text called the *Asclepius,* and other fragments in the collected works of Johannes Stobaeus (fifth century) and early Christian writers.

There has been a recent publication of a "Book of Thoth" written in Demotic, the late stage of the Egyptian language used for everyday documents; it was probably written in the first century, but it is preserved on a number of papyri from the second century. It contains a conversation involving Thoth, Osiris, and a student. Thoth imparts information regarding the netherworld, ethics, the sacred geography of Egypt, secret language, and mysteries. The theme of the tractate is decidedly netherworldly, though the genuinely Hermetic route to immortality leads to heaven. Yet the text displays many correspondences with Greek Hermetism, and a mention of a festival of Imhotep alludes indirectly to Asclepius. In one instance, the name of Thoth is qualified by a triple adjective "great" (*wer*), which is tantamount to "Trismegistus."

Along with Hermes Trismegistus, the aforementioned Asclepius—the deified incarnation of Imhotep (Greek Imuthes, Figure 8)—plays a prominent role in this text. In 1926, the discovery of a statue base of King Djoser

8. Imhotep seated with a roll
of papyrus on his knees.
Bronze statuette from the Late
Period. Private collection in
Geneva. Photo by Claire Niggli.

(c. 2650 B.C.E.) inscribed with the names and titles of Imhotep dispelled
any doubts that he was a historical figure. He was believed to be the author of the earliest work of wisdom literature and regarded as the prototype of sages in general. From Dynasty 26 on, he was a god in his own
right, with temples and priests, and people bore theophoric names containing his own. Later, as a healing god, he was equated with the Greek
Asclepius (Latin Aesculap).

The center of his worship seems to have been Memphis, and his tomb
presumably lies under the sands of the necropolis of Saqqara. The successful English archaeologist Walter B. Emery once hoped to find the

tomb; during the 1960s, its discovery was announced in the press nearly every year, but its location remains unknown to this day. There was another important cult center of Imhotep at the temple of Hatshepsut at Deir el-Bahari, which became a center for pilgrims in the Late Period; in the Ptolemaic and Roman Periods, his cult spread to Nubia. A characteristic piece of evidence is the so-called Famine Stela on the island of Sehel near Aswan, which dates to the Ptolemaic era (c. 200 B.C.E.). In the text, a famine causes King Djoser to turn to Imhotep, who belongs to the "priesthood of the Ibis," and in all haste, he obtains the needed information regarding the cause of the flood and conveys it to Djoser. Khnum, the god of the First Cataract, then intervenes and brings salvation, in return for which he receives a major donation.

In the year 46 B.C.E., during the reign of Cleopatra, Imhotep helped the high priest of Memphis Psherenptah and his wife Taimhotep to obtain the son they so longed for, and the infant was named after the god. Previously, the couple had called upon Imhotep in prayer as "he who grants a son to the one who does not have one." At this late date, Imhotep was more highly regarded at Memphis than Ptah, its erstwhile chief god.

In a Greek horoscope from the year 138 C.E., Hermes and "Asclepius, who is Imuthes" are named together, and "Asclepius the Imuthes" is also mentioned in the Hermetic tractate *Kore kosmou*. Clement of Alexandria (*Stromateis* I, 21) knows "Hermes the Theban and Asclepius the Memphite" as men who became gods as a result of their earthly renown, and there is a similar formulation in the writings of Cyril of Alexandria in the fifth century C.E. "Asclepius of Memphis" also appears in a Greek magical papyrus (no. 131) in the British Museum, and Ammianus Marcellinus (XXII, 14, 7) and Hieronymus (348–420) still knew the cult of Aesculap at Memphis. We may also note that Synesius (c. 400) connected his praise of baldness with Asclepius, who as a healing god knew what was healthy and beneficial and who was always represented without the usual divine wig.

The iconography of Imhotep as a seated scribe with a papyrus roll in his lap influenced the representation of Hermes Trismegistus in art. In his monograph on Imhotep (p. 115), Dietrich Wildung cites a description from the so-called Book of Krates (ninth century):

> I saw an elderly person, the most beautiful of men, seated in an armchair;
> he was wrapped in white garments, and in his hand, he held a tablet, on

which a book lay. . . . When I asked who this old man was, I received the answer, "It is Hermes Trismegistus, and the book before him is one of those books containing the explanation of the mysteries that he has concealed from humankind."

There is a more detailed and involved description of this vision (ibid., pp. 110–11) by the Arab alchemist Ibn Umail (900–60). It takes place in a temple, and Ibn Umail begins by describing the winged protective beings on the ceiling and then the reliefs on the walls, whose figures are turned toward a stone image seated in the interior of the temple. On his lap, the seated figure holds a tablet with the picture of two birds that form a circle, like the *ouroboros*, along with the sun and the moon. The statue and its tablet are depicted again and again in alchemic works from the sixteenth and seventeenth centuries. In addition to this ideal depiction of a wise man, there was the fantastic dragon figure of Mercurius (= Hermes Trismegistus) published by Giovanni Battista Nazari in his *Della tramutatione metallica* (On the transmutation of metals) in 1589, depicting Hermes as a mythical mixed form.

The tractates of the *Corpus Hermeticum* purport to be direct communications from Hermes Trismegistus, dialogues of Hermes with his son Tat (Thoth!) or with Asclepius, and there are also dialogues of Isis with her son Horus, as in alchemic tractates. Cosmocritical elements in Platonism are elaborated, and there are considerable similarities to gnostic doctrines (Hermetism has often been designated "pagan Gnosis"), and in the corpus found at Nag Hammadi, along with the gnostic tractates, there was an *Asclepius* and a Hermetic tract on the subject of the Ogdoad (Codex VI). According to a note in this codex, innumerable Hermetic texts in the Coptic language were circulating in Egypt around the middle of the fourth century.

The assumption of a principally Iranian origin of Hermetism, as proposed by Reitzenstein and others, has been generally abandoned, along with a derivation from Greek philosophy. Bruno H. Stricker in particular has favored an Egyptian origin, and he has gone so far as to think that Ptolemy I ordered the recording of old, esoteric Egyptian priestly doctrines, just as the Old Testament was translated into Greek at that time. In any case, it is clear that the *Asclepius* and its apocalyptic prophecy stand in an age-old Egyptian tradition that began with the Admonitions of Ipuwer, the Prophecy of Neferti, and similar texts from the Middle Kingdom and continued down into the Ptolemaic Period with the Potter's Oracle. There are also direct allusions to ancient Egyptian religion. According to the tractate *Kore kosmou*, which above all glorifies Isis, Isis and Osiris found the books of Hermes Trismegistus and passed their contents, the seeds of all culture and religion, on to humankind; the end of the tractate enumerates their beneficent deeds for the world and its inhabitants. Tractate VI 6 from Nag Hammadi was supposed to have been "composed for the temple of Diospolis (i.e., Thebes) in hieroglyphs" and carved on stelae at the behest of Hermes Trismegistus.

There was no single, binding Hermetic doctrine, but a cornerstone of Hermetism was the insight that all knowledge is obtained through revelation, and not reason. Tractate XVI of the *Corpus* is directed against the "verbal din" of Greek philosophy. The concern was to attain the secret lore that had once been revealed by the ancient masters, and the master of all masters was Hermes Trismegistus. The age-old knowledge therefore had to be carefully protected, even though it was no longer comprehensible, for the original revelations were there to be grasped in it. "Practical" Hermetism was thus largely a science of compiling that collected its building blocks from ancient factual knowledge and passed them along; its practitioners thus bustled about like zealous workers in the quarry of knowledge that had accumulated over the millennia.

According to the *Kore kosmou*, the gods endowed the priests of Egypt with three arts: philosophy and magic for the soul, and medicine for the body. The rest is gnostic salvation doctrine. The first human was formed by Nous, the creator of the world. The man himself functioned as a creative demiurge, but he descended through the zones of the planets to the earth, where he was ensnared by matter. Only those who know themselves can free themselves from these bonds, leaving their bodies and reascending through the zones of the planets to the eighth region of the Ogdoad. The highest attainable incarnation is located below the gods of the fixed stars. The gnostic Savior is missing—humans free themselves—and we do not encounter the dualism of the gnostic texts in the *Corpus Hermeticum*. There is a distinction between creator and demiurge, but the latter is not the "evil god" of Gnosis. In the Coptic *Asclepius*, there is an entirely un-gnostic assertion that the cosmos is good (*agathos*), and all of nature is viewed as divine. The goal is formulated thus in *Corpus* I, 3: "I wish to comprehend being and understand its nature and know God."

Hermetism purported to be a religion without temple or cult (in contrast to the Gnostics, who developed cult forms of their own), but it endorsed the still-existing Egyptian temples. László Kákosy has suspected that in the Egyptian temples of late antiquity, there were Hermetically oriented circles that continued to cultivate the worship of Imhotep (as Asclepius). In any case, Hermetic texts were being read in Upper Egypt, as was shown by the discovery at Nag Hammadi. "Books of Hermes" are first mentioned by Plutarch (46–120 C.E., *De Iside* 61), and then by Clement of Alexandria (*Stromateis* VI, 4, 35–37); according to the latter, there were forty-two such books.

Since Hermes Trismegistus was considered to be a man, not a god, even Christian writers could acknowledge him and make use of his doctrines. For Lactantius in the third century, who made extensive use of Hermetic sources, he was a wise pagan who heralded Christ, while for Tertullian, he was the "teacher of all students of nature." We shall return later to Augustine.

The Sabaeans in Harran, who were without a sacred scripture under Islam, in order to count as a "people of the Book," elevated the *Corpus Hermeticum* into such a holy book in the ninth century, thereby contributing to the continued existence of Hermetic texts among the Arab writers. M. Ullmann has published an example of such a tractate, the Serpent Book of Hermes Trismegistus, a dialogue of Hermes with Asclepius. In this text, we are informed, among other things, that his grandfather, the "Hermes of Hermes," built the temples of Egypt and deposited timeless knowledge in them. Other Arab writers offer similar accounts; al-Idrisi (d. 1165) stresses that this was Hermes' way of keeping his knowledge alive after the Flood. In particular, the temple of Akhmim was constructed by Hermes "several years before the Flood" (Ibn Duqmaq, d. 1407), and on its walls, "all the Egyptians' knowledge of alchemy, magic, talismans, medicine, astronomy, and geometry were set down" (al-Maqrizi, d. 1442).

The *Tabula Smaragdina* (Figure 9), also called "Kybalion," which was supposedly discovered in the tomb of Hermes Trismegistus under a statue of Hermes (the discoverer was reputedly Balinûs, that is, Apollonius of Tyana), is today held to be the work of an Arab alchemist of the eighth or ninth century. Its Latin text was first published in 1541, and no less a figure than Isaac Newton composed a commentary on it at the end of the seventeenth century, in connection with his alchemic studies and experiments; it remains unpublished, however, and the manuscript is kept at

Sol pater, LunaMater,
ventus portavit in ventre fuo, terra eius
nutrix eft.

9. Illustration for the Tabula Smaragdina, added to a 1775 Dutch edition published by G. von Welling, *Opus mago-cabalisticum.* Bibliotheca Philosophica Hermetica, Amsterdam. Photo by Thomas Hofmeier.

King's College, Cambridge. Betty J. F. Dobbs, who has drawn attention to this commentary, says regarding the text of the *Tabula,* "Even though this compressed and cryptic composition is world famous, it remains virtually incomprehensible." This ambiguity is entirely artificial.

Despite—or precisely because of—its ambiguity, this brief text counts as a "credo" of alchemy and of all of Hermetism. In it, we read, "true, without lie, sure and most true: what is below is the same as what is above, and what is above is the same as what is below. . . . And just as all things were created by One, all things spring from this One. . . . His father is the sun, his mother is the moon; the wind bore him in her womb, his nurse was the earth."

EGYPT OF THE MAGICAL ARTS

In the Old Testament, Egypt was already a land of magic, a reputation it bears to this very day. There have been attempts to connect all the great magicians with Egypt. Pythagoras has been credited with knowing the Egyptian magicians' art of bringing birds down from the sky, in his case, an eagle. Waking the dead was no problem for an Egyptian conjurer like Zatchlas, of whom Apuleius (II 28–29) writes; the prototype for this activity was the resurrection of Osiris.

There was a particular motif of competitions in conjury, already quite popular in the pharaonic period. We first encounter it in the stories of Papyrus Westcar, and then in the Old Testament competition between Moses and Aaron and the Egyptian magicians (Exodus 7), and finally in the Demotic Second Story of Setne. A Demotic fragment among the Carlsberg papyri in Copenhagen relates a contest in magic between Imhotep and a foreign queen; with Imhotep = Asclepius, we again find ourselves in "hermetic" territory. Saints also triumph over pagan magicians in Christian legends, as when a young Christian maiden defies and converts Cyprian, the great magician and devil worshiper.

Nubians—or "Ethiopians," as they were called—were supposed to be especially adept at magic. In a letter from Amenophis II to his viceroy Usersatet, which the latter "published" on a stela, the king admonishes his old fellow soldier, "Do not trust Nubians, beware their people and their magic." In the Second Story of Setne, Pharaoh himself is magically transported to Nubia, where he is afflicted with 500 blows of the whip; Thoth was obliged to intervene personally to help the Egyptians get revenge by doing the same to the Nubian chieftain. Plutarch related that a "queen from Ethiopia" participated in Seth's conspiracy against Osiris, which surely involved magic.

But the most effective magic was that which came from Thoth himself. It was for this reason that magical names had to be written with "Hermes ink" (PGM I 14), and the First Story of Setne is about the search for a book of magic written by Thoth with his very own hand:

> Two spells are written in it. If you [recite the first spell you will] charm the sky, the earth, the netherworld, the mountains, and the waters. You will understand what all the birds of the sky and all the reptiles are saying. You will see the fish of the deep [. . .]. If you recite the second spell while you are in the netherworld, you will again assume your earthly form, you will see Pre appearing in the sky with his Ennead, and the Moon rising as usual.

Magic came to play an increasing role in medical texts as early as the New Kingdom. Along with love charms, healing spells were the most popular form of magic. But first and foremost, these spells were intended to afford protection, and this goal was served by stelae depicting Horus, which made their appearance in the Ramesside Period and became widespread in the Late Period; the most famous example is the Metternich Stela (Figure 10) in the Metropolitan Museum of Art in New York. Here, as Shed ("savior"), the youthful Horus becomes the vanquisher of all dangerous animals, in particular, the serpent, the scorpion, and the crocodile. The effectiveness of the magic employed by Isis to protect her constantly threatened child, Horus, was supposed to be continually put to the test. A statue of the nursing Isis (*Isis lactans*) in the collection in Vienna has a Horus stela on its back. In the texts on these magical stelae, the speaker is often Thoth, who takes credit for saving Horus.

In one episode from the Metternich Stela, Thoth emerges from the sun barque to help Isis, whose distress had brought the sun to a standstill. This halting of the sun—and thus of time—is still to be found in Christian texts as the *ultima ratio* of the magician, and we also note the tenacious persistence of the old motif of the magician threatening to bring about the end of

10. Magical divine figures on the Metternich Stela in the Metropolitan Museum of Art, New York. From W. Golenischeff, *Die Metternichstele in der Originalgrösse* (Leipzig, 1877), pl. 3.

the world to achieve his goal. Sacred animals were drowned in order to put their dead souls at the service of a desired goal, whether to gain the love of a woman, or to help someone to emerge victorious in a chariot race. "Take a cat, and make it into Osiris by putting its body in water," as it is put in a magical instruction (PGM I 33–34); to this end we also find the invocation of the "cat-faced one," an old form of manifestation of the sun god. In temples, books of magic played a greater role in later periods than they had earlier, for in part, at least, magical protection was obliged to replace the former protection of the state.

New in the magic of the Ptolemaic and Roman Periods was the conjuring up of the dead; there is an example of this in the First Story of Setne. Necromancy had not had a place in ancient Egyptian religion; the dead were left in peace, or at most, letters were addressed to them. Also new were the form and name of Abraxas / Abrasax, who appears on magical gems as a figure with the head of a rooster and serpents for feet; already in the tomb of Ramesses VI, the sun god had been depicted with serpent feet. Abrasax, whom Carl Gustav Jung called a "fearsome" deity in his *Septem Sermones ad Mortuos*, was also a solar god, identical to the supreme deity Iao, the Old Testament Yahweh; the numerical value of the Greek letters of his name, 365, also identified him with time. The origin of Acephalus, the "headless" god who appears in Greek magical papyri and on amulets, is uncertain; Preisendanz wished to see him as Osiris-Onnophris (a form of Osiris). Frequently, we encounter the young Harpokrates ("Horus the child"), as well as the symbols of the *ouroboros* (Figure 11), especially on magical gems, and the *udjat*-eye, with its age-old apotropaic effect.

Especially delightful is a further innovation of later texts intended to gain a serviceable soul, a sort of *ushabti* (mortuary servant) for the living. In papyrus Berlin P.5025 from the fourth or fifth century, an angelic being is conjured up out of a shooting star by means of a falcon's head, and it is now at the disposal of the magician. It repels other people from the magician or subjects them to him, creates wind, provides financial resources, opens doors, makes things invisible, prepares splendid banquets, arouses the love of men, women, and many other beings, and after the magician dies, the helpful spirit takes his soul into the sky, for he is a spirit of the air.

11. Nine-headed cosmic god inside an *ouroboros*-serpent. From the description in a magical papyrus, c. 300 B.C.E. Drawing by Andreas Brodbeck.

In his later years, Lucian (c. 120–85) was a Roman official in Egypt. In his *Philopseudes* ("lover of lies"), he takes up the motif of the "sorcerer's apprentice." He portrays the knowledgeable Pancrates, who had learned the art of magic from Isis herself and could ride crocodiles. He could make objects of daily use come alive and serve him. He would outfit them in human garb, and, like servants, they would fetch water, go shopping, and prepare meals. When their work was done, they would be turned back into inanimate objects by means of another spell. His adept Eucrates took note of the first spell, and in Pancrates' absence, he succeeded in animating a rolling-pin and making it fetch water. But he did not know the spell to make it stop working, with the result that the entire house was flooded with water. In his distress, Eucrates split the rolling-pin with an ax, but now he had two servants incessantly fetching water. Only the return of Pancrates and the correct spell brought the emergency to an end. Goethe immortalized this pretty story in his "Sorcerer's Apprentice" (1797), though for the sake of rhyme, he changed the rolling-pin into a broom.

In the Roman Period story of the deception of Nectanebo, Pseudo-Callisthenes stresses the magical abilities of the last native pharaoh, Nectanebo, from whose reign we in fact have an especially large number of magical texts, among them the Metternich Stela. According to this version, after the Persian reconquest of Egypt, he did not flee to Nubia, but rather to Macedonia. There, his magical arts and astrological knowledge won the trust and the love of Queen Olympias, and, disguised as the god Ammon, he lay with her and engendered the future Alexander the Great.

From time to time, the power and influence of magic led to countermeasures. As early as 33 B.C.E., on the initiative of Agrippa, who was at that time serving as aedile, magicians and astrologers were expelled from Rome (Dio Cassius 49, 43, 5), and according to Suetonius, 2000 books of magic were burned in the year 13 B.C.E. at the bidding of Augustus. In the year 16 C.E., there was another expulsion under Tiberius (Tacitus, *Annals* 2, 32). On his visit to Egypt in 130 C.E., however, the emperor Hadrian met with the renowned magician Pachrates, with whose arts he was quite impressed. In 172, on his campaign to the Donau, Marcus Aurelius profited from the miraculous rainfall caused by the Egyptian magician Harnuphis, for which he showed his gratitude to Mercury (thus Thoth!) by having coins struck. When he visited Egypt in 199, Septimius Severus attempted to remove books of magic from general use by shutting them up in the tomb of Alexander the Great. Even Constantius II (r. 337–61) lived in constant fear of the secret power of the conjurers and the old gods. There were many attempts to stamp out magic, and book burnings as well, which were perhaps the cause of the cache of texts at Nag Hammadi.

Christian Egypt did not eschew the traditional art of magic; characteristically, the famous fifth-century Coptic abbot Shenute viewed Jesus above all as a great magician and miracle worker who, for instance, conjured up a ship for him in the midst of the desert. Jesus had already been invoked in pagan magical spells, even as Jesus Anubis; later, we shall note the equation of Bes and Christ in a Coptic magical text. In another text from the seventh century, as "Jao Christos Pantokrator," he is evidently equated with the mighty god Petbe, embodiment of "requital," for after allusions to his birth, death, and resurrection, the text describes him as a being with the forepart of a lion and the hindpart of a bear, with the form of a falcon and the face of a dragon (Kropp II 152)—only in this fearful form was he believed capable of the magical effect that was desired. The animal-headed deities of the ancient Egyptians also continued to make their appearance in Christian magic.

There was an obvious analogy between the Horus child and the baby Jesus and the care they received from their sacred mothers; long before Christianity, Isis had borne the epithet "mother of the god." The mixing of disparate elements that characterized Hellenism continued into Christianity in magic. Thus, in one magical spell, demons are expelled in the name of the God of Abraham, Isaac, and Jacob (Old Testament), and in the name of Jesus and the Holy Spirit (New Testament), and in the texts that follow on the same papyrus, with the help of the Greek Aphrodite, the Egyptian sun god Re, and the constellation of the Big Dipper (originally Chaldean!). Even the Sumerian goddess Ereshkigal received renewed veneration in Hellenistic magic.

The power of Egypt's magic, along with the ancient Egyptian gods, were conjured up in the temptation of St. Anthony, who resisted and overcame them. The entire problematic of the tenacity of the pagan deities emerged yet one more time in his battle with the demons.

Adolph Erman assigned an eighth century c.e. date to a find of Coptic magical papyri in the Faiyum, in which, among other things, a fully Egyptian story is told about Horus, who climbs a mountain and catches birds: "He cut it (the bird) open without a knife, cooked it without fire, and ate it without salt." Small wonder that he comes down with a stomach ache and calls on his mother Isis for help. Wishing to send a demon messenger to her, he asks each demon, "How long will it take you to go, how long to come back?" The first needs two hours each way and is naturally too slow. Only the one who answers, "I go with the breath of your mouth and come back with the breath of your nose" is fit for use. He finds Isis like an alchemist at a copper oven on the mount of Hermopolis, and she tells him the incantation that will heal her son. By way of a Christian alibi, the speech of Isis is followed by the assurance, "It is I who speak, the lord Jesus, who grants healing."

Even in Coptic love charms, the magician slips into the role of Horus and complains to his mother Isis about how he found seven maidens by a spring: "I wanted, but they did not want," and "I wanted to love NN, the daughter of NN, but she would not receive my kiss"; at the end is the incantation that NN "spend forty days and forty nights joined to me, like a bitch to a hound, like a sow to a boar" (Kropp II 6–8). In other spells, there is yet again the threat of an end to the world if the spell does not succeed, the sun and moon will be halted in their course, and the magician is even prepared to descend into the netherworld (Amente). New, however, is the threat to call on Satan for help—the Egypt of old had certainly not known this "counter-god."

In the Quran, Egypt often makes its appearance as a land of powerful sorcerers, and many medieval Arab authors viewed the Egyptian temples as structures dedicated to the teaching and practice of magic. Among Muslim Egyptians, widespread fear of protective spirits and their vengeance contributed much toward the preservation of ancient Egyptian monuments from destruction.

The medieval cabala, which often conjured up powerful spirits, purported to be a magical art. According to a famous passage in the Talmud, of the ten measures of magic that had come into the world, Egypt received nine and all the rest of the world only one (Qid 49b). Small wonder that even in the sixteenth century, Amun of No, that is, the Theban Amun, was still being conjured up as a sort of supreme devil. Already among the magical words in the Greek papyri, along with the many incomprehensible names, we find that of Amun, which also appears as Ammon in the Hermetic tractates. As early as the New Kingdom, Papyrus Leiden I 350 had stated, "the crocodile is powerless when his name is pronounced" (chapter 70).

In Johannes Spies' *Volksbuch* about Doctor Faust (1587), the great magician is credited with a visit to Cairo; because of the mention of an "Egyptian sultan," this must have been before 1517. Anubis, with a spotted dog's head and floppy ears, is one of the seven supreme devils with whom Faust has to deal. Even the crowning act of ancient Egyptian sorcery, the ability to reattach a severed head, occurs in the book. Within a few years, it experienced many editions and translations, one of them (1588) into Low German by Johann Balhorn, who parodied it.

A fine example of the enduring prestige of the magical land on the Nile is the comedy *A Bold Stroke for a Wife* by Susannah Centlivre (1667?–1723), which was performed in 1718 in Lincoln's Inn Fields Theatre in London. Among the guises of its hero, Colonel Fainall, is that of an Egyptian globe trotter equipped with a magical belt that makes its wearer invisible. In his collection of folk tales entitled *Dschinnistan* (1786–89), Christoph Martin Wieland presented a caricature of an Egyptian sorcerer with the pompous name of Misfragmutosiris, who wears a pyramid-shaped hat and a star-studded cloak. We may also mention the Egyptian sorceress Aithra in Hugo von Hofmannsthals' libretto for the opera *Die ägyptische Helena* (1926) and the magical scene with Tabubu in Thomas Mann's *Joseph*.

A recent example of ancient Egyptian magic is the modern belief in "Pharaoh's curse," which credits the ancient Egyptians with unimaginable magical powers that work their effect to this very day, spreading death and terror. This belief was sparked by the sudden death of Lord Carnarvon in 1923, after his discovery of the tomb of Tutankhamun. But the motif is already to be found in the work of Arthur Conan Doyle (1859–1930), the creator of Sherlock Holmes, in his thriller entitled *The Ring of Thoth* (1890). The novel tells of a mummy's return to life and a "ring of Thoth"—thus, once again, Hermes Trismegistus.

A typical representative of modern belief in Egyptian magic is Philipp Vandenberg, with his book *Der Fluch der Pharaonen* (1973; trans. into English by Thomas Weyr as *The Curse of the Pharaohs*, Philadelphia, 1975), which bears the brazen blurb, "Licht in das Dunkel der Fluchlegende" (Light on the darkness of the legend of the curse). We read further: "Six thousand year old papyri tell of arcane matters: the number of those who died mysteriously while building the pyramids was legion." The most important peg for the curse is the aforementioned Lord Carnarvon, who cut himself shaving and died of blood poisoning, in fact shortly after the discovery of Tutankhamun's tomb; when he died, the lights went out in Cairo, though anyone who travels to Egypt has experienced power failures often enough. And when Vandenberg lists, among those who—according to the jacket copy of the English-language edition—"died an untimely (or) inexplicable" death after the discovery (along with Breasted and Winlock), Sir Alan Gardiner (p. 24), he makes a grave error, for Gardiner did not die until 1963, at the age of eighty-four. Sir Flinders Petrie, who died "unexpectedly and mysteriously" (p. 223) at the age of eighty-nine (!), is also not exactly a good example; in 1963, his assistant, Margaret A. Murray, published her autobiography, which was entitled *My First Hundred Years*. All in all, there is so little raw material for the alleged "curse" that Vandenberg is obliged to pad his book with every anecdote he can find from the long history of ancient Egypt and its modern rediscovery, including the supposed mummy on the *Titanic* and the medium Rosemary—amusing, but trivial, and all in all, best shelved among the detective novels.

Egypt has proved to be a peculiarly attractive and fertile theme for thrillers. Along with Conan Doyle and (of course) Agatha Christie (*Death Comes as the End*, 1932), who also wrote a play about the famous pharaoh Akhenaten, we must also mention the genuine Egyptologist Elizabeth Peters and her novels *The Jackal's Head* (1968, with an attempted murder in a royal tomb), *Crocodile on the Sandbank*, or *The Last Camel Died at Noon*. At this writing, I have just seen the announcement of a new detective novel, *Die Osiris-Morde* (The murder of Osiris), by Morten Harry Olsen, in which it takes an Egyptologist to solve the case of a serial killer. Egypt will surely continue to be a productive source for this genre.

THE SPREAD OF EGYPTIAN CULTS

Isis and Osiris

The beginnings of the "Isis mission," as it has been called, can be placed no later than the fourth century B.C.E. A temple of Isis at Piraeus is attested as early as 333–32, but the worship of the Libyan Ammon, the oracular god of Siwa Oasis, came to Greece as early as the sixth century. Pindar (c. 520–446) composed a hymn to him (fragment 36), and we have many attestations from fourth-century Athens and Attica. We must view this situation as the background of Alexander the Great's visit to Siwa to confirm his status as son of Ammon. At a later date, veneration of Jupiter-Ammon flourished in Italy and Spain, where he was sometimes also identified with Sarapis.

Under Ptolemy I, Sarapis (Figure 12) was "imported" to Alexandria; his cult statue was purportedly brought there from Sinope in Asia Minor because of a prophetic dream. From the very beginning, he was the personification of Osiris, who was at this time not only ruler of the netherworld and the dead but also the sun god. In the Roman Period, his identification with Zeus and Jupiter made him into the *cosmocrator*, the "all-lord." He was represented as a Greek god, but occasional depictions of him with the head of Zeus wearing an Egyptian *atef*-crown show that he embodied the two great gods, Zeus and Osiris. Important stimuli toward his worship also came from his association with Isis, who was now also garbed in Hellenistic style, while her escort, the "yapping Anubis" (Vergil), tended to her "exotic" element.

12. Head of Sarapis bearing a basket with ears of grain wound around it (*kalathos*). Ancient painting on wood, c. 180 C.E. J. Paul Getty Museum, Malibu. Photo courtesy of Archiv für Kunst und Geschichte, Berlin.

In Egypt of the Late Period, Isis had already achieved the status of a universal goddess who absorbed the essence of many others, such as Nut (the sky goddess), Hathor, and Maat. In an inscription from Capua, Isis is called *una quae est omnia*, "the one who is all," and according to a hymn of Isidorus of Narmuthis (first century B.C.E.), she was worshiped by all peoples under various names. As "Mistress of the Sky" and embodiment of cosmic order, she controlled the power of fate itself, thus achieving supreme importance for all who desired to escape the relentless forces of destiny. Zeus had no power against fate, but Isis did! She also guaranteed success and prosperity in her old role as protective goddess and helper of those in need. As the *victrix* who had overcome the enemies of Osiris, she bestowed victory and triumph upon all, thus attracting the worship of ordinary Roman legionaries. The epithet *regina* designated her as queen of the universe. She was also the divine mother of the child Horus (*Isis lactans, Isis nursing*), and many statuettes and amulets depict her as protectress of mother and child.

As Isis-Sothis riding on a dog, she was guarantor of the Nile inundation and thus the fertility of Egypt and all the Roman world. Her ancient significance for the Egyptian calendar was reflected in her role as mistress of the New Year. New, however, was her function as *Isis pelagia* (maritime Isis), protectress of seafaring and mistress of the sea, for the sea had played no particular role in the Egyptian concept of the world.

In the Greek aretalogies (texts in which a deity proclaims himself or herself) attested from the first century B.C.E. on, Isis makes statements such as, "I was raised by Hermes" and "I invented writing with Hermes." But Thoth had little to do with the late cult of Isis. This had in part to do with the fact that Anubis had assumed the functions and attributes of Hermes-Thoth, to the point of making his appearance as "Hermanubis." Some scholars have seen a precursor of this phenomenon in the figure of Thoth wearing "jackal slippers," but the latter are probably to be connected with the jackal-god Wepwawet ("Opener of the ways").

The worship of Anubis was well established in the sanctuaries of Isis, with the god in third place, ranking behind Isis and Sarapis. As guide of the souls of the deceased, he connected this world with the next, where he also functioned as gatekeeper and ferryman. From the New Kingdom on, he was also considered to be son of Osiris and thus often appeared in the role of Horus. The latter's role was practically confined to that of Harpokrates ("Horus the child"), whose childish gesture, with his finger to his mouth, was interpreted as a mystical gesture of silence; but Harpokrates was also identified with Eros and with the club-wielding Heracles, with whom he shared the function of overcoming dangerous animals.

Osiris, who had been replaced as *cosmocrator* by Sarapis, retained his status as ruler of the afterlife. His discovery and worship were represented in the Iseum (Isis sanctuary) at Pompeii. His identification with the Nile, which became more important at this time, took concrete form in the cult image of Canopus, a jug with the head of Osiris, which appeared on coins of the first century and was once again venerated in the Renaissance; the jug's designation as Canopus goes back to Herwarth von Hohenburg (1553–1622), and it was subsequently adopted by Athanasius Kircher. Statuettes of Osiris are attested from throughout the Roman world.

The Apis bull, in his capacity of god of fertility, was also worshiped in the temples of Isis. Further, we must take note of the Nile as a deity who was popular in Rome as provider of grain provisions. Vespasian had a statue of the Nile set up in the temple of Pax at Rome, and both the Nile and the Tiber were venerated in the Iseum Campense.

Outside Egypt, freed of its connection with the central figure of Pharaoh, the Isis cult developed new forms. Alongside the priests and their assistants, there now appeared a congregation, something lacking in Egyptian religion, which was organized as a state cult. The deities were clothed in Hellenistic garb, so as to "modernize" them, or they were represented as legionaries or on horseback, and Anubis was sporadically depicted as an emperor mounted on a horse.

The spread of the cult of Isis began in the fourth century B.C.E. That was when, as already mentioned, a temple was founded at Piraeus and another circa 300 at Eretria; others followed on the islands of Delos, Rhodes, Cos, Samos, Lesbos, and Cyprus, and also at Ephesus. At Athens, the cult of Isis lasted until the fourth century C.E. In the western Mediterranean, Sicily was first to have an Isis cult, followed in the second century B.C.E. by the Italian mainland, in particular Pompeii; at this time, Pozzuoli already had a Serapeum of its own. The cult of Isis is attested at Rome as early as Sulla (88–78 B.C.E.), and Isis sanctuaries were gradually established in nearly all the provinces of the Roman empire. In particular, it spread via river valleys that were important trade routes, such as the Rhone valley in Gaul, and in Germany, the Rhine valley as far as Cologne. It eventually reached northwest Holland and England (there was an Iseum in London and a Serapeum in York), and Hungary in the northeast; additionally, it spread to north Africa and Spain.

In 1997, the great Isis exhibit in Milan impressively documented that goddess' sanctuaries in Italy. Best known, of course, is the rich material from Pompeii, where the wall reliefs of many houses display Egyptianizing motifs and even Greek myths were given Egyptianizing touches, such as Io as Isis, Europa's bull as Apis, and Narcissus as the drowned Osiris.

The fact that an Iseum or Serapeum was often outfitted with original works from Egypt provided further stimulus for the transport of monuments from Egypt, which became intensive immediately after the conquest of the land by Augustus in 30 B.C.E. This involved not only obelisks (the first two were taken to Rome in 12 and 10 B.C.E.) and statues but also objects of more modest size that served as visible proof of Egypt's religious charisma. From as late as the reign of Constantine, we have a Horus stela that was set up next to a statue of Isis-Fortuna on the Esquiline Hill; it testifies to the enduring belief in the healing power that emanated from such magical stelae, and others have been found outside Egypt, in places such as Byblos, Meroe, and Axum. A new phenomenon was the erecting of "Egyptian" buildings in Rome and other places in Italy; the early Augustan pyramid that served as the funerary monument of the praetor and tribune of the plebs Gaius Cestius Epulo (Figure 13), along with the other pyramids of Rome, served as models for the depiction of pyramids in the Middle Ages and the Renaissance. Thanks to these Roman models, Egyptian pyramids were for a long time represented as being too steep.

Trips to Egypt became fashionable in the immediate wake of the conquest of the land. Vergil probably accompanied Maecenus to the Nile as early as 29–28 B.C.E., and Strabo went there a little later. In 19 C.E., Germanicus even went to Thebes, where he was guided by an elderly priest. Seneca had a rather long stay (19–31 C.E.) with his uncle, the prefect Gaius Galerius. At the beginning of the second century, Juvenal commanded the Roman garrison at Aswan. Later, as we learn from the graffiti they left behind, visitors came from all parts of the Roman empire, even from Gaul and Spain. One of the last prominent travelers was Ammianus Marcellinus, who journeyed to the Nile in the 370s. The center of their interest was the Valley of the Kings, where innumerable graffiti left by ancient tourists have been found in some of the tombs, but the pyramids were also visited—in 1335, Wilhelm von Boldensele was still able to copy a Latin inscription on the pyramid of Cheops that stemmed from the time of Trajan or Hadrian.

Further developments were stamped by the differing attitudes of the individual Roman emperors toward eastern cults. Augustus was rather put off by them, with his bitter enmity toward Cleopatra of course playing a role in shaping his attitude. But that did not prevent him from associating his tomb and the Ara Pacis with a gigantic sundial, which Edmund Buch-

13. The pyramid of Cestius in Rome. From an engraving by Giovanni Battista Piranesi, *Le antichità romane* (Rome, 1784), vol. 3, pl. 40.

ner has styled "the largest clock of all times"; its gnomon was an obelisk of Psammetichus II from Heliopolis, to be found today on the Montecitorio. Buchner was able to find part of the sundial's network of lines in the cellars of Roman houses. The entire layout was a huge horoscope filled with cosmic symbolism that centered on the conception and birth of Augustus.

Augustus' daughter Julia was wild about Egyptian motifs, which she used in the decoration of her villa at Boscotrecase. Tiberius was staunchly opposed to all eastern religions, including Judaism; the affair of Mundus and Paulina led to a first persecution and to the destruction of the Iseum Campense on the Campus Martius. But Caligula did a complete about-face, passing himself off as a pharaoh (to the point of marrying his sister Drusilla!) and even considering making Alexandria his new capital. He brought another obelisk to Rome, the one that now stands in front of the Vatican; it was actually intended by the first prefect, Gaius Cornelius Gallus, as a victory monument. Caligula was also the first emperor to plan a journey to Egypt, but he was assassinated before he could embark.

Claudius was also positively disposed toward Egyptian religion, and Nero expressed interest in the sources of the Nile. Nero also had an Egyptian teacher, Chaeremon, who saw to the dissemination of Egyptian knowledge at Rome. According to Suetonius, Otho (69 C.E.) was the first Roman emperor to participate publicly in the cult of Isis. Notwithstanding his well-known stinginess, Vespasian dedicated a large statue of the Nile to Rome, after a Nile miracle occurred during his visit to Alexandria in the year 69. Together with his son Titus, he spent the night before their triumph over Judea (71 C.E.) in the temple of the Roman Isis, which was first depicted on Roman coins that year. Titus is probably the anonymous "pharaoh" depicted in front of the Apis bull in the catacombs of Kom el-Shuqafa in Alexandria. From the reign of Domitian on, Apis was represented on imperial coins.

In his youth, Domitian had escaped Vitellius' pursuit disguised as a priest of Isis, so he had every reason to declare his gratitude to the goddess. During his principate, the Iseum of Beneventum was erected, with Egyptian artists collaborating in its decoration, and the Iseum of the Campus Martius was renovated and embellished with a number of statues of Egyptian origin. Domitian had himself represented as a pharaoh in reliefs and statues, and the hieroglyphic inscriptions on the two small obelisks in Beneventum were composed in his honor.

Trajan and Hadrian were represented in the temple of Esna doing a cultic dance before the lion-goddess Menhyt; the dance was part of a ritual aimed at propitiating this dangerous deity. As Serge Sauneron has demonstrated, the temple experienced an intellectual heyday at this time. Hadrian promoted Alexandrian religion, as shown especially by coins; yet the small Serapeum at the temple of Luxor, which was erected in 126 C.E., also stems from his reign. When he visited the resonating Colossus of Memnon at Thebes, it was still known that it dated to Amenophis (III); a papyrus from Tebtunis testifies that in the reign of Antoninus Pius, knowledge of the ancient writing system was still a prerequisite for admission to priestly office.

But above all, after the voluntary sacrifice of his lover Antinous in the Nile during his visit to Egypt in 130 C.E., Hadrian founded Antinoopolis in the Hermopolitan nome, the nome of Thoth-Hermes, to whom one of the four sides of the obelisk of Antinous was dedicated. Erich Winter has demonstrated that the sacrifice of the Bithynian youth and his representation on the obelisk of Antinous at Rome, where he appears before the gods three times instead of Hadrian, were connected with concepts regarding the age-old Egyptian *sed*-festival, which served to rejuvenate and renew Pharaoh ("Hadrianus ren(atus)" on coins). Statues depict Antinous, who was certainly no emperor, as a pharaoh. The deification of Antinous had an effect down into the fifth century and in the Renaissance, Raphael Christianized him as Jonah.

Egyptian motifs continued to appear on Alexandrian coins under Hadrian's successor, Antoninus Pius, and the Isis cult received considerable state support under Commodus, who personally carried the statue of Anubis in festival processions. In 199 C.E., after his war against the Parthians, Septimius Severus visited Egypt; he was the last emperor to make a stay in Thebes, where he had the Colossus of Memnon repaired, thus silencing its resonating at dawn. According to Dio Cassius (75, 13), "he took all the books with secret content (magical and alchemic texts?) from nearly all the sanctuaries," and he evidently had them shut up in the tomb of Alexander the Great, "so that in the future, no one would be able to catch a glimpse of his body or read what is written in those books." The emperor was successful in both respects: knowledge of the tomb and the writings was lost.

Caracalla had himself represented as a pharaoh in his statuary; Sarapis appeared on Roman coins during his reign, and Alexander Severus was also a devotee of Sarapis. Afterward, there was a general decline; other eastern cults became prominent, and Christianity gained ground. Diocletian, who decorated his palace in Split with sphinxes and other Egyptian works of art, distrusted the secret lore of the Egyptians and had their alchemic writings burned; but in the fourth century, Isis and Sarapis were still being worshiped. Julian the Apostate enjoyed playing the role of Sarapis, and in the year 362, he had a last Apis bull enthroned with all due pomp. Eusebius reports that during the final struggles between Christianity and paganism, Licinius surrounded himself with Egyptian soothsayers, magicians, and priests.

The cult of Isis, one of the last bastions of paganism, came to an end after Theodosius forbade the practice of the pagan cults in 391 C.E., the very year that the Serapeum of Alexandria was pillaged and closed. Nevertheless, their zealousness against paganism did not prevent the Christian emperors of Rome from continuing to decorate their capitals with obelisks; the Lateran obelisk was erected in the Circus Maximus in 357, and in 390, the obelisk in the hippodrome of Constantinople was set up by Theodosius. As late as the fifth century C.E., we hear of the existence of pagan temples in Egypt, and of an Isis festival celebrated by peasants in the north of Italy. Political considerations kept the temple of Isis at Philae open into the sixth century, and it was not closed until the reign of Justinian, between 535 and 537. It is from Philae that we have the last hieroglyphic and Demotic inscriptions.

NINE

MEDIEVAL TRADITIONS

The triumphal spread of Isis and Hermes, which had reached its apogee, was slowed down by the triumph of Christianity, though the early Church fathers, beginning with Clement and Tertullian, still sought to make use of the authority of Hermes Trismegistus and remained captivated by Egyptian wisdom. But it is thought that when the Hermetic writings were collected in the Byzantine era, there was a negative selection, and much Egyptian and other pagan material was eliminated, with the result that it has been lost to us, and the *Corpus Hermeticum* probably took on a somewhat different coloring. Nevertheless, the Hermetic tradition remained alive in the Middle Ages, thanks especially to Arabic (and also Armenian and Syrian) authors and to alchemy, which was tolerated because it continued to be interesting and promising.

Notwithstanding its superficial rejection of everything pagan, early Christianity was deeply indebted to ancient Egypt. In particular, the lively picture of the ancient Egyptian afterlife left traces in Christian texts; thus, among the Copts, and later in Islam, we encounter a fiery hell quite like that of the Egyptians (Figure 14). The *descensus* of Jesus, which played no role in the early church, was adopted into the official Credo after 359, thanks to apocryphal legends that again involved Egypt. Christ became the sun in the realm of the dead, for his descent into the netherworld had its ultimate precursor in the nightly journey of the ancient Egyptian sun god Re; the daily rebirth of the god from the sky goddess Nut lived on in the Christian motif of the Madonna Platytera.

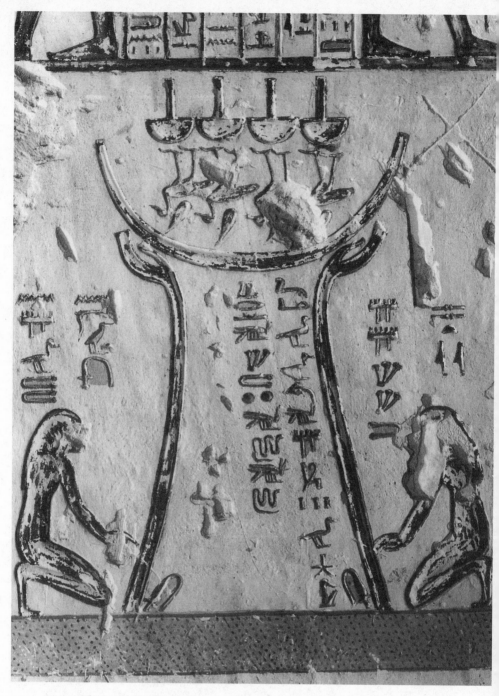

14. Punishment of the flesh, souls, and shadows of sinners in a cauldron. Book of Caverns in the tomb of Ramses VI (1140 B.C.). Photo by E. Hornung.

In the gnostic *Pistis Sophia*, sins are punished in the "outer darkness," which makes its appearance as a huge, twelve-part (!) *ouroboros* dragon, and the places where the punishment takes place are ruled by animal-headed archons. There was also St. Anthony's struggle with the demons of ancient Egypt, which were ever and again the great "temptation." The Christian slayer of the dragon had its model in the triumph of Horus over Seth, and there was a smooth transition from the image of the nursing Isis, *Isis lactans*, to that of *Maria lactans*. The miraculous birth of Jesus could be viewed as analogous to that of Horus, whom Isis conceived posthumously from Osiris, and Mary was closely connected with Isis by many other shared characteristics.

It was only in the long term that the doctrines of the official church were able to prevail over the cherished customs of popular belief. Mummification thus continued in Christian circles, and it was only Islam that brought it to an abrupt end. What the famous abbot Shenute (d. 451) had to say about the intactness of the body at the resurrection is characteristic: "Even if your eyes are put out, you will rise up with your eyes at the resurrection. . . . Even if your head is cut off, you will rise up with it . . . the little finger of your hand will not be missing, or the little toe of your foot." This perfection of the body, immaculate in the narrowly Egyptian sense, was retold in many Coptic martyr legends.

Devotion to the folk god Bes was especially tenacious. Amulets bearing his image have been found in Christian graves, and Bes and Christ are equated in a Coptic magical papyrus (Kropp III 10, Pl. 3). Bes was still a mighty and popular oracle god at Abydos around 500. Even in the twentieth century, the inhabitants of Karnak believed in a Bes-like *afrit* (spirit) who would dance at night in the ruins of the temple.

On another amulet, one side depicts the head of Christ and scenes from the New Testament, and the other a winged, youthful god (Horus-Shed) as tamer of crocodiles and scorpions, surrounded by an *ouroboros*, with a mention of the "seal of Solomon" in the text. There was also an association of the passion of Jesus with traditions regarding Osiris, especially in the apocryphal Gospel of Nicodemus, with its detailed description of a descent into Hades.

Many legends grew up around the sojourn of Jesus and his parents in Egypt (Figure 15). He was greeted by dragons and lindworms, whom He affectionately caressed, He caused His mother to wade through a stream without getting her feet wet, commanded a salted fish to leap back into the water, healed the sick with the touch of his diaper, bade graven images to fall from their columns, and so forth. Entirely "ancient Egyptian" was the miracle of the tree, in which a palm bowed down before Mary and her child, so that they might conveniently eat of its fruits, just as the tree goddess in tombs of the New Kingdom had offered her gifts to the deceased. These legends lie outside the "canonical" gospels, but they were often illustrated in Christian art of the late Middle Ages, as on the ceiling of the Church of St. Martin in Zillis, Switzerland. For centuries, Christian artists inserted the Holy Family into a fully European landscape; Nicolas Poussin ("Rest on the Flight into Egypt," 1658) was probably the first to show that the scene took place in Egypt by including an obelisk and elements derived from the Nile mosaic of Palestrina, which had been discovered around 1600.

Naturally enough, Coptic Christians had many legends about Jesus' stay in their land. The goal of the Holy Family was the monastery with the Church of the Holy Virgin at Deir el-Muharraq, nearly forty miles north of Asyut, where they supposedly stayed for three-and-a-half years. But their route continued through Matariya, where an old tradition located the sacred tree, and Hermopolis, the sacred city of Thoth, where they spent a night in the forecourt of the temple. During the night, the idols set up within the temple fell from their bases with a thunderous crash—another favorite motif of Christian iconography. The family was supposed to have embarked at Maadi, which is today a suburb of Cairo, so as to continue their journey to Upper Egypt, but most of their route was covered on foot and by donkey. There arose the question of who sat on the donkey: according to eastern custom, the husband did this, and thus Joseph, but according to Exodus 4.20, Moses had earlier placed his wife and sons on the donkey.

As early as Origen's *Contra Celsus* (I, 28), we enounter the claim that it was in Egypt, and specifically as an adult laborer, that Jesus had learned all the magical arts with which he worked miracles and on which he based his divinity. This tradition also occurred in early rabbinic literature, but it was of course suppressed in official Christianity, and it was Morton Smith who did the service of shedding fresh light on this "Egyptian" background of Jesus' deeds through his careful research. In his book *Jesus the Magician* (1978), he demonstrated how motifs from Graeco-Egyptian

15. "The Flight into Egypt," by the Master of the Passion (c. 1460). Oil on wood. Wawel Royal Castle, Cracow. Photo courtesy of Archiv für Kunst und Geschichte, Berlin.

magical texts are to be found even in the Gospels. He suspects that Matthew's legend of the "flight to Egypt" was directed against these non-Christian legends, while the remaining evangelists make no mention of the Egyptian connection.

The Christian chronologists all relied on the Egyptian priest Manetho and his precise chronological information. But they had no inhibitions about twisting the data as needed to bring it into line with biblical chronology, with the result that they equated Menes with Adam.

The early Church fathers still knew the ancient Hermetic literature, and Augustine, who himself had a gnostic and Manichean past, dedicated several chapters of his *City of God* to Hermes Trismegistus (VIII, 23, 24, and 26; XVIII, 8). He often cited from the *Asclepius*, including the famous passage according to which Egypt was "the temple of the entire world." Augustine criticized the fact that although Hermes already preached "the one true God," he could not free himself from the worship of idols and mourned the approaching end of the (pagan) cults, which he correctly predicted. Though he thus "mixed false with true," for Augustine, he was a "wise man" (VIII, 24) and essentially a precursor of Christian faith:

> He was renowned as master of many arts, in which he also instructed his fellow man, as service for which, after his death, it was desired or believed that he was a god. (XVIII, 8)

We have already made mention of the *Physiologus*, which was probably written in the mid-second century, and its connections with the later Horapollo; Egyptian animal symbolism was spread in the Middle Ages by this collection of tales about animals both real and fantastic, for it was widely read as a sort of popularizing book. Another important author was Plutarch, for his allegorical explanation of the myth of Osiris made the latter acceptable to the Christian Middle Ages. In Boccaccio (*De claris mulieribus*, On famous women), who relied on Diodorus and the Isis aretalogies, Isis was pictured as a culture bearer who taught humankind agriculture, writing, and law. Of the Hermetic writings, the *Asclepius* was available in Latin and read throughout the Middle Ages. Nevertheless, the influence of Egypt was far less at this time than it had been in late classical antiquity.

For the theologians of the twelfth and thirteenth centuries, the "philosopher" Trismegistus was an authority whose opinion they cited. In his *Theologia christiana*, Peter Abelard (1079–1142) knows Hermes Trismegistus as a celebrated philosopher of great antiquity, while for Albertus Magnus (c. 1200–1280), the "Egyptian Hermes" was above all a leading authority on astrology. Adelard of Bath, whom Ursula Sezgin drew to my attention, acquired a knowledge of Arabic in Sicily and made his appearance in twelfth-century England wearing a green mantle and an emerald ring, the colors of Hermes Trismegistus. It is striking, however, that Hermes Trismegistus is missing from the fourteenth century wall painting in Santa Maria Novella in Florence, which depicts St. Thomas Aquinas (c. 1225–1274) surrounded by eminent representatives of philosophy (including Pythagoras and Zoroaster), though Hermes Trismegistus was a philosophical authority for Bonaventura and Thomas as well. The concept of God as an infinite sphere whose periphery is nowhere and whose center is everywhere, which we find in Nicholas of Cusa, Marsilio Ficino, and again in Giordano Bruno, was associated with Hermetic tradition as the "circle of Trismegistus." Belonging more to folk belief were the unlucky "Egyptian days," which went back to the ancient Egyptian valuation of days (calendars of lucky and unlucky days) and played a role in the trials of heretics in the thirteenth century. Hermetic alchemy finally enjoyed so great a popularity that in 1317, Pope John XXII forbade its practice.

Gnosis was a subculture that persisted through the entire Middle Ages. The first heretic martyr, Priscillian, who was condemned by a synod at Saragosa in 380 and executed at Treves in 385, had spread gnostic doctrine in Spain about an evil primal being who created the physical cosmos. He was followed by the Euchites (who were described by Michael Psellus), the Paulicians, and, beginning with the tenth century, the Bogomils, who viewed Satanael as the firstborn son of God who sent the Flood and gave the laws to Moses. From Bulgaria, the Bogomils spread to Bosnia and Dalmatia; they were sometimes influential at Byzantium.

Gnostic groups sprang up in Germany and northern Italy in the eleventh century. The twelfth century saw the rise of the Cathari (the name is attested from 1163 on, but similar heretics are known from Cologne in 1143), a religious movement that clearly adhered to gnostic-dualistic notions. The world was created by an evil being, the demiurge of the Old Testament; for the Cathari, he was a manifestation of Satan, to be avoided like the Cross, an instrument of torture.

These groups were concerned with freeing the soul, which entered new human or animal (thus they were all vegetarians) incarnations, from the prison of the body, and they also believed in the power of destiny and magic. In southern France, this popular movement was supported by the nobility, especially by the Count of Toulouse, and it was defeated only after prolonged struggles. There was a first Crusade against them in 1209, and another in 1255—notwithstanding the considerable distress of the Christians in the Holy Land! The armed movement of the Albigensians, as they were also called, was not ended until the capture of the castle of Quéribus in 1255. The movement continued to flourish into the fourteenth century in the Pyrenees; the village of Montaillou and the documentation of the inquisition that took place there are now well known, thanks to the analysis by Emmanuel LeRoy Ladurie in a study published in 1975. In the Balkans, the gnostic groups died out only in the fifteenth century, under Turkish rule.

We can deal only marginally here with Jewish mysticism, the cabala (literally, "tradition"); it flourished in the thirteenth century but especially after the diaspora of 1492, when the Jews were expelled from Spain. We have already mentioned (chapter 7) the use of the name of Amun in writings of the sixteenth century as establishing a direct link to ancient magical literature. Cabala attempted to furnish an esoteric key to the Bible, indulging in particular in mysticism involving numbers and letters of the alphabet, *gematria*. The fundamental elements of the cosmos were the ten creative numbers (*sefirot*) and the twenty-two letters of the Hebrew alphabet. If, for example, the witness (*ed*), the judge (*dayan*), and the formulation "the righteous and the unrighteous" all have the numerical value 74 (so Abraham ben Samuel Abulafia), for the cabalist, this demonstrates the comprehensibility of the coherence of the world, just as it was demonstrated for the ancient Egyptians by wordplays based on the assonance of certain words. But the level of abstraction reached by cabalistic thought was foreign to the Egyptian mindset. Nevertheless, in later esoterica, we constantly find a link between Egyptosophy and cabala, and the connection between Moses and Egyptian wisdom to be found in many Christian writers is also relevant to our theme.

Even in antiquity, Jewish tradition viewed Moses as an Egyptian and

identical to Hermes (so first Artapanus in the third century B.C.E.) or someone close to him. He was the inventor of writing and philosophy; according to Acts 7.22, he was "educated in all the wisdom of the Egyptians,"
and for Philo Judaeus, he was initiated into the "symbolic" philosophy of
the ancient Egyptians. His identification as inventor of writing was imposed by the fact that he was the first person in the Old Testament to make
use of written material. Just as Thoth held his scribal palette, Moses carried the tablets bearing the Ten Commandments, and the Greeks knew
him as Musaeus. For Apion, against whom Josephus wrote, Moses was an
Egyptian from Heliopolis; according to Josephus, he was raised by
Princess Thermutis (the goddess Renenutet!) and commanded an Egyptian army in Ethiopia. Manetho, Strabo, and Tacitus also considered him
an Egyptian; Manetho polemicized that he was the leader of the lepers
who raged in Egypt for thirteen years before they could be driven out—a
complete reversal of the bondage in the Exodus narrative and the biblical
tradition overall. Jan Assmann has brought this anti-Jewish polemic to
light again, connecting it with the continued existence of Akhenaten's revolution in the "collective memory."

Cosmas, Bishop of Jerusalem in the mid-eighth century, viewed Moses
and Hermes Trismegistus as contemporaries who were initiated together
into Egyptian wisdom, thus rejecting the widespread assertion that the
two were identical. The temporal juxtaposition of the two teachers was
taken up again in the Renaissance, somewhat to the detriment of Moses'
Egyptian origin, though the latter was again featured prominently by Sig-
mund Freud. Jan Assmann has treated this tradition, from classical antiquity down to Freud, in his *Moses the Egyptian*. Freud was the first to connect Moses with Akhenaten and his founding of a monotheistic religion.
"If Moses was an Egyptian, and if he communicated his own religion to
the Jews, it was that of Akhenaten, the religion of Aten," wrote Freud in
Moses and Monotheism (1939). According to Freud, this identification explains the Jews' rejection of the netherworld, in which they followed
Akhenaten, and he explains the custom of circumcision as a borrowing
from Egypt. Kathleen Jenks goes still further in her novel *The River and the
Stone: Moses' Early Years in Egypt* (1977), having Moses derive his wisdom
directly from Kia, the widow of Akhenaten; it was only a short time earlier
that this lesser wife of the "heretic king" had been discovered by Egyptologists.

In the works of the Arab writers of the Middle Ages, Hermes Trismegistus appeared in alchemic texts but also in connection with the pyramids. He was viewed as the builder of the pyramids, with the assonance of the words *haram* and Hermes surely playing a role. Abdellatif had read in Sabaean documents that the two Great Pyramids were the tombs of Hermes and Agathodaimon, and Maqrizi imputed a whole family to Hermes. According to Ibn Batuta, Hermes, sagely foreseeing the Flood, stored all his wisdom for posterity in the Great Pyramid. We shall turn to other Arab traditions in our treatment of the mystique of the pyramids (chapter 17).

We also encounter Hermetic traits in the Grail legend transmitted by Wolfram von Eschenbach (c. 1170–1220); in all probability, Wolfram already had knowledge of the "ars nova," alchemy. The name of the recluse Trevrizent ("threefold knowledge") points to the "thrice great" Hermes. He tells Parzival the story of the Grail, which in one place is defined as "a stone" (469, 3), surely the Philosopher's Stone; but as a sacred vessel, it stands in the tradition of the Isis cult and the veneration of Osiris as Canopus. The formulation *des trachen ummevart* (483, 12) used by Wolfram already points to the image of the *ouroboros*-dragon of alchemy. The piebald Feirifiz, Parzival's half-brother, visits the east, traveling ultimately to India, where the priest-king Johannes acts as his son.

THE RENAISSANCE OF
HERMETISM AND
HIEROGLYPHS

The thirteenth century saw a renaissance of pyramids and sphinxes. Pyramids appeared on Christian graves in Bologna, while sphinxes served, inter alia, as the bases of columns in the cloister of St. John Lateran (after 1222, one of them bearded) and in Viterbo. The Egyptian lions (of Nectanebo I) in front of the Pantheon were another oft-copied model. It has been concluded that the Crusades aroused fresh interest in the east, and in Egypt in particular. For Europe, they opened a new door to the east, through which forms and ideas could work their influence; and in the Hohenstaufen "Renaissance," new attention was paid to the many Egyptian monuments in Italy. In the thirteenth century, the first western representation of the pyramids appeared in San Marco in Venice, but they were believed to be the granaries of Joseph, and thus not part of an esoteric tradition.

The new encounter with Greek literature, particularly in the framework of the Platonic Academy in Florence, awakened fresh interest in the classical accounts of Egypt and its superior wisdom. There was a special focus on late antiquity, an epoch that was thoroughly imbued with Egypt, while classical antiquity remained in the shadows.

Scholars drew on Plato, along with Plutarch, Diodorus, and Iamblichus, and there were also new discoveries: Ammianus Marcellinus and his obelisk translation, discovered in a German monastery in 1414 by the book collector Poggio Bracciolini; Horapollo, whose *Hieroglyphika* was found by Cristoforo Buondelmonti in June 1419 on the island of Andros; and especially the Corpus Hermeticum, which was regarded as the work of a unique wise figure of remote antiquity, Hermes Trismegistus. In 1460, Brother Leonardo of Pistoia brought a codex containing fourteen tractates of the Corpus from Macedonia to Florence, where a new Platonic Academy had been founded the year before at the court of the Medici to resume the traditions of the Athenian Academy closed by Justinian in 529.

In 1463, even before there was a Latin translation of Plato, the director of the Academy, Marsilio Ficino (1433–1499), translated the Greek tractates of the Corpus Hermeticum into Latin at the behest of Cosimo de' Medici. This made sense, for Ficino took the Hermetic writings to be evidence of a philosophy older than that of Plato. He even composed a genealogy of wisdom, leading from Hermes, through many intermediaries, down to Plato. Under the title *Liber de potestate et sapientia Dei* (On the power and wisdom of God), his work first appeared in print in Treviso in 1471 (this was the first heyday of book publishing!), and it experienced sixteen printings, through the end of the sixteenth century, along with many translations. In 1497, he produced a translation of Iamblichus' "Egyptian Mysteries," and his *Opera omnia* (Complete works) were printed in Basel in 1561. The original Greek text of the Corpus Hermeticum was first published in Paris in 1554.

In Ficino's philosophy, which shaped the Platonic Academy of Florence, Plato was the heir of Hermes Trismegistus, Moses, Orpheus, and Pythagoras. In his commentary on the first chapter of Genesis (*Heptaplus*, 1489), Giovanni Pico della Mirandola (1463–1494) assumed that Moses and the Greeks had obtained their learning from the Egyptians, though he also stressed the importance of Chaldean wisdom and cabalistic magic. In his famous speech *De hominis dignitate* (On the dignity of man), he frequently mentions Hermes, along with Zoroaster and the Chaldeans; in his opinion, "all wisdom spread from the barbarians to the Greeks." One had only to look into the traditions of the classical writers, and especially those of late antiquity, who were at that time being newly appreciated and widely read, to rediscover the "ancient theology" (*prisca theologia*). Thus, along with the Bible, there was an even older revelation that could be consulted. For Pico, Agrippa von Nettesheim, and others, even magic had its place in this revelation.

This original revelation and wisdom found pictorial expression in the famous mosaic on the floor of the dome of Siena, created in 1488 by the artist Giovanni di Maestro Stefano. It depicts Hermes Trismegistus as a contemporary of Moses and a lawgiver in Egypt, dressed in eastern costume—a great, dignified, bearded man wearing a miter, called "Hermes Mercurius Trismegistus, Contemporary of Moses." The writing tablet next to him is borne by winged sphinxes. Only a few years later, there were the frescos by Pinturicchio in the Vatican (see the following paragraph); they, too, depict Hermes in the company of Moses and also of Isis. Even more important for pictorial concepts was the bronze tablet called the *Mensa Isiaca* (Figure 16), which appeared in Rome in 1527 and was acquired by Cardinal Bembo; also thus called the *Tabula Bembina*, it is today in the Egyptian Museum in Turin. Its somewhat unusual representations clearly go back to original Egyptian forms, though the hieroglyphs have congealed into pure decoration and yield no comprehensible sense. The *Mensa* was

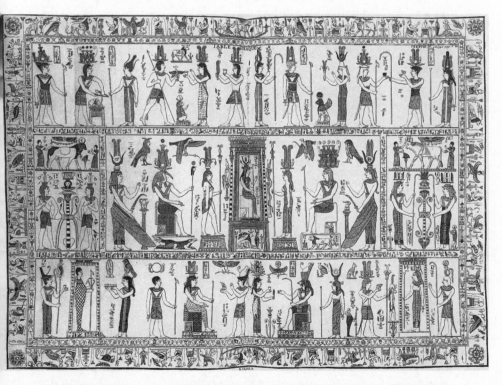

16. The *Mensa Isiaca*, now in the Turin Museum. From B. de Montfaucon, *L'Antiquité expliquée et réprésentée en figures* (Paris, 1719), vol. 2, pl. 138.

apparently prepared in the first century C.E. and was part of the decoration of a Roman Isis sanctuary. Its decorative program, which included the enthroned Isis at its center and many other divine figures, exercised a great influence on the innumerable imitations of Egyptian art that now came into fashion.

In Diodorus Siculus (I, 14–16), we encounter the couple Osiris and Isis as the deities who brought culture to humankind, a point already picked up by Boccaccio. The Dominican Annius of Viterbo (Giovanni Nanni, 1432–1502), secretary to Pope Alexander VI Borgia, included them in a work on the history and chronology of early humankind, so as to circumvent Greece and establish a direct influence of ancient Egyptian culture on Italy and to prove it by means of "inscriptions" that had been discovered. These ideas are also found in the frescos by Pinturicchio in the Sala dei Santi (1495) in the Vatican, which transplant the myth of Osiris to Italy and even equate the Apis bull with the heraldic bull of the Borgia family; in them, we also find Isis teaching science and law. The protagonists of the myth also appear in contemporary Renaissance wall paintings; only Hermes was orientalized by means of a turban when he was admitted into the Vatican.

Even before the first printed edition of a Latin translation of Horapollo's *Hieroglyphika* by Aldus Manutius appeared in Venice in 1505 (one of the earliest Latin translations, by Bernhard Trebatius from Vicenza, was printed in Basel in 1518), a genuine enthusiasm for hieroglyphs had broken out in Europe. In his book on architecture (*Ars aedificatoria*, 1485), Leon Battista Alberti had supplied an impetus to the creation of new hieroglyphs, especially on medals; his symbol of the winged eye is especially well known. He also drew fresh attention to the aesthetic aspect of the hieroglyphs, which had long been forgotten in the fixation on their symbolic meaning. There was also the Dominican Fra Francesco Colonna (1433–1527), with his *Hypnerotomachia Poliphili*, the "dream love battle of Poliphile."

This book, "so often cited and so seldom read" (E. Wind, p. 124), is a celebration of antiquity in the form of a novel that was printed only in 1499, though it was known before then and was probably completed in 1467. It takes place in a fantastic architectural landscape filled with pyramids, obelisks, and colossal statues, with the author making constant use of the accounts of Egypt by classical writers. The woodcuts from the school of

Mantegna used in the printed version became the building blocks of a new hieroglyphic that now sought to encode entire inscriptions, such as a citation from Sallust, "Through peace and harmony (symbolized by a serpent staff), small things (ant) grow, through discord (fire and water), the largest things (elephant) are diminished." Another picture puzzle was supposed to represent a dedication of the Egyptians to Julius Caesar. The motif of an elephant bearing an obelisk (after a Roman original in Catania) was often copied, and pictorial citations from the novel are still to be found in the work of Fischer von Erlach (1721) and even of Salvador Dali (elephants and ants in "Apotheosis of Homer," 1944–1945). The *Hypnerotomachia* was widely circulated in Europe in its day, and it continued to exercise an influence for a long time thereafter. And the hieroglyphic pictures newly created by scholars in the Renaissance were later recopied as "genuine" Egyptian hieroglyphs in the seventeenth century.

Albrecht Dürer (1471–1528) prepared a series of drawings for a Latin translation of Horapollo by his humanist friend Willibald Pirkheimer, which appeared in 1512; as an example, we may cite the "Eater of Hours," which goes back to Horapollo I, 42: "They indicate the *horoskopos* (observer of the hours) by a man eating the hours . . . for meals are prepared for men at designated times." Around 1515, with the help of Pirkheimer and Emperor Maximilian I, Dürer fashioned his monumental (138" × 117") woodcut of an honorary gateway whose purpose was to lend emblematic praise to Maximilian's life and work. It was also provided with a mysterious representation and a detailed titulary of the emperor—according to Pirkheimer, a "mystery of the ancient Egyptian letters, stemming from King Osiris"; the animals that surround the Kaiser are all taken from Horapollo. Hieroglyphs played so great a role in Dürer's work that there was soon a warning: "one must take care not to regard every lion, dog, crane, and so forth in a drawing by Dürer as a hieroglyph." We may also note that in the sixteenth century, hieroglyphs also gained importance for the *Ars memorativa*, a mnemonic technique that employed pictures, especially in the work of Francesco Panigarola (*Trattato della memoria locale*).

Until 1997, the only German translation of Horapollo was that of Johannes Basilius Herold (1514–1567) from Höchstädt, who worked as a proofreader for printing firms in Basel but was not admitted to study at the university because of his low birth. His translation (he also produced a number of historical works), which was printed in Basel in 1554, unfortunately was based on an incomplete Latin translation of the Greek text. It was not until 1997 that Helge Weingärtner published a new German translation, one based on the good Latin rendering of Jean Mercier.

In the year 1556, Henric Petri in Basel issued the work *Hieroglyphica* (Figure 17) by Piero Valeriano (1497–1558), from Belluno in northern Italy; it was the most important collection of the hieroglyphic lore of its time, and it greatly influenced all succeeding work on the hieroglyphs. There were further printings in Basel in 1567 and 1575, and there was a total of sixteen printings down to 1678, as well as a French translation by Gabriel Chappuys in 1576 and a German translation in 1615. Valeriano dealt with Horapollo, and with the *Mensa Isiaca* as well, but he also drew his explanations from the Bible and even made use of the newly-created "hieroglyphs" of the *Hypnerotomachia*, for "moderns, too, have devised many hieroglyphic signs." Around 1530, Giulio Romano included original Egyptian hieroglyphs in the decoration of the Palazzo Tè in Mantua. These "genuine" hieroglyphs played no role in the work of Valeriano, who preferred to translate descriptions by classical writers into visible pictures. An example is the supposed inscription in the temple of Neith at Sais mentioned by Plutarch and by Clement of Alexandria: "Oh, you who are born and die, God hates shamelessness" (Figure 18). But Valeriano had no clear concept of the appearance of a hippopotamus, which embodied shamelessness in Plutarch's account, while for Clement, it was a crocodile. For Valeriano, hieroglyphs constituted a pictorial script that could only be read symbolically, like our own concept of "symbol," which did not come into its own until the work of Georg Friedrich Creuzer.

Basel played a role again in 1574, when Johann Fischart received a doctorate in law there and in the following year published his "Affentheurlich Naupengeheuerliche Geschichtklitterung," a German version of Rabelais' *Gargantua*. Imitating the original, he derides the widespread fashion of making hieroglyphs that "change names and disarrange words," such as a bone (*Bein*) for "pain" (*Pein*), a bed without a teston (*lit sans ciel*) for "licentiate" (*Lizenziat*), an A plus a Moor for *amor* ("love"), or a loaf (*Laib*) of bread plus a goat (*Ziege*) for Leipzig, and so forth.

From Italy, Renaissance Hermetism quickly spread to England, where Thomas More wrote a biography of Pico della Mirandola and depicted a religion with expressly Hermetic traits in his *Utopia* (1516) and also propagated the idea of religious freedom. In Germany, however, Hermetism

17. The hieroglyph for "adoration." From Pierio Valeriano, *Hieroglyphica* (Basel, 1567), sheet 46.

18. Obelisk with a hieroglyphic inscription derived from Plutarch: "O you who are born and die, God hates shamelessness," or, in Valeriano's interpretation, "We are born and we die, we live and we die according to the discordance [represented by a hippopotamus!] of Nature." From Pierio Valeriano, *Hieroglyphica* (Basel, 1567), sheet 219.

found no fertile soil among the Lutheran Protestants. Let us cast a brief glance at some major personalities connected with Hermetism.

Paracelsus (1493–1541), actually Theophrastus Bombastus von Hohenheim, became the city doctor of Basel in 1527–1528, and the first edition of his collected works was published there in 1589–1591. There are constant references to his having made a stay in Egypt, which was supposedly "a chief source of his astounding skills" and in particular, the origin of his magical knowledge. He himself once states, "All such is originally Egyptian." But he seems to have had no connection with real Hermetism apart from the general principle of the correspondence of microcosm and macrocosm. Still, he was regarded as a great authority by the Rosicrucians and by all who were not in agreement with traditional learning, and his adherents constantly referred to traditions that went back to Hermes Trismegistus. Paracelsus attempted to introduce alchemy (as "chemiatry") into the preparation of medicines. His philosophy of nature was summarized by Oswald Croll (c. 1560–1608) in his *Basilica Chymica* (1609, thus on the eve of the Rosicrucian movement), which proved to be a highly influential work.

His great contemporary Nostradamus (Michel de Nostre-Dame, 1503–1566) concerned himself with ancient Egyptian wisdom and with hieroglyphs prior to writing his prophecies in the *Centuries* (which first appeared in 1555); around 1545, he wrote an *Interprétation des hiéroglyphes de Horapollo*, a version of the ancient work on the hieroglyphs in the form of epigrams. In 1968, P. Rollet published the work, based on a manuscript in the Bibliothèque Nationale.

In outlining his new, heliocentric view of the cosmos, Nicolas Copernicus (1473–1543) in one place cited Trismegistus as an authority; the ancient Hermetic writings had already ascribed a central position to the sun, while according to Macrobius, all great deities could be traced back to a *single* solar divinity. In the Corpus Hermeticum, Tractate XVI in particular stresses the central role of the sun, and according to the *Asclepius* (chapter 29), it is even "the second god." For Copernicus, the prestige of Hermes Trismegistus was an important confirmation against the Church, which itself for the most part acknowledged his authority.

Giordano Bruno (1548–1600) went further still, bemoaning the destruction of the "good religion" of the Egyptians by Christianity, which replaced it with "the cult of dead objects, absurd rites, bad moral conduct, and never-ending wars." He defended Ficino against the "grammatical pedants" of his day, and his idea of a boundless, cosmic All was born of the Hermetic spirit. Bruno also picked up the notion of the transmigration of souls through all the realms of the living—human, animal, vegetable, and mineral. In Egypt, Moses had drawn on Egyptian wisdom and magic, and for Bruno as for Manetho, the Jews were driven out of Egypt. The religion of the "all-knowing Egyptian Mercury" was second only to God's original knowledge, and the contemporary French statesman and Protestant, Philippe du Plessis Mornay (1549–1623), also pointed to the conciliatory power of this religion, as opposed to the growing discord of the Christian confessions and their bloody religious wars.

Many other contemporaries revered Hermes Trismegistus as one of the great founders of a religion, but he also had his place among the great natural philosophers. In 1612, G. Crosmann put the likenesses of the ten most famous naturalists, physicians, and alchemists in the bay window of the town pharmacy in the old Hanseatic city of Lemgo. Here, we find Dioscorides, Aristotle, Galen, and Hippocrates; the sixth is the turbaned Hermes Trismegistus, and the tenth is Paracelsus—a beautiful example of how Hermes continued to be treated as a historical personage.

Great art sprang from the soil of these new Hermetic mysteries in the Renaissance, art that took great joy in symbolic encoding. The works "were intended for the initiated, and they thus require an initiation" (Wind, p. 26) Overall, the artists sought to discover or express a secret meaning, and there must have been hermetically-oriented secret societies as early as the sixteenth century, long before the Rosicrucians. Raphael was one of the first Renaissance artists to take up, once again, the timeless forms of the pyramid and the Egyptian sphinx (wearing a headcloth). He also paid fresh honor to the many-breasted goddess Multimammia, who had already been taken to be a form of Isis in late antiquity. His personification of philosophy in the Vatican, visibly displaying the "breasts of Nature," is based on her.

ELEVEN

TRAVELS TO EGYPT

Wonder upon Wonder

There was a seamless transition from the ancient travelers who left graffiti throughout the land to Christian pilgrims who, from the fourth century on, flocked to Jerusalem in such throngs that it was "as though the Holy Spirit were abundantly present only among the inhabitants of Jerusalem, but unable to find its way to us," as Gregory of Nyssa (d. 394) reproachfully noted. The nun Egeria (381–84) and others trod in the footsteps of Moses and Aaron, whom they recognized in a pharaonic double statue in the eastern delta, but they came into contact with the land of the Nile only en route to Sinai and Jerusalem, and they no longer penetrated into Upper Egypt. For the European world, the latter fell into oblivion and would not be rediscovered until the end of the sixteenth century. Even Arab writers seldom mentioned the monuments of Thebes, though the temple at Akhmim, which lay on the pilgrimage route to Mecca, attracted a great deal of interest.

Especially holy to the Christian pilgrims was the Sinai, where Moses received his revelation, and where they believed they saw traces of the ancient Hebrews in the rock inscriptions, which had already been mentioned by Egeria. They knew exactly where the manna had rained, where the Israelites had drunk the pulverized remains of the golden calf, and where the wrathful Moses had smashed the tablets engraved with the Ten Commandments.

The stream of pilgrims did not dry up after the Arab conquest of Egypt and the Holy Land, though trade interests and traveling merchants stepped ever more into the foreground. The pilgrims, diplomats, and merchants were followed by the first real tourist in the person of Pero Tafur from Cordova, who was in Egypt in 1436–1437, and thereafter in various European lands. Like many before him, he reverently viewed the pyramids as the granaries of Joseph, though they remained the southernmost point of his visit. He was followed by many other gentleman-travelers, from the sixteenth century on, who often had scholarly interests. By way of an example, Cyriacus of Ancona, who traveled to Egypt for the third time in 1436, was not only a merchant but also a humanist who zealously collected manuscripts. From the end of the fifteenth century on, Hermes Trismegistus played a role for these travelers, thanks to his rediscovery by the Renaissance. Felix Fabri, the Dominican from Zurich who stayed in Egypt in 1483—where, among other things, he thought he saw a representation of Isis in the Sphinx—spoke of Hermes, but he also used Boccaccio's *Genealogy of the Gentile Gods* as a manual.

Knowledge of the classical writers on the one hand, and of the Old Testament on the other hand, provided many travelers of the centuries that ensued with a preconception that decisively stamped their encounter with Egypt. In this regard, Othmar Keel has made an excellent account of the difference that can be perceived after the Enlightenment and the French Revolution: French travelers brought along their Herodotus, Diodorus, and Strabo, while in general, Englishmen and Americans followed in the footsteps of the Bible, on the lookout, like the early pilgrims, for confirmation of the biblical tradition.

The epochal year of 1492 saw a new motif: the missionary movement of the Bohemian Brothers sent Martin Kabátnik to the east to find the "unspoiled" church that was no longer to be seen in the west. His description of his travels, which appeared in 1518, saw numerous reprintings, and many other travel accounts proved to be best-sellers in their day, bringing Egypt closer to the European public. Within a century, the *Itinerario* of Lodovico de Varthema, which appeared in Milan in 1510, was reprinted about fifty times and was translated from Italian into seven other languages. Many of these travelogue authors did not hesitate to copy from one another.

The Bohemian Brothers were followed by many other missions but with different goals. For the most part, these had to do with establishing contact with the Ethiopian church. In 1622, a Capucine mission was dispatched to Cairo to convert the Copts; they did not achieve their goal, but they were quite active until the end of the century, providing European scholars such as Nicolas Fabri de Peirese with useful information and Coptic manuscripts.

As early as the sixteenth century, we find travelers with distinctly archaeological interests, such as the physician Pierre Belon (1517–1564). Nevertheless, the representations of pyramids (much too steep) and sphinx (as a female bust) in the accounts of their travels had little to do with reality. Among the wonders being brought from Egypt to Europe at that time were mummies. From the thirteenth century on, they were used medicinally as a substitute for the rare and costly mineral bitumen that was employed in wound care. The trade in mummies was especially lively in the sixteenth and seventeenth centuries, and pulverized *mumia* is even mentioned as a remedy in the writings of Paracelsus. The large demand led to formal "excavations" and also to counterfeits: freshly deceased persons, appropriately prepared, were peddled to Europeans as mummies. In 1616, Pietro della Valle (1586–1652) from Rome, who supplied Athanasius Kircher with Coptic manuscripts, dug in a mummy field near Cairo (Figure 19), where the bodies lay in the sand, "one on top of the other, just like macaroni and cheese"; two of the mummies eventually made their way into the antiquities cabinet of Augustus the Strong in Dresden in 1728 via the collection of Count Chigi in Rome.

In 1622, Andreas Gryphius published a study, *Mumiae Vratislaviensies*, about three mummies that had ended up in Wroclaw, testifying to his interest in the rites and sacred customs of the ancient east as well as in the phenomenon of death. The use of *mumia* as a remedy declined in the eighteenth century, yet the price list of the firm Merck in Darmstadt included *mumia vera aegyptiaca* ("genuine Egyptian mummy") as late as 1924. In the meanwhile, mummies had become exotic curiosities, indispensable to any of the collections that were being formed as witnesses to ancient Egyptian culture.

Other objects also found their way to Europe. As early as the sixteenth century, Istanbul was a market for Egyptian antiquities—it was there that for 200 ducats, the imperial ambassador Ghislain de Busbeck (d. 1592) purchased a naophoric statue (a statue of a man holding a shrine) still to be found in Vienna. In 1632, two beautiful Late Period sarcophagi came

19. Excavation of mummies near Cairo in 1616. From Pietro della Valle, *Reise-Beschreibung in unterschiedliche Theile der Welt* (Geneva, 1674), p. 104.

The Sepulchres of the Kings of Thebes.
To the Honourable William Herbert.

20. The Valley of the Kings. From Richard Pococke, *Description of the East*, part I (London, 1743), pl. 30.

directly from Egypt; Kircher made drawings of them, and Lafontaine sang their praises, and they are now in the Louvre. From nearly the beginning, originals were accompanied by fakes and imitations. As early as 1635, Archbishop Laud presented the Bodleian Library at Oxford with both a genuine *ushabti* (mortuary figurine) and an obvious forgery.

But the travelers were interested in more than just mummies and grave goods. They were interested in the still unreadable hieroglyphs, which were presumed to contain the secret lore of the ancient Egyptians. Relatively accurate renderings of inscriptions were produced at an astonishingly early date. One of the earliest examples is the drawing of an inscribed block statue made by Claude Duchet in 1573; it is depicted by Baltrusaitis, and it is essentially more accurate than the renderings made of it in the eighteenth century, such as that by Montfaucon. Here, we are at the threshold of genuine scholarly concern with ancient Egypt, which took notice of the reports of contemporary travelers like Pococke (Figure 20) and Norden, though at first, the scholarship was thoroughly imbued with Hermetism. Michael Vansleb, who acquired manuscripts in Cairo in 1672–1673, was interested in magic, and in 1712 and the following years, in the monastery of St. Anthony, Claude Sicard encountered monks who had devoted themselves to alchemic work. Even Napoleon Bonaparte's scholars were still interested in the esoteric dimension of Egypt.

TWELVE

TRIUMPHS OF ERUDITION

Kircher, Spencer, and Cudworth

It would be impossible to conceive of the beginnings of modern learning without citing Hermes Trismegistus, though shortly thereafter, it turned against him. In 1614, Isaac Casaubon (1559–1614), from Geneva, published his late dating of the Corpus Hermeticum in the framework of his comprehensive critique of Cardinal Cesare Baronius' history of the Church; for Casaubon, the Corpus was a fake created by early Christianity. Hermetism quickly recovered from this blow, and Cudworth (see below) soon objected that Casaubon had generalized too freely; Cudworth maintained that Casaubon's late dating did not apply to the entire Corpus and that the *Asclepius*, for example, contained original Egyptian theology. But Francis Bacon renounced the now dubious Hermes in his Platonically inspired utopia *New Atlantis* (1624), citing only Moses as a lawgiver; the "House of Solomon" also made its appearance in the work as a sort of Academy of Sciences and a predecessor of the Royal Society.

Another major opponent of the Hermetists was Hermann Conring (1606–1681), with his work *De hermetica Aegyptiorum vetere et Paracelsicorum nova medicina liber unus* (On the ancient Hermetic medicine of the Egyptians and the new medicine of the Paracelsists, 1648); a new edition appeared in 1669 under the title *De hermetica medicina* (On Hermetic medicine). In it, he declares that all the books claiming to have been authored by Hermes Trismegistus are fakes. There had probably never been a man of that name, and in any event, the medicine and the other sciences of the

Egyptians had been pure superstition that had been thoroughly super-seded by the Greeks, as was also true of philosophy. With their cult cere-monies and their colorful hieroglyphs, the ruling priestly class had duped the people so as more easily to control them. The motif of priestly decep-tion would constantly play a role in the literature that followed.

Among the portraits of the most important scholars in history that adorn the Aula Leopoldina in Wroclaw (1728–1732) is that of the "Ger-man Archimedes," Athanasius Kircher (1602–1680). Born at Geisa in Hesse, Kircher first attended the Papal Seminary in Fulda; in 1618, he be-came a novitiate in the Jesuit order in Paderborn, and he made use of his studies in Paderborn, Cologne, and Mainz to absorb nearly all the knowl-edge of his time. His first teaching position was correspondingly univer-sal: in 1629, he became professor of ethics, mathematics, and oriental lan-guages (i.e., Hebrew and Syriac) in Würzburg. After the Jesuits were expelled from Würzburg by Gustav Adolf, he taught the same subjects in Avignon, where he came into contact with the French scholar Fabri de Peirese (1580–1637), who had a collection of Coptic manuscripts at his disposal and was interested in the hieroglyphs. A brief intermezzo in Vi-enna as the court mathematician of Emperor Ferdinand II created a last-ing connection with the Austrian royal house, but in that very same year 1633, he became professor of mathematics, physics, and oriental lan-guages in Rome.

As chance had it, in February of the following year, 1634, a typical Baroque festival took place in the Piazza Navona in Rome; it included an "Egyptian" masquerade, and the new professor surely did not miss it. Long known only from a description written in 1635, the festival and the drama were finally brought to light again in 1939, in Ragna Enking's study of Dinglinger's Apis Altar (see below). According to the plot, the itinerant Sir Tiamo of Memphis (he is the hero of Heliodorus' *Aethiopica*, who is there called Thyamis, but now he bears the eloquent name Tiamo) draws the wrath of the gentlemen of Rome down on himself by loudly proclaiming his love for Rosinda. The gentlemen compete against him in a tournament, and then, in a dramatic speech, they inform him that silence is the first commandment of all lovers—but this barbarian from Memphis cannot know that, for he comes from a land where the din of the cataracts has deafened the inhabitants, where Anubis barks like a dog, and where people worship the sacred cow guarded by the hundred-eyed Argus. Four

Egyptian knights of Isis come to help the Romans, and Rome once again triumphs over Egypt, as it had under Augustus.

In Rome, Kircher spent decades in immensely fruitful activity and became the center of the learned world of his day—whoever visited Rome also felt obliged to see Father Kircher and his "museum." Here, under the spell of the obelisks of Rome, Kircher began to grow increasingly interested in the Egyptian writing system and language. He had no great problem in penetrating into Coptic, the latest stage of the ancient Egyptian language, written with the Greek alphabet; Nicolas Fabri de Peirese, Claude de Saumaise, and others had already worked in this area, and in 1629, Coptic type had already been prepared for use in propagating the faith.

The first fruit of those studies was the *Prodromus coptus sive aegyptiacus* (Coptic or Egyptian messenger), which appeared in 1636 and contained the first Coptic grammar. It was followed in 1644 by the *Lingua aegyptiaca restituta* (The Egyptian language restored), which long remained the basic Coptic dictionary; it built on the work of Peirese and the manuscripts collected by Pietro della Valle. Kircher was wrong in his opinion that the Coptic letters were the prototype of the Greek alphabet, but he correctly recognized that Coptic was the ancient Egyptian language. Of his later works, we may mention in particular the *Oedipus Aegyptiacus* (1652–1654) and the *Sphinx mystagoga* (1676). When he died in November 1680, Kircher could look back on thirty-two works written in Latin, comprising 14,000 pages printed in folio format! Lichtenberg rightly proclaimed that "when Athanasius Kircher took pen in hand, a folio volume would flow from it."

In his work, Kircher brought together a remarkably large amount of original Egyptian monuments and made relatively exact descriptions and depictions of them, such as all the obelisks known to him in 200 pages of his *Oedipus*, and even monuments in Egypt that he never saw but of which he had the descriptions made by travelers. His *Oedipus Aegyptiacus* also contained a description of the temple of Isis Campensis in Rome, a chapter "Alchymia hieroglyphica," and a section on the "imitators of Egypt"; this book remained the fundamental, oft-consulted work on Egyptian art, science, culture, religion, and language until the appearance of the *Description de l'Égypte* prepared by Bonaparte's scholars. His collection, the well-known *Musaeum Kircherianum*, which he opened in 1651, was not published until 1790, by F. Bonanni. Kircher's museum was but one of the collections of Aegyptiaca in Rome, which had already begun to be formed in the sixteenth century. In particular, there was that of Queen Christina of Sweden, who settled in Rome after her abdication and built up a collection in the Palazzo Riaro; it was purchased in 1724 by the king of Spain and wound up in the Prado in Madrid.

Kircher believed that he had deciphered the meaning of the hieroglyphs and boasted of his ability to restore missing portions of obelisks and the like. He even drafted "new" hieroglyphic inscriptions, such as the one on an obelisk in honor of Emperor Ferdinand III (Figure 21), a confused mixture of ancient Egyptian sign forms and others of his own devising. The emperor was supposed to be glorified as *Osiris Austriacus* and *Momphta Austriacus* and as a "supporter of the mercurial arts," that is, a follower of Hermes Trismegistus.

For Kircher, the inscriptions contained the philosophical lore of the ancient Egyptians, with the result that he branded as false the obelisk translation of Ammianus Marcellinus, which correctly renders a historical inscription. A. Grimm had some of his "translations," which were composed in a somewhat difficult Latin, rendered into German. These samples can be found in the catalogue of the Munich exhibition "Theatrum Hieroglyphicum: Ägyptisierende Bildwerke des Barock" (Hieroglyphic theater: Egyptianizing works of the Baroque), which was on display in 1995. Here are two examples:

From here, a hidden activity of the holy fish pond distributes matter, through secret motion, to the conception of forms in the nature of things, through the movement of Sol, who pours his sympathetic power out into the fourfold region of the world, whereby the fruitful realm of Momphta (an invention of Kircher!) or the Canubic spirit is bound to the life that benefits the world through the beneficent power of moisture, which the twelve-towered area pours out.

By plan (and) virtue, Thaustus or Osiris will fill the subterranean temple chamber of the sacred Nilotic vessel with an overflow of (all) necessary things, and the fourfold world will be overturned by the fallen owl Bebonia, life will be connected with the overflow of the (Nile) inundation, the moist substance of the world of the twelve-towered area and the great subterranean temple chamber will fall under the rule of the fourfold world.

Elogium hieroglyphicū
FERD·III·CÆSARIS
immortalitati
huius erectione obelisci
æternum consecrauit
A·K·S·I·

21. Obelisk with an inscription honoring Emperor Ferdinand III. From A. Kircher, *Oedipus Aegyptiacus*, vol. I (Rome, 1652), Elogium 27.

For Kircher, Hermes Trismegistus, whom he dated to the time of Abraham (*Oedipus Aegyptiacus*, I, 103), was the inventor of the hieroglyphs and prophet of the *one* God. Kircher's books employ many citations from the Corpus Hermeticum and the *Asclepius*. In ignoring Casaubon's late dating, he writes as a representative of the Catholic Counterreformation against the Protestant Casaubon.

In his book *The Search for the Perfect Language* (Oxford, 1995), Umberto Eco maintains that Athanasius Kircher was the founder of Egyptology. But Jan Assmann has pointed to two other early "Egyptologists" who were contemporaries of Kircher: John Spencer (1630–1693) and Ralph Cudworth (1617–1688). In his 1670 dissertation, Spencer collected, much more critically than Kircher, all available classical information about Egyptian religion for the purpose of shedding light on the Egyptian background of the Mosaic laws and institutions. For him, Egyptian culture was older than Moses, and his contemporary John Marsham seems to have been the first to have tried to fix the chronology of Hermes Trismegistus; he placed him 100 years after Menes and 800 years before Moses and the Exodus, about 2270 B.C.E. (*Canon chronicus Aegypticus, Ebraicus, Graecus, et Disquisitiones*, 1672). Marsham believed he had found the name of the Egyptian god Thoth in the Atothes of the king lists, and thus in Dynasty 1, just after Menes, with whom the succession of historical kings commences.

In his book *The True Intellectual System of the Universe*, Ralph Cudworth promoted the notion of an original monotheism, which was already to be found in the work of Lord Herbert of Cherbury in 1624. For Cudworth, too, Egypt was the original home of knowledge. Relying on Clement of Alexandria, but also on Plutarch and Horapollo, Cudworth opined that in Egypt, there had been an esoteric monotheism for the kings and certain of the priests, into which Moses had also been initiated. It was thus that monotheism came to the Israelites and was proclaimed to an entire people and not just to a small circle of initiates, which is why it had to be safeguarded by strict legislation. According to Cudworth, along with their multiplicity of deities, the Egyptians worshiped "One Supreme and All-encompassing Deity," to whom the formula *Hen kai Pan*, "One and All," could be ascribed. There was thus both a polytheistic popular religion and a monotheism of the learned initiates, a distinction that still had an influence on Georg Friedrich Creuzer as late as 1810. Cudworth also made a detailed treatment of the inscription from Sais rendered by Plutarch, to which we shall return in our discussion of the picture of Egypt in the Romantic period; from the late seventeenth century on, it was the starting point for many representations of the "unveiling" of Nature.

Many seventeenth-century scholars held Osiris and Isis in great esteem. These deities were universal culture bearers who, for example, bestowed the art of brewing beer upon the mythic king Gambrinus. In particular, scholars saw etymological assonances everywhere and connected Paris and many other place names with supposed Isis cults. They even believed they could recognize the Egyptian Thoth in the Tao of the Chinese and in the *teotl* ("god") of the Mexicans and Pharaoh in the Indian king Poros. To this day, much nonsense continues to be perpetrated with such similarities between words!

In the seventeenth century, the rendering of Egyptian motifs continued to be oriented toward classical models, and not original materials from the pharaonic period, of which much too little remained known, notwithstanding the efforts of Athanasius Kircher. Isis was thus depicted in the knotted garment of the Hellenistic Isis, Anubis with floppy ears (Boissard), and Osiris with a falcon's head; the sistrum was changed into an astrolabe, and so forth. Many ancient coins served as models, but in the case of Anubis, there was probably St. Christopher, with his dog's head.

This Hellenistic picture also included the Nile mosaic of Praeneste (Palestrina, Figure 22), which was excavated around 1600. The only things still lacking were the paintings in the temple of Isis in Pompeii, which was first excavated in 1765–1766. Nicolas Poussin included elements from the Praeneste mosaic in his painting "Rest on the Flight into Egypt" (1658). We have already noted (chapter 9) that he was the first artist to place the endlessly-depicted motif of the flight to Egypt in an Egyptian setting, employing temples and an obelisk; as early as 1645, in "The Finding of Moses," he provided the painting with a background that included little temples and obelisks, and he also used a sphinx to make it clear that the locale was Egypt.

The *Mensa Isiaca*, which even Gotthold Ephraim Lessing admired in the Turin Museum, exercised a strong influence on everything Egyptianizing until the beginning of the nineteenth century. The high point of this phase in which classical models of Egypt were imitated was the Apis Altar made

22. Detail of the Praeneste mosaic in the Palestrina Museum. Photo courtesy of Paul Rehak and John G. Younger.

in Dresden by Johann Melchior Dinglinger in 1731 under the commission of Augustus the Strong, with a depiction of the introduction of a newly-discovered Apis bull into Memphis at its center. Here, however, we shall not go into detail regarding the history of art and the ways in which it treated Egypt but rather turn to the Rosicrucians.

THIRTEEN

"REFORMATION OF THE WHOLE WIDE WORLD"

The Rosicrucians

When the Rosicrucian movement appeared at the beginning of the seventeenth century, it was at first a purely fictitious fraternity. We know its mythical and also its actual founder. Christian Rosenkreuz (or Rosencreutz), who was allegedly born in 1378, was supposed to have been in Egypt and also to have spent three years among the Sabaeans of Yemen, who were especially well versed in Hermetism and astrology; he learned Arabic there and also in the city of Fez in Morocco. The supposedly miraculous discovery of his tomb and the secret book it contained stands entirely in the Hermetic tradition.

The fraternity was first made known by the Swabian theologian Johann Valentin Andreae (1586–1654), whose father had already been keenly interested in alchemy and theosophy. He might have written his *Chymical Marriage of Christian Rosenkreuz in the year 1459* as early as 1607, but the book was not published until 1616, thus later than the printing of the first manifesto of the new "order" in Kassel in March 1614. The latter bore the ambitious title *General Reformation of the Whole Wide World. Also the Fama Fraternitatis of the Meritorious Order of the Rosy Cross, Addressed to the Learned in General, and the Governors of Europe*; it was presumably authored by Tobias Hess of Tübingen (1563–1614) and his circle of friends; Hess was a jurist, theologian, and physician, and also a follower of Paracelsus. Its model was a satirical work by the Italian Traiano Boccalini, which appeared in Venice in 1612 and critically ripped apart the then-widespread proposals for bettering the world. There followed a flood of further pamphlets, more than 400 of them between 1614 and 1625, and as early as the book fair at Frankfurt in 1614, the first "real" Rosicrucians were believed to have been spotted, but their appearance was awaited in vain in the years that followed. In chapter 5 of their *Confessio*, it is stated that God had "compassed us about with his clouds," so that "no longer are we beheld by human eyes, unless they have received strength borrowed from the eagle." As late as 1623, Johannes Kepler wrote that he "knew none of the good brothers," and Descartes also searched in vain for them. They made an appearance in Paris in 1623, but contrary to their hopes, Cardinal Richelieu did not receive them. The political failure of the "Winter King" Frederick V of the Rhineland in 1620 surely contributed to the fact that the fraternity continued to remain a fiction and was not "officially" constituted.

A comparable fiction of this period, one that went back to a supposed Hebrew manuscript of 1387, is connected with the name of Abraham of Worms and his "Book of the True Practice of Ancient Magia," the oldest copies of which date to 1608 and are rather indebted to the cabala. Somewhat later is the supposed document written by Abraham to his son Lamech concerning "the sacred magic of Abramelin," a fictitious personality whom Abraham claimed to have met at the end of the fourteenth century in an Egyptian oasis. A 1725 printing made in Cologne describes it as "the great Egyptian revelations . . . together with the spiritual and miraculous power that Moses learned in the desert from the burning bush, including all the hidden lore of the cabala." The work draws especially on the magical literature of the sixteenth century and aims at subjecting infernal spirits to one's will. Abramelin's magic is still highly regarded by modern Hermetists.

It has come to light through the research of Carlos Gilly that the Rosicrucian manifestos were already in circulation years before they appeared in print. A first response by the Tyrolean teacher, musician, and alchemist Adam Haslmayr (1562–1630), who was "a befuddled head" to his opponents, was published as early as 1612, and it led to his arrest and trial. He was obliged to spend four-and-a-half years as a galley slave in the harbor of Genoa, but even during this period, his prodigious production of Paracelsian and alchemic works continued.

In Rosicrucian symbolism, the Christian Passion (the cross) is connected with life renewed from death (the rose). The two had already been associated with one another by Martin Luther.

The teachings of Paracelsus (for Haslmayr, the "German Trismegistus" and "mysteriarch"), cabala with its numerical mysticism, Hermetism, and alchemy are strangely mixed in Haslmayr's work, and an appeal to Egypt was soon added. As early as 1617, the physician and alchemist Michael Maier traced the Rosicrucians back to Egypt in his *Silentium post clamores* (Silence after the clamors), in which he oriented himself in particular to Plutarch. Andreae also drew on the *Hypnerotomachia Poliphili* of Francesco Colonna, and the Rosicrucians also made considerable use of Baroque emblems. In particular, we find in the *Confessio* of 1615 the widespread expectation of the last days; the world had "nearly reached the eve of fire" and would return to the beginning, but first it had to be renewed from the ground up. The brothers' polemic was directed first and foremost against the Pope and the "false alchemists" who took the people's money, while the Rosicrucians themselves "promise(d) more gold than both the Indies bring to the King of Spain," as is stated in the *Fama fraternitatis*.

The *Chymical Marriage* purports to be the autobiography of the fictitious founder of the order, Christian Rosenkreutz, who undertakes a pilgrimage at a very advanced age in order "to be present at this mysterious and hidden Wedding" to which he has been invited; this is the gnostic "calling" that has issued to him. The tidings, which an angel has given him with the blast of a trumpet, are followed by a dream in which the narrator beholds himself in a dark dungeon from which he gains release only with great difficulty. Sticking four roses in his hat, he proclaims himself to be a "Brother of the RED ROSIE CROSS." With Hermes accompanying him as guide, he journeys eastward, seeing many wondrous things along the way. At sunset, on a tall hill, the pilgrim enters the castle in which his initiation awaits him, and where the worthy will be separated from the unworthy, in particular, the false alchemists. The new garments that pertain to the transition from the profane to the sacred realm are intimated by new shoes and a tonsure. On the third day of his journey, he withstands all sorts of tests on the golden scale of virtue, thereby also completing the alchemic opus of which the fraudulent, the alchemists devoted only to making gold, are incapable; harsh punishments are imposed, the most horrible of them being carried out on those guilty of fraud.

On the fourth day, the maiden Alchemy leads the pilgrim to the fountain of quicksilver, which is guarded by a lion holding a tablet with a message from Hermes in his paws. We cannot help but think of Rilke's verses:

And the lion, like a shield-supporter,
sat at the edge and held the stone.
("The Egyptian Mary," 1908)

Additionally, a gleaming white unicorn emerges from the dark trees of the garden and reverently kneels down. A comedy in seven acts (the seven stages of the opus), which is now enacted as the wedding festival in the "House of the Sun," unites Alchemy and Salvation. After that, the narrator and his fellow pilgrims are allowed to dine at the royal table for the first time.

On the following day, the fifth, Christian is led to a subterranean room of the castle, where he beholds the naked Venus (in alchemy, she represents copper) lying inert on a bed. Another vision (already at the end of the fourth day) leads him into a long room in which three royal couples who differ in age lie in state and are beheaded by a black man wielding an ax—the *mortificatio* of the alchemic process, which is already to be found in the visions of Zosimus. In their coffins, the murdered royal couples voyage on a lake (here there are surely Osirian overtones!) and land on a square island on which stands the seven-storied Tower of Olympus, where the alchemic opus is finally concluded by a rebirth and a mystical marriage. They return in jubilation and rejoicing, and all the participants are appointed "Knights of the Golden Stone," and because of his adventure with Venus, Christian is obliged to serve as gatekeeper. The tale concludes midsentence; the final pages of the work are supposedly missing, and readers are invited to bring it to a conclusion through their own efforts.

Andreae intended more than a comedic mystification of his contemporaries with his fictitious fraternity, which had at first supposedly been kept secret but was now in part made known. It also had to do with an intense longing for the unity of divided Christendom, which a few years later was plunged into the horrors of the Thirty Years War, and there was a widespread feeling that a new and general reformation was urgently needed; Kepler expressed the same hope in his "Detailed Account" of the comet of 1607. This new Reformation was supposed to transform not only religion but also science and its attitude toward nature. Signs in the heavens—the nova of 1604 and the aforementioned comet—seemed to portend an immanent new millennium. Rosenkreuz' message thus met the chiliastic expectations of the age: "Europe is with child, and will bring forth a strong child," as the *Fama Fraternitatis* puts it. But like any myth, that which Andreae and others created with their writings quickly began to take on a life of its own.

The idea soon gained a foothold in Europe, and Robert Fludd (1574–1637) wrote apologies in defense of the Rosicrucians, who had been attacked in many broadsheets; an example is his *Tractatus apologeticus Societatis de Rosea Cruce defendens* (Apologetic tract in defense of the Society of the Rosy Cross, 1617). The attitude was more critical in France, where Gabriel Naudé and François Garasse published attacks in 1623. In the same year, there appeared a broadsheet by Marin Mersenne against Fludd, from which we learn, among other things, that Paracelsus and Hermes Trismegistus (!) had been condemned by the Parisian High Theological Faculty.

Typical of the many other attacks that were written is the title *Kurtze und Trewherzige Warnung, für dem Rosencreutzer Ungezifer* (Brief and true-hearted warning concerning the Rosicrucian vermin) by Philipp Geiger, which appeared in 1621. In 1619, there was an initial Inquisition against Rosicrucians by order of Count Moritz of Hesse. But many societies of the seventeenth century made reference to the Rosicrucian fiction, with the result that the idea took on ever more concrete form. It was probably in the wake of this development that there flourished a new literature about Hermes Trismegistus, such as *De Zoroastro bactriano, Hermete Trismegisto* (On the Bactrian Zoroaster, and Hermes Trismegistus) by Johann Heinrich Ursinus (1661), *Hermetis Aegyptiorum et chemicorum sapientia* (Wisdom of the Hermes of the Egyptians and of the chemists) by Olaus Borrichius (1674), *Conjectaneorus de germanicae gentis origine, ac conditore, Hermete Trismegisto, qui S. Moysi est Chanaan . . .* (Conjectures regarding the origin of the Germanic tribes and their founder, Hermes Trismegistus, who is St. Moses in Canaan) by Wilhelm Christoph Kriegsmann (1684), claiming that Hermes was the founder of the German people (!), and *Ovum hermetico-paracelsico-trismegistum* (The Hermetico-paracelsico-trismegistic egg) by Johann Ludwig Hannemann 1694). In Philipp von Zesen's *Assenat* (1670), a novel about Joseph, Hermes Trismegistus is identified as the inventor of obelisks and their obscure picture writing. Laurence Sterne testified to his high regard for Hermes as late as the eighteenth century, in his *Tristram Shandy* (1760–1767); for him, Trismegistus, the king, lawgiver, philosopher, and priest, was "the geatest of all earthly beings" (Book IV, chapter 11).

In 1710, the Silesian priest Samuel Richter, writing under the pseudonym Sincerus Renatus, claimed that the fraternity of the Rosicrucians had "several years ago gone to India so as to live in better peace," but he also referred to Hermes Trismegistus and Raimundus Lullus. Many other authors also wrote in this vein about the prehistory and the contemporary activities of the Rosicrucian movement. In the eighteenth century, the members of the Knights Templar were made into early Rosicrucians or Freemasons, thus beginning a new esoteric tradition that endures to this day, especially in France. According to this tradition, the early fourteenth century had seen the decline of the order—in 1306, the very year in which all the Jews had been expelled from France, charges were raised against the Knights Templar; all its leaders in France were arrested on October 13, 1307, and on March 19, 1314, Jacques DeMolay, the last Grand Master, was burned. This fiery death was later connected with the phoenix legend in Masonic circles.

The movement of the "Gold and Rosy Cross of the Ancient System" emerged in the latter half of the eighteenth century (it can be traced back to 1757), and for a time, it even gained political influence, especially in Prussia, where Crown Prince Friedrich Wilhelm became a member in 1781. The new order proved to be attractive to many Freemasons, and it made its appearance with a written history of the order, whose beginnings can be found in the *Aurora Philosophorum* (1615) and in later legends. The history leads from Adam immediately to Moses, who was initiated into Hermetic lore in Egypt, and then to Solomon and the prophets, and, of course, to Hermes Trismegistus as well. A novelty is an Egyptian priest from Alexandria named Ormus (from Ahuramazda, the old Persian god of fire) who was baptized as a Christian by the evangelist Mark, after which he cleansed the secret lore of Egypt of everything heathen and founded the school of the Wise Men of the Light. There followed an "Order of the Builders of the East"; supposedly founded in 1196 by three brethren from Scotland, it was ultimately absorbed by the Brotherhood of the Gold and Rosy Cross.

Alchemy (sometimes with life-threatening experiments) and cabala were enthusiastically practiced in the order, and from the seventh (of nine) degree of initiation on, the brothers believed they were in possession of the Stone of the Sages. But it is indicative that these circles also practiced necromancy, yet another root of later theosophy, and all this in the age of the Enlightenment and rationalism! In any event, these were people who were dedicated to the struggle against the areligious Enlightenment. As was only fitting, the highest degree was that of "magus," and the highest magus of the order was supposedly a Venetian living in Egypt. The system of high degrees was taken over by the Freemasons, with whom the new order was closely connected.

Of the many published attacks, *Der Rosenkreuzer in seiner Blösse* (The Rosicrucian in his nakedness) by a "Master Pianco" (1781) proved to be particularly effective. The importance of the order dwindled quickly after 1787, and official interdictions (1793 in Austria, 1800 in Prussia) definitively brought it to an end. For a somewhat lengthy period, the Rosicrucians played a role only in literature, but after 1865, a series of societies began to make reference to the Rosy Cross and sought to connect themselves with the legendary history of the origin of the order, though they otherwise differed considerably in their concepts, many focusing on the cabala and others on alchemy.

The first of these new associations was the *Societas Rosicruciana in Anglia*, founded by Robert Wentworth. Especially indebted to ancient Egypt was the Ancient and Mystical Order Rosae Crucis, called AMORC for short, founded in 1915 by the American Harvey Spencer Lewis (1883–1939). Since 1927, it has been centered in San Jose, California, with a delightful group of buildings in Egyptian style, the winged sun disk as its publisher's mark, and a collection of Egyptian antiquities that in the meanwhile has become genuinely important; for a long time, the Belgian Egyptologist Jean Capart was in charge of it. The current Rosicrucian Museum building (Figure 23), which was designed by Earl Lewis, dates to 1967.

The AMORC makes reference to an age-old tradition dating back to about 1500 B.C.E., that the Rosicrucian order was founded by Tuthmosis III, and that it was the source of Akhenaten's impulse to found a new religion. The pyramids were of course not royal tombs, but "places of study and mystical initiation." Thales, Pythagoras, and many others journeyed

23. The Rosicrucian Egyptian Museum in San Jose, California. Photo by Fabienne Haas.

to Egypt and were inducted into the schools of the mysteries, after which they brought their deepened knowledge back to the western world. Thanks to the Library of Alexandria, the Arabs could continue to hand down the mystical teachings, which were once again communicated to the west through the Crusades. All the important alchemists were of this opinion, including Rosenkreuz, and to this day, alchemy is part of the order's program of instruction. Among others, Albertus Magnus, Paracelsus, Roger Bacon, Descartes, Leibniz, and Newton are claimed to have been Rosicrucians. In 1694, Rosicrucians came to settle in North America, where they exerted influence on some of the Founding Fathers of the United States of America.

Spencer Lewis, the founder of the AMORC, made many trips to Egypt, and in 1936, he published a book entitled *The Symbolic Prophecy of the Great Pyramid*, which included precise plans of the subterranean passageways and columned halls beneath the Great Sphinx and the pyramids, "made from secret manuscripts possessed by archivists of the mystery schools of

Egypt and the Orient . . . telling of the ancient forms of initiations held in the Sphinx and the Great Pyramid." Here we encounter the Abbé Terrasson and his pyramid initiation, to which we shall return in the following chapter, but the author also makes reference to the then-ongoing actual excavations by Selim Hassan at the Sphinx of Giza. The most recent speculations concerning the immense age and importance of the Sphinx fall basically along the same lines.

In Europe, the foreground of the Rosicrucian movement is occupied by the "Lectorium Rosicrucianum," which was founded in 1925 by Jan van Rijkenborgh (1896–1968). Its center is in Haarlem in the Netherlands, and there is a German center with a "Christian Rosenkreuz Temple" in Calw. This "International School of the Rosy Cross," which continues the tradition of the "Gold and Rosy Cross" of the eighteenth century, understands itself to be "a gnostic-esoteric, Christocentric spiritual school" with no relations "with other secret societies that might bear the name of Rosicrucian, . . . for these strive for other goals." The epithet "gnostic" is underlined in the self-proclaimed task of this "mystery school" of "reawakening, in people who are searching, the prerecollection of the original realm of light that is not of this world." It thus sees itself as the "instrument of universal brotherhood, which since the Fall of humankind has been concerned to bring . . . the erring children of God back home" and strives to "awaken the primal recollection sunk deep in humankind" from "the bonds of this world" so as to enter the "celestial fatherland." Here, we are deep in the ideational realm of gnosticism. But the School of the Rosy Cross also deals "with the alchymical processes of renewing the world and humankind" and attempts a "transfiguration" of the human race. In both branches of modern Rosicrucianism, the symbolism of the Sphinx plays an important role; it is practically a "trademark" of modern esoterica.

The spiritual progenitors of the fraternity include, among others, the Buddha, Lao-Tse, Zoroaster, Orpheus, Plato, Pythagoras, Apollonius of Tyana, Jesus, Mani, and of course also Hermes Trismegistus. In the Introduction to Carlos Gilly's book about Haslmayr that was mentioned earlier, Joost R. Ritman, the founder of the Bibliotheca Philosophica Hermetica in Amsterdam, writes of the Hermetic-Christian tradition in Alexandria, "where their spiritual father, Hermes Trismegistus, worked and composed his *Corpus Hermeticum* and *Tabula Smaragdina*," and in the

Introduction to the exhibit catalogue of 1995, he sees the basis of Rosicrucianism "in Egyptian opinions about initiation in the priestly city of Memphis, which were set down in the library of Heliopolis." The order continued to call on the Cathari and the Albigensians, for they were all members
of "a universal chain that stretches from the dawn of time to the present."
"Original Egyptian gnosis" stands at the beginning of this "dawn," and in
its functions, the school constantly refers to the teachings of Hermes Trismegistus.

FOURTEEN

THE IDEAL OF A FRATERNITY

The Freemasons

Robert Fludd (1574–1637) and Elias Ashmole (1617–1692) count as forerunners of the Masonic movement; Madame Blavatsky viewed Ashmole as "the last Rosicrucian and alchemist." In 1646, Ashmole was admitted into a lodge in Warrington, Lancashire, that was known as the "House of Solomon," and later, he made his appearance in a lodge in London. Like him, other out-of-towners were admitted into the "lodges" of the building craftsmen in the seventeenth century. There is a widespread opinion that English Freemasonry had its origins in Rosicrucianism, uniting it with medieval traditions of the masons' guilds and the huts of these construction workers, where we also find the beginnings of a hierarchical structure. "Rosie Crosse" and "Mason word" occur in two successive verses of a poem published in 1638 by Henry Adamson of Perth (see the study by Edinghoffer cited in the bibliography of the preceding chapter). The designation "freemason" occurs in an English manuscript as early as 1376 (see the work by Nefontaine cited in the bibliography).

The idea of an ideal fraternity regardless of person or religion appears in many seventeenth-century writings, and it also stood behind the founding of the Royal Society in 1622. In 1641, the Czech scholar Jan Amos Comenius (1592–1670) published the blueprint for a *Collegium lucis* that was supposed to have its seat in England. The *Fraternitas* of the Rosicrucians was an important model, and the early Freemasons felt that they were affiliated with this fraternity. Though it began as an exclusively male association (and the idea still persists), the movement later opened itself to women as well, producing a multiplicity of diverse groups. Masonic symbols, such as the hammer, the square, the compass, and the apron, are derived from construction work. Before they had buildings to house their lodges, they gathered in taverns.

The Masonic movement's official date of birth is June 24, 1717. On that date, the four lodges of southern England chose Anthony Sayer (1672–1742) as the first Grand Master; this memorable event took place at the Goose and Gridiron tavern in St. Paul's Churchyard in London. Only three months later, on September 22, in the Apple Tree Tavern (Charles Street, Covent Garden), the pantheist John Toland (1670–1722) founded an order of druids, which led Helena Blavatsky to transpose the founding of the Masonic order to this tavern. But already in the preceding year, the Venetian dignitary Andrea Cornaro (1672–1742), whose uncle Giovanni II Cornaro was at that time doge of the republic, had commissioned a cycle of frescos containing Masonic themes and symbols, including Solomon's temple and the works undertaken by Hiram of Tyre. The cycle was executed in 1716–1717 by the painter Mattia Bortolani, who was only nineteen years of age, in the Carnaro villa in Piombino (Veneto) built by Andrea Palladio, and we may correctly suppose that there were gatherings of people sympathetic to the new movement in this rather remote locale.

The first "Constitutions" of the Freemasons, authored by the Scottish intellectual James Anderson (1684?–1739), was printed in London in 1723. This work was already provided with a legendary history that began with Adam and his sons; Noah kept the builders' art alive after the Flood, and his grandson Mizraim brought it to Egypt, where Moses was later active as Grand Master of the society. There was a new edition of the work in 1738, at the same time that the Grand Lodge of England was founded. Freemasonry then quickly spread throughout Europe, and lodges were founded as far away as Turkey, China, Indonesia, and America. The first French lodge was probably founded in Paris in 1725, and the first German lodge, called Absalon, in Hamburg in 1737.

Pope Clement XII issued a bull entitled *In eminenti*, against the new movement as early as 1738—the very year that the Prussian crown prince Frederick was inducted as a Freemason in Brunswick. There were further prohibitions, including one in 1744 by the city council of Geneva; in France, all the lodges had already been banned for the first time in 1737.

At first, the Freemasons displayed no interest in Egypt; rather, they sought, even in their symbolism, to attach themselves to biblical traditions, especially the temple of Solomon, and Hiram, who had it built. Nevertheless, in 1728, the seal of the Perfetta Unione lodge in Naples already displayed a pyramid and sphinx (Figure 24). Masonic usages and symbols were now reinterpreted. There were also influences from alchemy, for the stone that the mason symbolically worked was also viewed as the Philosopher's Stone. The Freemasons also adopted cabala and the teachings of the Rosicrucians, taking over the supposed history of the latter's origins, and they constructed a chain of traditions that led back, via temple masters, cabalists, gnostics, and Pythagoreans, to Solomon, whom they revered as the ruler of the spirit world, and finally, via Moses, to Adam. Even Hermes Trismegistus appeared in the name of an early German lodge in Landau. Along with him, Moses was already viewed as an authority; according to C. Ernst Wünsch (*Horus*, 1783), Moses was initiated into Hermes' arcana by the secret priestly society of Egypt. The Order of the Strict Observance also made reference to the medieval Knights Templar. After DeMolay's execution in 1314, some of the order's leaders had fled to Scotland and introduced their secret lore to the masons' huts there; this was also the origin of the system of higher degrees.

The Egyptian component was not elaborated until the latter part of the eighteenth century, at a time when the origins of all religion were often being sought in Egypt. A lasting influence was also exerted by the description of an "Egyptian" initiation in the novel *Séthos* by the Abbé Jean Terrasson, a Hellenist at the Collège de France who also translated Diodorus; his novel was published anonymously in 1731, after which it was widely reprinted and translated. As a young man of sixteen, the hero of the novel is initiated into the Isis mysteries inside the Great Pyramid of Giza; midway, he passes through all four elements, which are elaborately staged inside the pyramid. This trial by the elements renders Sethos worthy of participating in the "mysteries" of the great goddess Isis. Cagliostro, of whom we shall speak later, also took up such matters, but even earlier, there had been efforts to find an entrée into gnostic and Hermetic thought.

Antoine-Joseph Pernety (1716–1801) founded a "Rite hermétique" in Avignon in 1766; two years later, he was summoned to Potsdam to be the librarian of Frederick the Great. The mystical Freemasonry of Jacques de

Pasqually (1727–1774), who spent his last years living in Haiti, was more indebted to gnosis. In his writings, we encounter the gnostic doctrines of the fall of humankind and the creation of the world by a subordinate demiurge; his gnostic sexual magic would occur again later in a number of groups.

The Afrikanische Bauherren group, also called the African Lodge, was more strongly oriented toward Egypt and its supposed initiations. In 1766, under Carl Friedrich Köppen (1734–1797), it broke off from the mother lodge Zu den drei Weltkugeln in Berlin, leading to violent quarrels. From this circle emerged the brief (only thirty-two pages) but highly influential tract entitled *Crata Repoa: Oder Einweihungen in der alten*

24. Seal of the lodge "Perfetta Unione" in Naples (below), 1728, and a later imitation. From Ruggiero di Castiglione, *Alle sorgenti della Massoneria* (Rome, 1988), photo no. 8.

geheimen Gesellschaft der Egyptischen Priester (Crata Repoa, or initiations
into the ancient secret society of the Egyptian priests), which appeared
anonymously in 1770 and became the model for an "Egyptian" initiation.
The name *Crata Repoa*, which has yet to be explained, refers to the secret
priesthood of the ancient Egyptians, which was founded by Menes.

The authors of the tract (besides Köppen, there was also Johann Wilhelm Bernhard von Hymmen) based themselves on information about
Egyptian priests given by classical authors, with their dietary prohibitions
and other precepts, but out of this information, they constructed a complicated initiation path through a total of seven degrees. Through the gateway of the profane, the neophyte arrived at the first degree as a *Pastopho-
ris*, or apprentice. After being questioned by the hierophant, he had to
withstand the test of the four elements and also to pledge loyalty and secrecy. He was initiated into the sciences and into the "common hieroglyphic writing system" and then clad in an "Egyptian" fashion with a
pyramid-shaped cap (= white crown?), apron, and collar.

A period of fasting prepared him for the second degree of *Neocoris*.
There was also a test of love and a test involving a serpent, with a serpent
staff as an external sign. Moreover, like Osiris, he held his arms crossed
over his chest; the eighteenth-century travel accounts of Fredrik Ludvig
Norden and Paul Lucas were the origin of this detail. In the third degree,
that of *Melanophoris*, he passed through the door of death into a room containing embalmed bodies and coffins, with the coffin of Osiris in their
midst. Here, he had to answer the question of whether he took part in the
assassination of his lord, and he suffered a symbolic death that is a component of all initiations. Now he was familiarized with another kind of
writing system, the hierogrammatic. Guided by a rope, he then reached
the fourth degree, that of a *Christophoris*, was given a bitter drink and new
garments, and stood face to face with the royal lord of the association. The
password *yoa* was reminiscent of the gnostic name of God, and in the fifth
degree, that of *Balahate*, he received the password *chymia* and was familiarized with alchemy. In the sixth degree, as an *Astronomus*, he learned
about the stars and the divine, but he was warned away from astrology.
Through the portal of the gods and with the password *ibis*, which brings
us back to Hermes Trismegistus, he finally reached the seventh and last
degree, that of a *Prophet*.

Already in 1768, also anonymously, Köppen had published a brief tract entitled "Erklärung einer Egyptischen Spitz-Säule welche vor dem Lateran in Rom zu finden ist" (Interpretation of an Egyptian obelisk to be found in front of the Lateran in Rome). In it, he already had his sights on an "Egyptian" initiation: "By means of a raven atop a gallows (the royal Horus-name!), the tip of the pillar provides the concept of nature of a man who was more inclined to evil than to good, but who had a strong urge to broaden his knowledge through secret initiations."

A few years later, in 1775, Köppen, weary of the endless strife among the Freemasons of Berlin, resigned from the Afrikanische Bauherren, which would be formally dissolved in 1781, and from the Masonic movement altogether. But his *Crata Repoa* remained a fundamental document of esoterica and would enjoy great popularity among the Theosophists who surrounded Helena Blavatsky.

The actual founder of "Egyptian" Masonry was the controversial Count Cagliostro (Giuseppe Balsamo from Palermo, 1743–1795), who, after founding various "Egyptian" lodges, founded his "Rite de la Haute Maçonnerie Égyptienne" in the lodge La Sagesse Triomphante on December 24, 1784 (there had already been a "Rite de Memphis") and, as Master of the order, gave himself the title Grand Copht. "Egyptian" Masonry was introduced into Paris in the following year, but in 1785, the "Affair of the Necklace" brought a sudden end to Balsamo's work, and the false count sat in the Bastille for nearly a year. In Warsaw, where Calgiostro had given a stellar performance in 1780 and founded a Temple of Isis lodge, a stone bearing Egyptian motifs has been found, one that probably belonged to this "Egyptian" lodge, and in the Baltic States, where Cagliostro had been active in 1779, there was a lodge called Isis in Reval, with a Baron von Ungern-Sternberg as its Master (1784). Cagliostro had also founded an "Egyptian" lodge in Strasbourg in 1780, and from there, he brought his Egyptian Rite to Basel.

According to Johann Joachim Christoph Bode (see the book by Kiefer in the bibliography), Cagliostro said "that he had learned his secret knowledge in the subterranean vaults of the Egyptian pyramids, where, like Moses, he was instructed in all the lore of the Egyptians." In his autobiography, the "count" affirmed that he had been educated in the Arabian city of Medina, that he had made "the acquaintance of the priests of the underground temples" in Egypt, and that he was in possession of statues of Egyptian masons that Cambyses had found in the temple of Isis. His supposed teacher Althotas, who accompanied him on his early journeys, is probably taken from the teacher Amedes in the novel *Séthos*, though to judge from his name, he is also an adaptation of the god Thoth, with the Arabic article *al-* ("the"), and thus Hermes as teacher and guide.

In Mitau in 1779, Cagliostro had designated himself as the direct subordinate of Elias, who, together with Moses and Christ, had constituted the sublime board of directors of the globe; in the following year, he had recourse to his Egyptian wisdom in Warsaw. His fantasy-filled fabrications enjoyed one success after another with a gullible public. Even Friedrich von Schiller thought that "he has brought us the true chymia and medicine of the ancient Egyptians along with him" and designated him in this regard as a "new Paracelsus," though in his tale "The Ghost-Seer" (1788), he was inclined to unmask such practices as fraudulent.

Goethe, who became a member of the Anna Amalia lodge in Weimar on June 23, 1780, was more critical. In his comedy "The Great Cophta" (1791), he portrays Cagliostro as a wondrous figure after the manner of Apollonius of Tyana, "as old as the Egyptian priests, as sublime as the Indian sages," thus repeating the ancient connection between India and Egypt. But the scenery in which the Great Cophta wanders about is entirely stamped by Egypt, and the story also has an "Egyptian lodge" decorated "with Egyptian pictures and decoration," and we find the usual trappings of esoteric Egypt:

> My imagination immediately abandoned this cold, confined region of the world; it visited that torrid stretch of sky where the sun ever blazes over unutterable mysteries. Suddenly, I saw Egypt standing before me; a sacred half-light surrounded me; I wandered amidst pyramids, obelisks, enormous sphinxes, and hieroglyphs; a shudder came over me. (Act 1, Scene 4)

During his trip to Italy, Goethe had visited the Balsamo family in Palermo in 1787 to inform himself regarding the origins of the "count." When he wrote his play, Cagliostro had most of his long lifetime behind him. In 1791, the Inquisition in Rome condemned him to death as a "Restorationist and propagator of Egyptian Masonry," but Pope Pius VI commuted the sentence to life imprisonment, and in 1795, he died in the papal prison of San Leo near Urbino.

The story "Der Stein der Weisen oder Sylvester und Rosine" (The Philosopher's Stone, or Sylvester and Rosina), which appeared in 1786 in the first volume of Christoph Martin Wieland's collection of tales entitled *Dschinnistan*, is mainly directed against Cagliostro's fraud and his proclivity for alchemy and magic. Here, bearing the fantastic name of Misfragmutosiris, he appears as an "Egyptian adept from the genuine and secret school of the great Hermes"; the depiction on the title page (Figure 25) shows him wearing a cloak decorated with hieroglyphs and a pointed cap crowned by a sphinx. At the court of King Mark of Cornwall, he boasts of his adventures in the Great Pyramid of Giza, a theme that goes back to the Abbé Terrasson, though Wieland further embellishes it. A hieroglyphic inscription over the entrance to the first room explains the pyramid as a tomb of the great Hermes; the adept finds the divine old man, guarded by a dragon, lying on a magnificent bed in a "dome of black jasper."

Even independently of Cagliostro, Egypt had by now solidly anchored itself in Freemasonry. In 1784, the geologist and mineralogist Ignaz von Born (1742–1791) inaugurated the new *Journal für Freimaurer* with a fundamental essay, "Ueber die Mysterien der Aegyptier" (On the mysteries of the Egyptians). The year before, in his book *Horus*, C. E. Wunsch had proclaimed that the secret society of the Egyptian priests had initiated Moses into its arcana. Karl Leonhard Reinhold also stressed Moses' dependence on Egypt in *Die Hebräischen Mysterien oder die älteste religiöse Freimaurerey* (The Hebraic mysteries, or the most ancient religious Freemasonry, 1788), which he published as "Brother Decius"; he had already written several contributions on Hebraic and other "mysteries" for von Born's *Journal*. Also indicative is the title of a work by Johann Gottfried Bremer, which was issued by Karl Philipp Moritz in 1793: *Die Symbolische Weisheit der Aegypter aus den verborgensten Denkmälern des Altertums, ein Theil der Aegyptischen Maurerey, der zu Rom nicht verbrannt worden* (The symbolic lore of Egypt from the most hidden monuments of antiquity, a part of the Egyptian Masonry that was not burned in Rome). In it, the ceremonies of the "Egyptian" mysteries unfold in seven stages. When the work appeared, Calgiostro was already sitting in the papal dungeon, and his manuscript on "Egyptian Masonry" had been publicly burned!

Von Born, relying in particular on Apuleius' account, stressed the similarities between the initiation of an Egyptian priest and that of a Mason.

IV.
Der
Stein der Weisen
oder
Sylvester und Rosine.

In den Zeiten, da Cornwall noch seine eigene König hatte, regierte in dieser kleinen Halbinsel des grossen Brittanniens ein junger König, Nahmens Mark, ein Enkel desjenigen, der durch seine Gemahlin,

25. Christoph Martin Wieland, "Der Stein der Weisen oder Sylvester und Rosine," from *Dschinnistan oder auserlesene Feen- und Geistermärchen*, vol. I (Winterthur, 1786).

He drew chiefly on Diodorus and Plutarch for his depiction of the "condition, duties, and knowledge of the Egyptian priests"—ancient Egyptian sources were not yet known. He did not view the pyramids as places of initiation; rather, he thought that the knowledge of the ancient Egyptians was stored in them.

In the same year 1784, in which von Born's essay—and a little later, a parallel essay "Über die Mysterien der Indier" (On the mysteries of the Indians)—appeared, Wolfgang Amadeus Mozart was admitted into the Zur Wohltätigkeit lodge in Vienna, and it has been assumed that he memorialized Ignaz von Born, the Master of the Zur wahren Eintracht lodge and the spiritual head of the Viennese Freemasons, in the person of Sarastro. In 1779, Mozart had already composed his music for Tobias Philipp von Geber's drama *Thamos* (1773), which takes place in the "sun temple of Heliopolis" and was also inspired by Terrasson's *Séthos*; it even has a high priest named Sethos.

The culmination was Mozart's music for *The Magic Flute* (1791), which accompanied the text by his fellow lodge member Emanuel Schikaneder. The opera brought Masonic concerns onto the stage in Egyptian dress, down to the "mysteries of Isis" and initiation inside a pyramid (so the stage directions); Schikaneder had drawn on Wieland as well as Terrasson. The evil Queen Daluca of the novel *Séthos* lay behind the "Queen of the Night." In the early productions of the opera, the action took place in a fairy-tale Orient of Turkish inspiration. Later, the sets designed by Karl Friedrich Schinkel (1781–1841) in 1815 and Simon Quaglio in 1818 inserted the opera into splendid Egyptian scenery that would exert an influence for a long time to come.

A quick glance at the New World reveals that Freemasons played a decisive role in the Revolutionary War fought by the colonists against Great Britain. George Washington, Thomas Jefferson, Benjamin Franklin, and other Founding Fathers of the United States of America were Freemasons, and they infused the new republic with their humanitarian and religious ideals. To this very day, a pyramid stressing the Egyptian connection adorns the one-dollar bill issued by the Federal Reserve Bank; it is topped by a triangle containing a radiant eye that symbolizes the great Architect of the universe. And in the capital city of Washington, D.C., there is an obelisk nearly 560 feet tall.

When he was the American ambassador in Paris, Franklin joined the lodge Les Neuf Soeurs (referring to the nine Muses), and he became its Master in 1779. To this lodge, which was founded in 1776 (the Grand Orient de France was born in 1773), belonged a number of the leading personalities of the day, including Jean le Rond d'Alembert, the Marquis de Condorcet, the Marquis de Lafayette, and the later revolutionaries Camille Desmoulins, Georges Jacques Danton, and Emmanuel Sieyès, as well as the professor of medicine Joseph Ignace Guillotin, the sculptor Jean-Antoine Houdon, the painter Jean Baptiste Greuze, and the composer Niccolo Piccini. Its Secretary was Antoine Court de Gebelin, to whom we shall return in connection with the tarot. Franklin also brought the naturalist and world traveler Georg Forster into the lodge, and, on April 5, 1778, even the aged Voltaire.

But the machinations of shady characters such as "Count" Cagliostro, along with the secrecy of the lodges, also put many people off. Thus, Herder, who had been called by his Masonic friends to Riga, where he joined the Zum Schwert lodge in 1766, soon proved to be disappointed. The Order of the Strict Observance also provoked resistance, leading to a search for new forms of secret society. Among those searching was August Baron von Knigge, who in 1780 joined the order of Illuminati, which had been founded by Adam Weishaupt in 1776, and which exercised great political influence on Friedrich Wilhelm II of Prussia. In the following year, there appeared his vengeful *Über Jesuiten, Freymaurer und deutsche Rosencreutzer* (On Jesuits, Freemasons, and German Rosicrucians), in which all these "orders" were tossed into the same pot. In 1786, von Knigge denounced the Freemasons once again in his "Beytrag zur neuesten Geschichte des Freymaurerordens in neun Gesprächen mit Erlaubnis meiner Oberen herausgegeben" (Contribution to the most recent history of the Freemasons in nine conversations, published with the permission of my superiors). At that time, there was a widespread suspicion that the Jesuits (who had been banned from Austria in 1773) were seeking to gain influence over the Freemasons and Rosicrucians; accordingly, the abbreviation SJ (Societas Jesu) was interpreted as *Superiores Incogniti*.

Armed with insider knowledge, Georg Forster expressed the widespread skepticism and frustration in a letter to the Swiss historian Johannes Müller dated December 20, 1783: "Hold firm to your decision not to seek secret societies and sciences. I leave the question undecided whether or not there are legitimate secret sciences; but it is nevertheless agreed that most of this sort that is spread about in the world is false pretenses, lies and deception, or, to believe the least, pious self-deception.

In the nineteenth century, Egyptian influence was especially visible in the Egyptian style of many lodge rooms, in their architecture as well as their decor; we can cite examples from both the Old and the New World, from Boston (in Lincolnshire), Brussels, Edinburgh, Paris, Philadelphia, and many other places. Egyptian elements were even employed in the construction of synagogues and churches, so little were they seen as "heathen" at this time. The connections of the Freemasons with ancient Egypt were emphatically stressed by Alexandre Lenoire (1762–1839); in a work that appeared in 1814, he also attempted a "decipherment" of the hieroglyphs and included depictions of Terrasson's trials by the elements. Other "Egyptian" rites were founded, including one by the archaeologist Alexandre Dumège (1780–1862) in Toulouse ("Amis du Désert"), and later by the Ancient and Primitive Rite of Memphis and Misraim. In Egypt itself, many lodges appeared at this time, which in part aimed at directly taking up the tradition of the ancient Egyptian mysteries.

Even in more recent times, there has been no lack of attempts to concretize the "Egyptian" origins of Masonry. Thus, in 1905, C. E. Gernandt attempted to identify the "first temple of the Freemasons in Egypt" with the temple of Ramesses II at Abydos, and with its richly documented cults, Egypt remains an inexhaustible source, especially for the ritual components of Masonry. The orientation, however, is not toward the "Beautiful West" of the ancient Egyptian afterlife but rather toward the "Eternal East."

FIFTEEN

GOETHE AND ROMANTICISM

"Thinking Hieroglyphically"

When the young Johann Wolfgang von Goethe experienced a serious physical and psychological life crisis during the winter of 1768–1769, it was the world of Hermes Trismegistus that gave him health and fresh momentum. He described this period in Book 8 of his *Dichtung und Wahrheit* (Poetry and Truth), and Rolf Christian Zimmermann has shed light on its intellectual background in his study *Das Weltbild des jungen Goethe* (The Philosophy of the young Goethe); there, it is made clear that Goethe was not "converted" to Christianity but to a Hermetism with Christian traits. "Neoplatonism was its foundation, and Hermetism, mysticism, and cabala made their contribution, and so I built myself a rather strange world," wrote Goethe as he spent long winter evenings "in this solitude." His companion in these studies was Susanne von Klettenberg (1723–1774), a member of the Pietist circle in Frankfurt, whom Goethe immortalized in the "Bekentnisse einer schönen Seele" (Confessions of a beautiful soul). After studying Paracelsus and Basilius Valentinus, they ventured on alchemic experiments, which were also popular with the Freemasons and the Rosicrucians: "Now, strange ingredients of the macrocosm and microcosm were treated in a mysterious, wonderful way." The "Frankfurt interval" was followed by a stay in Strasbourg, where Goethe continued to pursue alchemy as his "secret mistress." Much of what he learned from these "Hermetic" studies found a place in his later poetry, especially *Faust*.

In these studies, Goethe encountered an Egypt refracted by Hermetism and on other levels by the Bible and the classical writers. But when he stayed in Italy from 1786 to 1788, he beheld Egyptian originals for the first time, "splendid Egyptian monuments," especially, of course, in Rome. The first sketch for Johann Heinrich Wilhelm Tischbein's famous painting *Goethe in the Roman Countryside* portrays the poet on a shattered obelisk covered with hieroglyphs that were later effaced. But in Rome, a clear distinction between originals and imitations was scarcely possible, and Goethe, who among other things sketched the pyramid of Cestius, was especially enthralled by a pyramid reconstructed by Louis-François Cassas (1756–1827): "This drawing is the most enormous architectural concept I have seen in my life, and I do not believe that anyone can surpass it." Cassas also provided his fantasy pyramid with columned halls, obelisks, and an alley of sphinxes.

In his capacity as Director of the museum in Weimar, Goethe ordered the preparation of squeezes of Egyptian originals in Rome, for "we must have these invaluable things." His own private collection of Aegyptiaca, however, which was published only in 1980, was of lamentable quality when contrasted to the fine Egyptianizing objects in the taste of his day that he possessed (Figure 26). But because of his Hermetic studies, what he saw behind them was the transfigured Egypt of classical antiquity. And in any case, in the eighteenth century, the vitality of the ancient Egyptians was to be seen principally in architecture.

In his latter years, in a letter to Rühle von Lilienstern dated August 12, 1827, Goethe once stated his "aversion to that desolate land of the dead." In recent years, he had devoted less attention to Egypt—"an all too solemn land that seems to have sealed the most wonderful writings forever." Under the influence of the older Johann Gottfried Herder, Goethe's attitude toward Egypt, originally so positive, had changed into an antipathy toward the Romantics and their fascination with Egypt. Thus, in his Strasbourg period, Goethe said that he anxiously sought to hide his "mystico-cabalistic chemistry" from Herder.

Herder had also experienced a change in this regard. In a 1768 paper about Winckelmann, he reproached him for seeing the Egyptians with overall Greek eyes and comparing them to the Greek ideal—"even Herodotus was scarcely as Greek." In Hermes Trismegistus, Herder saw the symbolic discoverer of numbers and letters; in 1801, he published a "Hermetic" dialogue between Hermes and Pymander in his journal *Adrastea*.

26. Egyptianizing cup and saucer from Goethe's estate. Used by permission.

But in his *Reflections on the Philosophy of the History of Mankind* (1784–1791), Herder fell into the same error as Winckelmann. In the estimation of Siegfried Morenz, he thereby blazed the trail for "accurate understandings of historical phenomena" and thus formulated many correct insights into the essence of ancient Egyptian culture. Yet in Egypt and its hieroglyphs, he saw only a "first rude infantile essay of the human mind," for even "the rudest savages of America had hieroglyphics," by which he meant the Mexicans and their picture writing. Today, probably no one would call the Aztecs or the Maya "rude savages." "But what poverty of ideas, what stagnation of the mind, do the Egyptians display, in so long retaining this imperfect mode of writing, and continuing to paint it for centuries with immense trouble on rocks and walls!" The hieroglyphs had blocked the Egyptians' path toward science; the pyramids were signs of superstition and imperial despotism; and "mummies show that the figure of the Egyptians was by no means beautiful"!

In a letter written in 1826, Goethe also expressed the opinion that mummies were not an "indispensable component of a museum," but a "fashion accessory, and fashion speaks: What many have, everyone must have. What it is good for, no one asks." In his late years, Egyptian antiquity, and Indian and Chinese as well, were "ever mere curiosities; it is good to make oneself and the world familiar with them; but they bear scant fruit for moral and aesthetic training."

The eighteenth century was fascinated with the idea of a universal language comprehensible to all periods and peoples. This language assumed material form in the Egyptian hieroglyphs invented by Hermes Trismegistus, as affirmed, for example, by Antoine-Joseph Pernety in his *Dictionnaire mytho-hermétique* (Mytho-Hermetic dictionary) of 1758. Hermes Trismegistus was also the inventor of the hieroglyphs in Johann Heinrich Zedler's (1730 ff.) representative *Grosse Universal-Lexikon Aller Wissenschaften und Künste* (Great universal dictionary of all the sciences and arts). But notwithstanding all the efforts of Kircher and others, the hieroglyphs remained undeciphered. The then-popular comparison with the Chinese writing system, knowledge of which had been communicated to Europe by Jesuit missionaries in China, resulted in no progress, though repeated attempts were made to shed light on the Egyptian writing system with the help of the Chinese.

The Abbé Jean Jacques Barthélémy, in particular, propagated the notion that Chinese culture was dependent on that of ancient Egypt, and some even suggested that the mythical kings Osiris and Sesostris had once conquered India and China, and that the Egyptians had established colonies in these distant lands. In 1758, Joseph de Guignes presented a paper to the Académie des Inscriptions in Paris in which he "demonstrated" that China was an Egyptian colony, while in Sir Isaac Newton's chronological framework, the appearance of conquering Egyptian kings at the Ganges River was dated exactly to the year 974 B.C.E.

In *The Divine Legation of Moses* (1737–1741), William Warburton (1698–1779), relying on Horapollo and other ancient writers, attacked Kircher's "insane attempts" to ascribe a philosophical meaning to the hieroglyphs. He mocked Kircher for having struggled with late classical Platonic writers and the fake tractates of Hermes, "which contain Philosophy not Egyptian to explain old monuments not Philosophical." Like Leibniz, he reckoned that the obelisks bore historical texts, for secret lore would not have been recorded on monuments erected in public places (similarly, later Herder: "secret matters are not written on towers and walls"). To Warburton, writing was invented for practical reasons of communication not for esoteric ends; as others would do, Diderot relied on Warburton's opinion in his article on hieroglyphs in the great *French Encyclopedia*.

The year 1775 saw the appearance in Göttingen of Georg Christoph Meiners' *Versuch über die Religionsgeschichte der ältesten Völker besonders der Egyptier* (Attempt at a history of the religions of the most ancient peoples, in particular the Egyptians), which articulated the growing criticism of Hermetism and paid fresh honors to Casaubon. Meiners banished Hermes Trismegistus "from the realm of history . . . into the vast realm of supposedly ancient Egyptian chimeras"; he concluded by summarizing the controversial opinions regarding Hermes as follows: "I hope that whoever takes all of this together will not think ill of me if I sincerely declare that I know nothing of what Hermes was and did, and that I doubt that anyone ever knew or will ever find out, and that I therefore hold all attempts on this point to be a most irresponsible waste of time." Later, in his *Briefen über die Schweiz* (Correspondence regarding Switzerland), Meiners became a passionate critic of Cagliostro, and we are also indebted to him for his essay on the "Geschichte der hieroglyphischen Schrift" (History of the hieroglyphic writing system) in the *Göttinger historischen Magazin* of 1789.

But Hermetism withstood this blow, as it had Casaubon's late dating of the Hermetic texts. Magic, belief in the supernatural, and alchemy continued to flourish, even after Antoine-Laurent Lavoisier laid the foundations of modern chemistry with his *Traité élémentaire de Chimie* (Elementary treatise on chemistry, 1789). In 1783, the Leipzig physicist Christlieb Benedict Funk had published a work on "Natürliche Magie" (natural magic) that "could be taught by professors," and in 1808, Johann Heinrich Jung-Stilling, whose *Heimweh* will concern us below, would write a "Theory of Pneumatology".

The Isis religion, which had once been the last major opponent of early Christianity, enjoyed another heyday in the French Revolution, recast as the cult of a goddess of reason or of nature, intended to replace Christianity. In his *Origine de tous les cultes* (Origin of all the cults, 1794), the archaeologist and politician Charles-François Dupuis (1742–1809) traced all religions back to an original worship of nature and the stars whose cradle was Egypt. There were also quite concrete speculations about a connection between Isis and the name Paris, and it was believed that the cathedral of Notre Dame was built on the ruins of an earlier Isis temple; Dupuis interpreted the cathedral itself as an Iseum. Under Napoleon, Isis would become the tutelary goddess of Paris. Egyptian forms such as the pyramid, the obelisk, and the sphinx were especially popular during the era of the Revolution, and they were in no way viewed as symbols of the ruling class.

The high point of this new veneration of Isis was the dedication of Jacques Louis David's *Fontaine de la Régénération* on the ruins of the former Bastille on August 10, 1793. Here (Figure 27), regenerating water streamed from the breasts of an enthroned Egyptian goddess of bronze-covered plaster. The goddess was adorned with the "obligatory" royal headcloth, and she also wore a king's loincloth. Hérault de Sèchelles delivered a speech in which he called her the embodiment of nature.

La Fontaine de la Régénération
Sur les débris de la Bastille, le 10 août 1793.

27. The Fontaine de la Régénération, 1793. From the exhibition catalogue *Ägyptomanie: Ägypten in der europäischen Kunst 1730–1930* (Vienna, 1994), p. 108.

Plans to turn the Strasbourg cathedral into a temple of reason began to take on reality with the erection of a statue dominated by a *multimammia*, a many-breasted goddess of nature assumed to be Isis. And the new revolutionary era that temporarily replaced the Christian era employed the Egyptian calendar, with its ten-day weeks and its months of uniformly (as suited the idea of *égalité!*) thirty days, though the epagomenal (five extra) days were now called *sans-culottides*. After the Concordat that Napoleon concluded in July 1801 with Pope Pius VII, France returned to the Catholic faith, and the remnants of the revolutionary cult disappeared. But in the meanwhile, the Romantic movement had already made Egypt its own.

The "moonlit, magical night" (Johann Ludwig Tieck) of the Romantics was best suited to pyramids and sphinxes. Its look at the night side of the world included Egypt, and we also find, quite the opposite of Herder, an openness to representations and especially to "hieroglyphs" of every sort.

Great influence was exerted by the supposed inscription in the temple of Isis at Sais, which was handed down by Plutarch (*De Iside*, c. 9) and used by Schiller in his poem "The Veiled Image of Sais" (1795), though in an abbreviated form and reinterpreted as referring to "veiled truth," though the lifting of the veil in the detailed version given by the neo-Platonic writer Proclus (410–85) clearly refers to sexual union. The poem states,

> I am what is, and what will be, and what has been,
> No one has lifted my veil.
> The fruit I bore was the Sun.

Schiller again used this text, which was found "on a pyramid at Sais," in his essays "The Mission of Moses" (1790) and "On the Sublime." And in his "Critique of Judgment" (1790), Kant states, "Perhaps there has never been a more sublime utterance, or a thought more sublimely expressed, than the well-known inscription upon the Temple of *Isis* (Mother *Nature*): 'I am all that is, and that was, and that shall be, and no mortal hath raised the veil from before my face.'" For Beethoven, who had it standing framed on his desk, and for many other contemporaries, this quotation was the embodiment of Egyptian wisdom. The hieroglyphs were now widely viewed as a shrewd means by which the Egyptian priests concealed their belief in divine unity and their knowledge of its deepest secrets from the superstitious masses.

Isis' veil is lifted by the hero of Jung-Stilling's *Heimweh* (Homesickness), which was written in 1793–1794. This hero, Christian von Ostenheim, travels to the east as a modern crusader, in the process coming to Egypt, where he is initiated into a secret order inside the Great Pyramid. At the center of this initiation is again the trial by the elements after the model in Terrasson's novel *Séthos*. According to Jung-Stilling, the "great wise men of the east" had turned to Egypt "and there joined with the few genuine descendents of the age-old students of Hermes"; he assumes there was a "hidden society of initiates" there.

A little later (the fragment is from 1798–1800), Friedrich Hölderlin expressed this longing for the east, and especially for Egypt, in his *Death of Empedocles*. There, Empedocles says to Pausanias,

> And if your soul will not rest, go
> to the other, more solemn stream,
> and ask them, the brethren in Egypt.
> There, you will hear the solemn Saite tune
> of Urania, with its changing tones,
> There, they will open the Book of Fate to you.

Hölderlin also sang the praises of the Nile in his poem *The Archipelago*:

> ... the aged, the first-born,
> He who concealed himself too long, your Nile, the majestic,
> Loftily striding from distant peaks, as with clangour of weapons,
> Comes victoriously home and with arms extended in yearning.

Around the same time, in 1798, there was another fragment, *Die Lehrlinge zu Sais* (The apprentices at Sais) by Novalis (Georg Philipp Friedrich von Hardenberg); the very title alludes to the attempt to lift the goddess' veil. The searching youths Novalis describes are "filled with yearning and thirst for knowledge ... in search of a trace of that lost, perished, primeval race, ... (of) that sacred language, ... the few words ... that might yet have been in the possession of some fortunate sages among our forefathers"; they turn to Sais and "its temple archive" to get information, and then

> In the distant East, it becomes light,
> grey times become new again.

Long before the Romantic period, Johann Georg Hamann (1730–1788), the "magus of the north," had longed "by crusades to the lands of the east and by reconstructing their magic" to endeavor to "bring the dead languages of nature back to life from the dead."

Rudolph, the hero of Joseph von Eichendorff's *Ahnung und Gegenwart* (Premonition and present, 1815), also stands in this tradition of esoteric yearning for the east. He travels "to Egypt, to the magi, here to penetrate into the essence of things," like the hero of the epic *Der Franke in Egypten* (The Frank in Egypt), by Karoline von Günderrode. Peter Schlemihl, in Adelbert von Chamisso's "wondrous tale" of the hero without a shadow (1814), makes his permanent residence in Egypt, specifically in the desert of the Thebais, for "it was suddenly definite and clear within me: here is your home," in the caves of the Christian inhabitants, from which he reconnoiters the rest of the world by means of his seven-league boots.

Along with their mystical attitude toward nature, thinking and speaking "hieroglyphically" was an ideal for many Romantics, and Clemens Brentano even spoke of "hieroglyphic footprints." In his *Bogs der Uhrmacher* (Bogs the watchmaker), he describes a mummy from which "hieroglyphs" become detached and turn into "living animals"; his mention of the ibis shows that Egyptian picture signs are meant, and a mummiform coffin with its decoration was probably his inspiration.

The Romantics continued the eighteenth century's search for a universal language that was binding for all, and they set themselves the goal of deciphering the "Book of Nature." Paracelsus and his disciples had already acknowledged nature as God's second revelation, next to the Bible. Now, hieroglyphs were included in the Romantic theory of art. As Novalis put it, "the first art was hieroglyphistic." In an anticipation of depth psychology, Gotthilf Heinrich Schubert (*Symbolik des Traums*, 1814) pointed to "a striking relationship" between "hieroglyphic picture language . . . and the picture language of dreams," seeing in it possibilities for a deeper insight into the natural world around us, "of which our usual natural history does not allow itself to dream."

Among these efforts were the "hieroglyphic" pictures (so designated by Joseph von Görres and Friedrich Schlegel) of Philipp Otto Runge (1777–1810); "Morning," with its swarm of children in a calyx, draws its inspiration from a passage in Plutarch. Goethe also saw "genuine hieroglyphs" in these pictures by Runge, "a veritable labyrinth of dark references, arousing a dizziness of sorts in the beholder with the near unfathomableness of their meaning." Among the highly concrete symbols that appear in the works of Novalis, Runge, and others are the venerable *ouroboros*, the serpent with its tail in its mouth, and interest in the Hermetic art of alchemy also remained alive. The natural symbolism of the Romantics would later exert an influence on Caspar David Friedrich.

In the meantime, the public had been acquainted with detailed descriptions and renderings of monuments in Egypt by the Danish naval officer Frederik Ludvig Norden (*Drawings of Some Ruins and Colossal Statues at Thebes in Egypt*, 1741) and the English traveler Richard Pococke, whose *Description of the East* appeared in 1743. But even the scholars who accompanied Napoleon's expedition had no feel for original Egyptian art, for their eyes had been trained by later fakes and imitations; even so, though the hieroglyphs had not yet been deciphered, they made quite useful text copies. In the wake of the French expedition, a continual flood of original works, fed especially by the European consuls in Egypt, flowed into the great collections that were now being formed in Europe. In the future, scholars would have more accurate material before their eyes.

In connection with the French expedition, there sprang up, *inter alia*, the legend that in August 1798, Napoleon and General Kléber were initiated into the so-called Rite of Memphis, at that time popular among the Freemasons, by a venerable old man, a descendant of the sages of ancient Egypt, inside the pyramid of Cheops. Here, we again encounter the role of the Great Pyramid as a place of initiation, which goes back to Terrasson, and the reputedly Egyptian origin of the Freemasons.

The Romantic turn to the night side of the world and the discovery of the unknown also led to a view of Egypt as a nightmare, a fact that is usually overlooked in treatments of western attraction to Egypt. This aspect is already evident around 1780 in the architect Jean-Louis Desprez' horrific scenery, in which, among other things, Death appears in the form of an Egyptian priest. In Ludwig Tieck's *Franz Sternbalds Wanderungen* (Franz Sternbald's wanderings, 1798), the pyramids of Egypt inspire "horror or dread" (III, 2), and in the novel's account of Ludovico's visit to Egypt (III, 8), there is no mention of the fount of wisdom that occupies the foreground of the works of other Romantics; pyramids, the Nile, and "sandy deserts with their pyramids" are conjured up on a purely superficial level. But even for Tieck, the land of the Nile was "the cradle of humankind" (III, 1).

Aleida Assmann has drawn attention to Egypt as an out-and-out trauma in the *Confessions of an English Opium Eater*, published by Thomas DeQuincey in 1822, the very year the hieroglyphs were deciphered. Here, terrifying images, in part derived from Giovanni Battista Piranesi's fireplace etchings, arise from the unconscious. Egypt is the embodiment of menacing alterity, along with India and now also China. DeQuincey felt that he was at the mercy of the divine world of the ancient cultures:

> I was the idol; I was the priest; I was worshipped; I was sacrificed. I fled from the wrath of Brama through all the forests of Asia . . . I came suddenly upon Isis and Osiris: I had done a deed, they said, which the Ibis and the crocodile trembled at. I was buried, for a thousand years, in stone coffins, with mummies and sphinxes, in narrow chambers at the heart of eternal pyramids.

And then, as the culmination: "I was kissed, with cancerous kisses, by crocodiles."

Immediately thereafter, he again sees himself confronting the "abominable head of the crocodile": "his leering eyes looked out at me, multiplied into a thousand repetitions: and I stood loathing and fascinated." Aleida Assmann comments on the crocodile's kiss as follows: "Here, the crocodile becomes the embodiment of the strange; in this cipher, the sublime plunges into physical loathing and dread."

But the crocodile also stood for a new view of Egypt that temporarily stepped into the foreground after 1830: an "exotic" Egypt in which crocodiles and lions romped among the old, familiar pyramids and sphinxes. In a 1971 essay, Martin Kaiser drew together various amusing instances of this exotic picture of Egypt in the works of poets such as Ferdinand

Freiligrath (1810–1876), Emanuel Geibel, Victor Hugo, and Gottfried Keller. In 1844, Keller received a stipend form the Zurich city government to travel in the east, but unfortunately, he used it only for a trip to Heidelberg. In Freiligrath's poem *Der Wecker in der Wüste* (The waker in the desert, 1838), the lion's roar in the desert wakes even the royal mummies in their pyramids:

> Camel and crocodile hear
> the raging roar of the king.
> It is heard in the background on the Nile's bank
> and at the wall of the pyramids;
> it wakes the royal mummy, brown and weary
> in the bosom of the pyramids.

Awakened, the mummy recalls its former glorious deeds,

> when banners of victory fluttered round me,
> when your ancestors brought me lions . . .
> and this sole, soft and dry,
> trod on the tangled hair of the Moor,
> trod on the Indians' amber brow
> and on the neck of the desert's children.

Heinrich Heine appropriately commented on this sort of poem in his *Atta Troll*:

> Is Freiligrath no poet?
> Who could sing of the lion better
> than his compatriot, the camel?

But when Freiligrath's volume of poetry appeared in 1838, Adelbert von Chamisso exuberantly stated, "Since he began to sing, all the rest of us have been sparrows," and Franz Brentano's opinion was also quite positive. There was a general valorization of the new, powerful language behind which the Romantic fuzziness lurked. Freiligrath himself described his verses as "poetry about a desert and a lion"; he carries the reader off to an exotic world that was surely fed by modern travelers' accounts and the colonialism that was just beginning but which still depended on the classical authors and their picture of the east for many motifs, such as Pharaoh as conqueror of India in Diodorus or the entirely un-Egyptian team of lions that Mark Antony supposedly drove. At this time, Egypt was a province of the Turkish empire, of the modern east, with traces of the pharaonic era still infused in it. The painters known as "Orientalists," who left their mark on France in particular in the nineteenth century, had a parallel vision. After that, during the course of the century, the work of Egyptologists succeeded in distinguishing pharaonic Egypt more clearly from the classical and Turkish east.

With that, there commenced a development that would lead far from the esoteric picture of Egypt. It was not until the last quarter of the nineteenth century that Theosophists again emphasized the Egypt of wisdom and initiation. They took up the traditions of the Rosicrucians and the Freemasons, but they were also able to make early borrowings from the discipline of Egyptology, which had been established in the meanwhile. Art now also received fresh stimuli, and the Symbolist painters were inspired in many ways by Helena Blavatsky's *Isis Unveiled*.

SIXTEEN

THEOSOPHY AND ANTHROPOSOPHY

We find mention of *theosophy* and *anthroposophy* as early as the sixteenth century. Jakob Böhme in particular has been designated a theosophist, but there were also Franz Xaver von Baader (1765–1841) and others. As early as 1783, a Theosophical Society was founded in London; it was influenced by another theosophist, the Swedish "ghost-seer" Emmanuel Swedenborg. Here, however, we shall concern ourselves with its later successor and with the anthroposophy of Rudolf Steiner (not that of Robert Fludd) that emerged from it.

The predecessor of the Theosophical Society founded in New York in September 1875 was the secret society called the Hermetic Brotherhood of Luxor, which not only displayed a twofold connection with Egypt in its name (Hermes and Luxor), but also used the *ankh*, the Egyptian symbol for life, as its publisher's mark. The seal of the new society also contained two ancient Egyptian symbols, the *ouroboros*-serpent and the *ankh*, and the names "Egyptological Society" and "Hermetic Society" were also considered as names, as Colonel Olcott informs us in his memoirs. From the very beginning, there was a strong connection with spiritualism, which constantly crops up in theosophy. The events of December 1847 in Hydesville, New York, were crucial to this development: two girls aged 12 and 13 entered into contact with the spirit world, setting off a veritable boom in mediums, who found credulity even in high society. The spiritual component of theosophy looked to India with *karma* and reincarnation ranking among its major tenets. An external sign of the Indian connection was the transfer of the society's seat to Bombay in 1879, and in December of 1882, to Adyar, a suburb of Madras. After the society nearly died out in New York, it suddenly spread. Until 1885, it was organized on the model of the Freemasons and grew to 121 lodges; after 1886, national Sections were formed.

At the society's center stood Helena Petrovna Blavatsky (1831–1891), daughter of Colonel Peter Hahn; born in Yekaterinoslav (Dnepropetrovsk), her mother was a Dolgoruki, and thus from a noble family. In 1848, Helena was married to Nikifor Blavatsky, the vicegovernor of Yerevan in the Caucasus. After only a few weeks, she fled to Constantinople; she is attested in Cairo in 1872, and later, she claimed to have spent seven years in Tibet, where she was initiated by Master Morya, though there is no mention of this episode in her book on Isis. From 1873 on, she lived in the United States of America, and in 1877, after the founding of the society, she published *Isis Unveiled: A Master-Key to the Mysteries of Ancient and Modern Science and Theology*, which saw many printings and also appeared in German translation in 1909. With this work, she intended to lift the veil of Isis, and she described the goal of the new society as "to experiment practically in the occult powers of Nature, and to collect and disseminate among Christians information about the oriental religious philosophies" (p. xli). She credited the ancient cultures with a superior knowledge (I, 6) that needed to be brought to light again—there was a need to search for truth in the most ancient texts (I, 444). Moses and Aristotle had been initiated into Egyptian wisdom, Pythagoras and Plato had learned all their philosophy from the books of Hermes Trismegistus (I, 144), and "Isis is but the symbol of nature" (I, 16).

She has a great deal to say about "Hermetic philosophy," and for her, Paracelsus was the first true initiate of modern times (II, 349); but along with the tradition stemming from Hermetism and Paracelsus (in I, 100 she mentions Paracelsus, Cagliostro, and Mesmer in one and the same breath!), she also attempts to make use of the Egyptology of her day. For her, as for its editor Georg Ebers, Papyrus Ebers was one of the six Hermetic books on medicine mentioned by Clement of Alexandria, and the Book of the Dead was the most ancient book of wisdom (the Pyramid Texts were not discovered until 1881); she used the translation by Birch in von Bunsen, *Egypt's Place in Universal History* (1867). But her source for an

Egyptian initiation was the Masonic "Crata Napoa" (sic!—for Crata Repoa) (II, 364–365). The pyramids were places of initiation, and the "sarcophagus of porphyry" in Cheops' pyramid was a "baptismal font" for the rebirth of the neophyte (I, 519). She wished to connect it with an "esoteric school" for an inner circle of initiates.

In Book I (p. 205), she lists the components of the secret sciences: alchemy, cabala, Pythagoras, magi, neo-Platonics, Indian gymnosophists, Chaldean astrologers, and magic as "ancient psychology" ("as old as man": I, 18); spiritualism is an additional, modern ingredient, and in other places, she mentions the secret gnostic teachings connected with Jesus. She thus presents a colorful mixture of highly diverse religious traditions. Additionally, she often stresses the spiritual relationship between India and Egypt. Theosophy was an attempt to distill the essence of all religions, and it should be viewed as a reaction to the materialism and the fossilized Christian theology of the modern era.

Helena Blavatsky's original contribution was her reconstruction of the early spiritual history of humankind, with the sunken continents of Lemuria (where Adam and Eve lived) and Atlantis at its center; this was the topic of her second book, *The Secret Doctrine* (1888). In this connection, she appealed to the so-called *Akasha Chronicle*, which also played an important role in the work of Rudolf Steiner; all spiritual activity had left its traces in this work, making it a sort of collective memory of the cosmos. Peter Paddon, a contemporary esoteric writer, informs us that it was the gift of Thoth Hermes himself (*Book of the Veil*, p. 107). While Atlantis was an ancient tradition that was being popularized in a number of books at that time, the continent of Lemuria, once a land bridge between southern India and Madagascar, was not "discovered" until 1874, by P. L. Slater. The continent was Slater's explanation of how it is that lemurs, which today are found only in Madagascar, once also existed in Europe and North America. Because of their nocturnal racket, this suborder of monkey-like animals is called by the Latin word for the dead souls that wander about as ghosts in the night. Thomas Mann mentions this sunken continent at the beginning of his novel *Joseph and His Brethren*.

After vehement controversies and scandals, Helena Blavatsky left India in March 1885 and traveled in Europe; in 1887, she settled in London, where she died on May 8, 1891. In England, the poet William Butler Yeats sympathized with the theosophists and became a member of the Society in 1887, though a little later, he transferred his membership to the Hermetic Order of the Golden Dawn, which was more committed to the fundamentally esoteric; later, the eccentric Aleister Crowley also became a member. George Bernard Shaw was also in contact with the theosophists; in *Arms and the Man* (1894), he portrayed the theosophist Annie Besant as Raina, who ultimately did not decide in favor of her Bulgarian war hero but rather preferred the less bellicose Swiss "chocolate soldier" Bluntschli.

Theosophists were strongly oriented toward the wisdom of the East. After a brief stay in Adyar, Franz Hartmann (1838–1912), an intimate of Helena Blavatsky, converted to Buddhism; he later headed an independent "Theosophical Society in Germany," with Theodor Reuss as vice president. Other important confidantes of Blavatsky were the Swedish countess Constance Wachtmeister (from 1884 on) and Annie Besant (1847–1933), a prominent feminist who became a member of the Theosophical Society in 1889; until Blavatsky's death in 1891, Mrs. Besant was her closest collaborator. In 1893, she also moved to India, and she even took the trouble to learn Sanskrit. In 1905, she published *The Ancient Wisdom: An Outline of Theosophical Teachings*, and (after the death of cofounder Henry Steel Olcott) from 1907 until her death in 1933, she was president of the Theosophical Society in Adyar. There, although she concentrated on Indian wisdom, she also published writings on Hermes Trismegistus, including a *Gospel of Hermes* by Duncan Greenlees (Madras, 1949). There were also ongoing connections with the Freemasons.

Beginning in 1909, Annie Besant, who was reproached for her "orientalizing" of theosophy, attempted to set up Jiddu Krishnamurti (1895–1986), who came from a Brahman family, as "World Savior," a reincarnation of the World Teacher, a development that led, among other things, to Rudolf Steiner's resignation from the Theosophical Society. Since the turn of the century, Steiner had given ongoing lectures, in particular on mystical experiences, to a theosophical circle in Berlin, and later in other places as well, and from October 1902 on, he had served as the secretary of the German Section of the Adyar society. In his book *Theosophie* (1904), he fully adopted its concepts regarding reincarnation and karma, but the "eastern way" of the Anglo-Indian movement was not practicable for him, especially after the "discovery" and propagation of Krishnamurti.

Growing differences led the German Section of the Theosophical Society to split from Annie Besant at the beginning of 1913. Immediately thereafter, an Anthroposophical Society was founded by Rudolf Steiner and his followers; in the same year, they began the construction of the first Goetheanum in Dornach. Steiner had otherwise already come into contact with theosophy in Vienna in 1888, in the persons of Maria Lang and Friedrich Eckstein (1861–1939), but he rejected the movement of Hartmann (who also stayed in Vienna for a time) and especially its spiritual excesses. He felt that along with the theosophists' openness to spiritual impetuses, there was also "triviality and dilettantism" (*Mein Lebensgang*, "My lifetime," p. 293). What he rejected was the propagation of Buddhism and Hinduism in Europe, where Christians already possessed a "kernel of wisdom." To him, Krishnamurti was merely "a Hindu lad" to whom he ascribed no importance.

Krishnamurti's father had been a member of the Theosophical Society since 1882, and in 1909, he and his two sons moved to Adyar. There, on the Madras shore, the fourteen-year-old boy was "discovered" by Charles Webster Leadbeater (1847–1934). The latter was a highly enigmatic and dubious character. A former Anglican priest, he was a theosophist who followed Helena Blavatsky to India. Leadbeater doubtless had certain parapsychological abilities, but he was constantly embroiled in homosexual scandals and sometimes excluded from society. He and Annie Besant, who collaborated closely, were purportedly initiated by two wise teachers in Tibet (whom Madame Blavatsky supposedly also saw); they constantly referred to the instructions and advice of these two gurus, who belonged to the "Great White Brotherhood," which guided the destiny of the world.

In the Theosophical Society at that time, there was a prevalent expectation—even this was an old esoteric tradition—of a new Messiah. Maitreya, who had previously been embodied in Krishna and then in Jesus, was making his way toward a fresh incarnation. Leadbeater was chosen to find a suitable boy, and he first struck it lucky in the United States of America with a fourteen-year-old. Brought to India with his mother by Mrs. Besant, the boy encountered the already (in April 1909) "discovered" Krishnamurti, to whom Annie Besant had paid homage and even adopted—a somewhat awkward situation. The team of Leadbeater and Besant constructed a history of the new Savior's incarnations, stretching back over forty-eight of them (once even as a pupil of the Buddha) to about 75,000 B.C.E., when the Manu, who would also play an important role in Steiner's works, led a chosen group from Atlantis to Arabia and then to central Asia. This did not prevent Leadbeater from "discovering" yet another Indian Messiah in 1913.

Krishnamurti and his brother took up residence in Europe in 1912, and later, they displayed a preference for California. He had trouble with English schools, and for a time, he was more interested in sports and motorcycles than in esoteric matters; it was not until he reached California that he had the experience of Kundalini yoga. To judge from many reports, he must have displayed a highly magical charisma. The death of his brother and fresh scandals involving Leadbeater (who had been active in Australia since 1914) triggered a change in Krishnamurti. In 1929, he dissolved the order of his followers, the Order of the Star, and in 1930, he resigned from the Theosophical Society with the remarkable explanation, "truth cannot be organized." Following World War II, he published philosophical writings and gave innumerable lectures, and after India gained its independence in 1947, he began to spend a great deal of time there. He never went so far as to deny being an embodiment of Maitreya, and he had again identified himself with him at the fifty-year jubilee of the Society in 1925. But here, as in the case of the seventeenth-century Sabbatai Zvi, the self-professed savior of the Jews who converted to Islam, we have the remarkable case of an apostate Messiah who was untrue to his calling.

We need not deal here with the further destiny of the Theosophical Society, for it had scarcely anything more to do with Egypt. Its membership greatly increased, but it also drew many critics; in the opinion of Papus (see chapter 19), though the Theosophical Society made diligent collective efforts, it afforded no true initiation. After the death of Annie Besant on September 20, 1933, George Arundale, an opponent of Leadbeater, became president of the Society, and he remained so until his own death in 1952. He was succeeded by a series of Indian presidents, beginning with C. Jinarajadasa, whom Leadbeater had "discovered" in Sri Lanka. The New Age movement that spread in the 1960s doubtless had deep roots in theosophy, with which it shared a predilection for eastern thought and religious syncretism.

Theosophy was introduced into Switzerland by Alfredo Pioda (1948–1909), who wrote a *Theosophia* (1889). In September 1889, he founded Fraternitas, Inc., with whose help he intended to build a lay cloister on Monte Verità in Ascona; C. Wachtmeister and F. Hartmann, who have already been mentioned as close associates of Helena Blavatsky, were involved in the undertaking. Nothing came of the scheme, and in 1900, Henri Oedenkoven and Ida Hoffmann inherited Alfredo Pioda's site on the Monte Verità, which in the following years became a place for experimentation with new lifestyles and with ideas that were highly radical in their time. Vegetarians, naturopathists, anarchists, and theosophists took over the "Mount of Truth," making it a shrine to alternatives and investing it with the "sacral topography" invoked by Harald Szeemann in his exhibit regarding Monte Verità in 1978.

Such was the environment that witnessed the birth of the Eranos conferences, which were founded by Olga Fröbe-Kapteyn; Rudolph Otto and Carl Gustav Jung served as advisors for this new type of conference, which also received stimulus from Martin Buber. Since 1933 these annual conferences have been held in Ascona, and since 1993, on Monte Verità. Their initial goal was to bring together eastern and western religiosity and spirituality, including "esoteric" matters. The psychologist Erich Neumann once dubbed them "a small part of the Golden Chain," the Hermetic Aurea Catena that began with Hermes Trismegistus. The conferences came to be held in ever higher regard, and the *Jahrbücher* (Yearbooks), in which the proceedings are published, now nearly seventy in number, furnish a rich store of material on all sorts of esoteric questions.

"Notwithstanding all rumors, Rudolf Steiner was never on Monte Verità. But he had many followers in Ascona, and they attended his lecture at the home of Elfriede Rathgen in Locarno-Monti on September 19, 1911"; so writes W. Schönenberger in the catalogue *Monte Verità* (p. 73). Nevertheless, Rudolf Steiner (1861–1925) came from the theosophical movement, and for him, too, Egypt was a spiritual homeland. In September 1908, he gave twelve lectures in Leipzig to members of the German section of the Theosophical Society; they were first published in 1911 under the title *Ägyptische Mythen und Mysterien* (Egyptian myths and mysteries). Steiner draws on Helena Blavatsky for the "complicated" topic of reincarnation in lecture 10, and already in lecture 1, he stresses that our souls were already present in ancient Egypt. "We ourselves probably once lived in ancient Egypt," he stated in another lecture a year later. But he also attempted to use "the means of occult research" to penetrate further, into even earlier cultures that thrived in the Lemurian and Atlantian eras. The

Leipzig lectures thus deal mostly, in purely theosophical tradition, with our cosmic past and with the various epochs that predated Egypt, with the Egypt of the third epoch living on in the current fifth epoch. "Our modern truths are reborn Egyptian myths," and "all modern culture seems to us to be a recollection of that of ancient Egypt," said Steiner in a lecture in Stuttgart in 1908; to demonstrate this notion of the transmigration of ideas, he offered the example of Copernicus, who was already incarnate in ancient Egypt, where he observed the prime importance of the sun. In his 1911 lecture on Hermes (see below), he stressed that "this culture . . . (has) a certain mysterious relationship with what present-day man desires and might set as his goal."

"Isis and Osiris are spirit beings on the moon, but we find their deeds on earth," states lecture 8 given in Leipzig. This reminds us of the Manichaean doctrine (expressed in the textbook *Kephalaia*, chap. 29) according to which the "third legate" had his place in the sun, while Jesus was at his side in the moon; ancient Chaldaean beliefs about these heavenly bodies might also be entailed here. The Manichaean path to salvation passed beyond the moon and the sun, which had already been Paradise to the Pythagoreans. Previously, in lecture 7, Steiner had recounted the Osiris "saga" essentially according to Plutarch, and he had relied on Diodorus for the animal cults. He returned to these matters ten years later in several lectures given in Dornach. For him, the Sphinx was a winged being, symbol of secret lore "from gray prehistory," and in other matters as well, he was indebted to classical traditions about Egypt not to modern Egyptology. His doctrine of humankind's sinking ever more deeply into matter until a new ascent from it began with Christ sounds Gnostic, especially when Steiner stresses that humankind will be led back up into the spiritual realm, so that man "will again gaze upon the world into which he had descended."

In lecture 9, we again encounter Zarathustra rubbing elbows with Hermes Trismegistus ("the Great Initiator"). Steiner devoted an entire lecture, which he gave in Berlin in February 1911, to Hermes. In it, Hermes was "that spirit who, according to ancient traditions, created the first records of the world's wisdom," though in fact we learn little of him as opposed to Moses, for whom Steiner made use of the Old Testament tradition. For him, Moses was "a student of the lofty Egyptian schools, of the mysteries," wherein he once again stood in the classical tradition. But in the foreground were Osiris and Isis, whom Steiner straightforwardly called "the mother of the Savior" and "Maria-Isis" in a lecture entitled "The Search for the New Isis, the Divine Sophia," which he gave in December 1920.

In "Der Seelen Erwachen" (Wakening of the souls, 1913), the fourth and last of Steiner's mystery dramas, scenes 7 and 8 constitute an initiation that takes place in an Egyptian temple ("a temple somewhat of the Egyptian sort," Figure 28). "The Egyptian woman" makes an appearance in scene 8, along with the earlier incarnations of all the actors in the play. Lucifer and Ahriman are present in this scene "in sphinx form"—in any event, as stone sphinxes that also have bull and angel components, for the form of the sphinx "should reproduce something that has been seen in an inspiration," as he put it in *Geheimnes der Trinität* (Mystery of the Trinity, 1922, p. 42). But it had already been claimed in the eighteenth century that

28. Depiction of a scene from the mystery drama "Der Seelen Erwachen," by Rudolf Steiner, c. 1932. Scene 8: a temple in Egyptian style. Sketch by M. and W. Scott-Pyle. Photo by Emil Gmelin.

the Egyptian sphinx (with an eagle's wings, a thoroughly un-Egyptian feature), incorporated the symbols of the four evangelists.

"We should not pursue Egyptian mythology in a didactic manner," says Steiner in the last of his Leipzig lectures, while in the eleventh, he offers a highly unconventional and very realistic explanation of animal deities. Darwinism represents a recollection of them; for him, it is "nothing other than our ancient Egyptian heritage in materialistic form." In the final lecture, he also speaks of Pharaoh and his initiation; the uraeus-serpent on Pharaoh's brow represents the spiritual power that he assumed within himself, and the forty-two judges of the dead are ancestors who had to be answered to. He repeatedly refers to the Judgment of the Dead, and he even quotes from Spell 125 of the Book of the Dead. Striking, however, is his complete silence regarding Akhenaten, the great worshiper of Light.

Steiner was especially fascinated by the form of the mummy, and to him, Egypt was a "mummy culture" plain and simple. Through the art of mummification, the Egyptians wished to prevent—according to Steiner—a second human descent into the world; the dead were supposed to remain in the spirit world, and by means of their mummies, the Egyptians could associate with powers of nature. Even the modern myth of the "curse of the pharaohs" entered into this belief: according to Steiner, there was always a "poisoned atmosphere" surrounding a mummy, for it was implanted with a threat through the power of words, a threat that remains effective to this day and kills people who come into contact with Egyptian mummies and tombs. Steiner delivered this explanation to the staff of the Goetheanum in Dornach in 1924, shortly after the discovery of Tutankhamun's treasure and the death of the Earl of Carnarvon.

In another Dornach lecture in 1918, he had dealt with the "star mysteries" of the pyramids, which were built by Iranian conquerors learned in astronomy and not by the Egyptians. Here, we are already close to the extraterrestrial, but Steiner derived some of what he had to say from *Der Kampf um die Cheopspyramide* (The struggle for the pyramid of Cheops, 1902), by the engineer Max Eyth (1836–1906), a book that was quite popular at the time.

In his approximately 5,000 lectures, Steiner made constant references to the "wisdom of Hermes." For him, Hermes Trismegistus was the second greatest initiate after Zoroaster, from whom Hermes derived various secret traditions. Significantly, the principle of secrecy, until then compulsory for all esoteric groups, was officially abolished in 1923, creating a marked distinction from other esoteric circles. And while Blavatsky and Besant constantly referred to their initiation by the great masters in Tibet, we hear nothing from Steiner about an actual initiation. He obtained several high degrees in the Masonic Rite of Memphis and Misraim, but he soon distanced himself from that group.

In Steiner's opinion, Christian Rosenkreuz was a historical figure like Hermes and Zoroaster, an initiate who had constantly been reincarnated. For Steiner, Rosenkreuz and the theosophist and occultist Louis-Claude de Saint-Martin (1743–1803) had preached an ancient, mysterious wisdom to which the "Philistines" of the nineteenth century had remained blind. Steiner thus took up this rather old tradition, and early on, he maintained connections with Masonic rituals.

In 1955, Ernst Uehli (1875–1959) offered a more detailed account of ancient Egyptian culture from an anthroposophical point of view, that is, from the perspective of a "mystery science." He proceeds from Steiner's thought, but he makes use of modern Egyptology to enhance it with a more detailed portrayal of Egyptian history and the principles of Egyptian art. For him, too, Hermes Trismegistus was the founder of the "Egyptian cultural epoch" (p. 251), the "original teacher . . . who received a training in the mysteries from Zarathustra" (p. 34)—but this was the elder Zarathustra, who belonged to the seventh millennium B.C.E., just as Hermes, the human propagator of the original wisdom, is to be distinguished from the god Thoth, the "ultimate source of this original wisdom" (pp. 64–65). This "elder" Zarathustra was in no way a discovery of Steiner or the theosophists but rather the result of a reading of Plutarch, who mentions the "magus Zoroaster," who "is supposed to have been 5,000 years earlier than the Trojan War" (*De Iside*, chap. 46) and therefore lived in the seventh millennium; it is to him that Plutarch transfers the dualistic teaching of the later religious founder. And even before Plutarch, Pliny had spoken of *two* Zoroasters (*Natural History*, 30, 8).

In Uehli's work, the "Heliopolitan priests of Hermes," whose initiates included even Imhotep, played an important role; they also supported Akhenaten, who opposed the Theban priests of Amun by preaching "the great solar mystery" of his faith in Aten. Uehli also endeavored to recover an anthroposophic picture of the creation of the world from the myth of Osiris, which he, too, recounted according to Plutarch, just as he depended on Arthur Weigall for Akhenaten; he also had no problem with using the Old Testament tradition (e.g., the story of Joseph) as a trustworthy historical source.

A person being initiated into the ancient Egyptian mysteries would be placed in the sarcophagus in the Great Pyramid, and the blocking stone would be lowered into place (an unpleasant sensation!); after three days, the person was admitted into the brotherhood of the initiated, with the "handled cross of Isis," the uraeus, and the headcloth as external signs—so Uehli, and he also claimed that the Sphinx of Giza originally had wings, for it was a combination of man, lion, bull, and eagle. Since Zarathustra had initiated his original pupil, Uehli, like Steiner before him, attempted to demonstrate the plausibility of an "Iranian" origin of the pyramids, specifically from the "Iranian astral mysteries" (pp. 144–146). In any event, he viewed the pyramids as places of initiation, and the Pyramid Texts and the Coffin Texts could only have been written by initiates (p. 195).

Steiner had already stressed the importance of the mummy as a means of posing questions to the divine and as a link to the spirit world; Uehli added the popular but lurid tale that a mummy on board the *Titanic* had caused the ship to sink in 1912. The anthroposophic poet Albert Steffen turned this story into a drama, "Fahrt ins andere Land" (Journey to another land), which was performed in the municipal theater of Basel in the autumn of 1938. The drama is centered on the mummy of a princess "of Dynasty 16" who brings disaster to all. In a prelude, we see a team of archaeologists under the direction of Professor Theodor Fisher (who believes, among other things, in reincarnation) working in the Theban tomb where the mummy is discovered. "Hieroglyphs all round," state the instructions for the set design, which also mention a Judgment of the Dead in which Hermes appears "with the head of an eagle (!)." "We hear the distant howling of a jackal, which becomes louder in the course of the action."

Professor Fisher brings the mummy on board the *Titanic*, where nearly all the members of the expedition are reunited. At the end of scene 3, the floating iceberg makes its appearance "in the form of a pyramid that grows to gigantic proportions." As the ship sinks, the professor makes an entrance with the mummy chest on his back, for he does not feel that the cabin is a fit burial place for an Egyptian priestess. "We carry ancient Egypt in our souls," he says. The mummy's coffin and its decoration offer consolation to those who are drowning, and at the end, it also saves an infant.

Frank Teichmann adopted and elaborated Rudolf Steiner's idea of Pharaoh's initiation, which itself goes back to formulations in the works of Clement of Alexandria and Plutarch. Teichmann represents a younger generation of anthroposophists, and he has examined ancient Egypt thoroughly, doing research of his own. In his book *Der Mensch und sein Tempel—Ägypten* (Man and his temple—Egypt, 1978), it is already a "fact that in Egypt, there were places for enacting mysteries in which the Egyptian pharaohs were initiated" (p. 8), and that in Egypt, no one could become king without being initiated (p. 67). In ancient tradition, according to Teichmann, the pyramids were the "places in which Pharaoh's coronation and initiation took place" (p. 99), and Rudolf Steiner had precisely described the practices of ancient initiation (pp. 90–91). Julius Evola (1898–1974), the noted Italian Hermetist, also described a royal initiation in ancient Egypt.

Teichmann went a step further in *Die Kultur der Empfindungsseele* (The culture of the sensing soul, 1990), in which he adopts Rudolf Steiner's distinction (which had an early precursor in the work of Robert Fludd) between three stages of human consciousness: a soul capable of sensation, one capable of understanding, and one capable of consciousness. Teichmann sees ancient Egypt as a typical example of the first stage, that of the soul capable of sensation, but his particular thesis is that Pharaoh's consciousness was fundamentally different from that of ordinary Egyptians. Erwin Horstmann had already stressed that in ancient Egypt, only initiates could think logically, and for Teichmann, the ultimate consequence is that Pharaoh was the only individual in ancient Egypt who could think: "the ordinary Egyptian had no thought" (p. 138). Elsewhere, however, he speaks of a "small group of men ... who were capable of analytic thought" (p. 84), though only Pharaoh could "perceive what happened in the spirit world" (p. 123). He received this insight by means of a momentary distancing of his *ka*-soul, and "this procedure in fact took place in a coffin" (p. 196; similarly Uehli and also E. Horstmann). The motif of placing the one to be initiated in a coffin appears again and again in modern esoterica—for the Freemasons, it is symbolic, not real, but in many contemporary sects, the sublimest experience seems to be to spend a night in the coffin in the pyramid of Cheops.

Teichmann's view of Egypt thus stands in an esoteric tradition that also includes reincarnation. The only thing missing is mention of Hermes Trismegistus; instead, we find the prominent figure of Imhotep (thus the later Asclepius), though in fact he was no pharaoh. The Books of the Netherworld are mystery texts intended to initiate Pharaoh into the mysteries of the course of the sun, and Teichmann therefore stresses the principal distinction between the decoration of royal tombs and those of officials. But in Dynasty 18, and especially after the Amarna Period, officials found other ways to involve the tomb owner in the mysteries of the sun's course—first, through solar hymns in the entrances to the tombs, and later through ingenious representations of the course of the sun in ever new variations in Ramesside Period tombs and Books of the Dead.

We must maintain that Steiner's attempt to found a *rational mysticism* remains questionable, for mysticism is always and above all irrational. The concept of a "mystery science" or "science of the mysterious" is thus also inherently self-contradictory and paradoxical. The problem is that scientific results must be capable of being checked and refined; if not, arbitrariness will rule. Science can therefore never be secret and reserved only for initiates or make use of purely intuitive insights, even if these happen to be entirely correct. It cannot be denied, though, that much fruitful guidance in practical life has emerged from the esoterica of anthroposophy.

SEVENTEEN

PYRAMIDS, SPHINX, MUMMIES

A Curse on the Pharaohs

Every traveler to Egypt, whether in antiquity, in the Middle Ages, or in modern times, has marveled above all at the Great Pyramids of Giza (Figure 29). They gave Diodorus the impression that some god (an extra-terrestrial!) had made them and set them in the desert sands (*Bibliotheca historica*, I, 63, 7), but Diodorus still knew that they had been built as tombs (64, 4). This knowledge was lost to the Christian, and to some of the Islamic, writers of the Middle Ages. For one group of Christian authors, as attested already in the eighth century, they were Joseph's granaries, and for another group, they were treasure vaults and powerful talismans for protection against the Flood. The Arab writers constantly referred to Hermes Trismegistus as the builder of the pyramids, for he saw the Flood coming and wished to rescue the cultural heritage of humankind from it.

The granary explanation seems to go back to Gregory of Nazianz (fourth century). Since tradition often referred to the pyramids only as *turris* ("tower"), even their shape fell into oblivion on some medieval and Renaissance maps. Yet, they were correctly designated as burial places by Isidore of Seville and, in the Carolingian period, in Hrabanus Maurus' *De universo* (On the universe).

The pyramids are depicted as granaries in the thirteenth-century mosaics of San Marco in Venice. Wilhelm von Boldensele, who traveled to Egypt in 1335, expressed doubts as to this interpretation, but it was not until around the end of the fifteenth century that criticism mounted to the

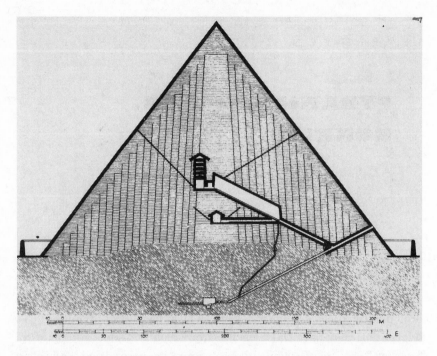

29. Cross section of the pyramid of Cheops. The main chamber is not subterranean, as in the other pyramids, but rather in the middle of the monument. The scale below shows Egyptian cubits. From L. Borchardt, "Einiges zur dritten Bauperiode der grossen Pyramide bei Gise," in *Beiträge zur ägyptischen Bauforschung und Altertumskunde*, vol. 1/3 (Cairo, 1932), pl. 1.

point that they were again viewed as tombs. Knowledge that they were tombs had remained alive among Arab authors, and we even find them explained as the tomb of Hermes Trismegistus and Agathodaimon (Mas'udi, d. 956; Abdellatif; al-Maqrizi); but around 985, writers such as Moqaddasî already knew the explanation that they were Joseph's granaries; in the Islamic period, there was always an interest in finding traces of Joseph's activity in Egypt.

Abu Ja'far al-Idrisi (1173–1251), who came from the region of Dendara, drafted a thorough work on the pyramids; in 1989, Ulrich Haarmann produced a critical edition whose flowery Arabic title, translated into English, reads *Book of the Lights of the Superior Heavenly Bodies: On Revealing the Secrets of the Pyramids*. To Idrisi, the pyramids were the pinnacle of the wondrous things that the faithful could and should see, and for this reason, they were a popular stopover for north African pilgrims journeying to Mecca. Idrisi thus tells us of a Moroccan pilgrim who was immediately sent back on his way by his *sheikh*, for he had neglected to have a look at this Wonder of the World.

Nearly a quarter of Idrisi's text is devoted to the question of whether the pyramids were built *before* or *after* the Flood, with the overwhelming majority of sources favoring the option *before*. Al-Halabi (d. 1267), a friend of al-Idrisi, went so far as to connect their construction with pre-Adamites, the inhabitants of an earlier earth, a notion that again brings us close to "extraterrestrials." According to a fourteenth-century manuscript, the Sphinx had once stood atop the pyramid of Cheops, whence it had been hurled and smashed by the might of the Flood. Arab writers supply various figures, ranging from one to twenty, regarding the controversial question of how many camels could fit on the upper surface of the Great Pyramid, for by the Middle Ages, the tip of the pyramid was already missing. Idrisi recounts early efforts to make precise measurements of the two largest pyramids. There were also thoughts on how they were built, and just as in modern times, writers marveled at the perfect art of the pharaonic stonemasons, which bordered on magical power; according to Maqrizi, it derived specifically from magic. But "Allah knows best!" The geographer and historian Ibn Fadlallah al-'Umari (d. 1348) originated the well-known saying, "Everything fears Time, but Time fears the pyramids."

According to al-Maqrizi (1364–1442), who wrote the other detailed account that has survived, the pyramids were built by King Surid because of the impending Flood and were filled with "talismans, wonders, treasures, idols, and the corpses of their kings," and they were inscribed with the secret sciences of the Egyptians. The material and intellectual treasures of the ancients were thus preserved through the Flood, and each pyramid was assigned a special, fearsome guardian. The astrologer Abumasar (787–886) had already ascribed the construction of the pyramids to a dream of King Surid.

Al-Mas'udi (d. 956) and other writers mention a Queen Daluka who, after Pharaoh perished in the Red Sea, came to the throne and built a wall around all of Egypt. (The earliest account is probably that of Ibn Abd al-Hakam in the ninth century; he relied on earlier sources dating back to a son of Amr ibn al-As, the conqueror of Egypt.) This queen was renowned for her wisdom, and she also built the temples of Egypt, where she stored the secrets of Nature. Later, the pyramids also made their appearance as the work of Queen Daluka in the accounts of seventeenth-century European travelers such as George Sandys (1610) and John Greaves; we shall deal with the latter below. In his *Admiranda ethnicae theolgiae mysteria propalata* (The wondrous and manifest mysteries of pagan theology, 1623), Johann Georg Herwart von Hohenburg also seems to have been aware of the Arab tradition according to which the pyramids and the Sphinx were built as bulwarks against the (Nile) flood. This tradition continued, and we encounter Queen Daluka (spelled Daluca) in the Abbé Terrasson's novel *Séthos* (1731). With regard to this novel, however, it must be maintained that none of these early travelers viewed the pyramids as places of initiation; in the sixteenth and seventeenth centuries, there was a widespread view that Cheops' sarcophagus was the intended burial place of the pharaoh who drowned in the Red Sea at the time of the Exodus. The pyramids were also often assigned an astronomical purpose.

In 1637, John Greaves, Professor of Astronomy and Mathematics at Oxford, contributed a new, scientific attitude with his investigations and measurements; he even mentioned the "air channels" in the pyramid of Cheops. His *Pyramidographia* (1646) and *Pyramidologia* (1663) long remained the basis for all treatments of these monuments; his efforts were complemented by the meticulous investigations of the French consul Benoît de Maillet, beginning in 1692. Many eighteenth-century travelers zealously made measurements in and around the Great Pyramid.

But there was also a flowering of pyramid mysticism. The naturalist Thomas Shaw, who visited Cairo in 1721, thought that the interior of Cheops' pyramid was not suited to be a tomb; he therefore took it to be a temple, and he also believed there were subterranean passages linking it to the Sphinx and the other pyramids. He viewed its sarcophagus (Figure 30) as an implement for the mystical worship of Osiris. He was followed by the physician Charles Perry, who published his *A View of the Levant* in 1743. Perry also believed that the Great Pyramids were intended for religious mysteries. The pyramids also loomed in mystical dimensions, literally higher than the clouds, in the visions of the artists of the period, such as Fischer von Erlach (1721), and especially Hubert Robert in his oil painting of 1760, which was recently on view in the "Egyptomania" exhibit (no. 22). In it, the pyramid, contrasted by tiny humans at its base, rises steeply

30. The sarcophagus chamber in the pyramid of Cheops. From Luigi Mayer, *Views in Egypt* (London, 1801).

into infinity, high above a dramatic mass of clouds. In these visions, the Roman pyramid of Cestius, with its acute angles, is combined with ancient accounts of the mighty constructions of King Moeris.

In his *Recherches philosophiques sur les Égyptiens et les Chinois* (Philosophical researches on the Egyptians and the Chinese, 1773), Cornelius de Pauw expressed the opinion that the pyramids were not tombs but rather temples for the worship of "the Being who filled the universe with light" (a typical Enlightenment formulation), though he viewed the chambers in the pyramid of Cheops as the tomb of Osiris. Moreover, the pyramids had their origin in a grandiose job-creation scheme (de Pauw was a Prussian court official!) by means of which the Egyptian kings created work for their subjects. He thus had an economically more positive view of the pyramids than that of Toynbee in his *Study of History* (1934–1939), wherein the modern, rationalistic view of history celebrates a triumph; for Toynbee, the pyramids symbolized the fetishism that allegedly afflicted Egypt, and they were built by the forced labor of an enslaved people for the purpose of immortalizing their lord. To this day, slavery plays a role in discussions of the building of the pyramids, though it was not an economic factor in the Old Kingdom.

Meanwhile, as already mentioned (chapter 14), the Abbé Terrasson had raised the notion that the pyramids had served as places of initiation, in his novel *Séthos* in 1731. The idea was quickly picked up by the Freemasons and then by many esoteric groups. As impressively described by Terrasson, the initiate had to wander through lengthy subterranean passages within the pyramid; a raging watercourse was one of the barriers he had to overcome.

Giovanni Battista Caviglia, who conducted research at the pyramids beginning in 1816, embraced a special mysticism regarding these monuments, one that aspired to find hidden passageways and chambers everywhere. Additionally, he propagated a secret society called *Fratres lucis* ("Brothers of Luxor"), which went back to the ancient mysteries of Isis and supposedly held nocturnal meetings in the Pyramid of Cheops. Caviglia even attempted to introduce Champollion into this circle when the latter visited Cairo.

James St. John, who was at Giza in 1832, took the pyramids there to be temples that Cheops and his successors had built to Hathor (= Aphrodite). He based his conclusion on the fact that cattle bones had been found in the sarcophagus in the Chephren pyramid when Belzoni first opened it in 1818; St. John wished to explain them as having to do with the cow-goddess Hathor.

Next, work of fundamental importance was done in 1837 by Colonel Richard N. Howard Vyse, with measurements supplied by the engineer John S. Perring. Their three-volume work, *Operations Carried on at the Pyramids of Giza*, long remained the "bible" of pyramid researchers; in the second volume, Vyse supplied a still-useful collection of earlier opinions regarding the pyramids. At about the same time, Mimaut, who was the French consul from 1829 to 1837, found himself obliged to counter Viceroy Mohamed Ali's proposals to use the pyramids as a quarry for the dam he planned to build north of Cairo! Vyse himself was not exactly squeamish, and he went so far as to use gunpowder in the course of his investigations.

After Terrasson raised the idea that the Great Pyramids were places of initiation, Edmé-François Jomard, who wrote the chapter on the pyramids of Memphis for Napoleon's *Description de l'Égypte* (the first volume of which appeared in 1809), connected this notion with the opinion that knowledge of ancient Egyptian science was deposited in the pyramids. Around 1800, there was evidently a widespread feeling that the pyramids were witnesses to a lofty science that had perished. "Count" Cagliostro, who propagated his "Egyptian" Freemasonry, also believed that they stored the treasure of human science and knowledge, which is why he claimed to have learned the secret sciences in their subterranean vaults.

The English book dealer John Taylor took an interest in Jomard's assumption that a special unit of measurement had been employed in the pyramids. He included the pyramid inch in his book *The Great Pyramid, why was it built and who built it* (1859), and it was taken up and further defended by the Scottish astronomer Piazzi Smyth (1819–1900), even against Isaac Newton, who had already determined the correct length of the ancient Egyptian cubit. From the relationship between the height of the Great Pyramid and the circumference of the earth, as supplied by Taylor, Smyth worked out a relationship between the height of the pyramid and the distance from the earth to the sun, and he also believed he could derive the specific weight of the earth from the measurements of the sarcophagus, along with further key data of astronomy. Smyth and many others after him tried to derive all of biblical history and its aftermath from the measurements of the interior spaces, and Smyth saw a result of divine revelation in all these relationships.

Smyth's measurements at the site itself in 1865 led to the multivolume *Life and Work at the Great Pyramid* (1867), which became a source for mysticism centered on the pyramid, along with his earlier work, *Our Inheritance in the Great Pyramid* (1864). A son of his collaborator Petrie, William Flinders Petrie, went to Egypt at the end of 1880 to substantiate Smyth's theories through further measurements. Nothing remains of these, and at the end of the Introduction to his *Pyramids and Temples of Gizeh* (1883), Petrie cites an American adherent of pyramid theories who visited him and after some days sadly remarked, "Well, sir! I feel as if I had been to a funeral."

But the patient was not really dead, just in suspended animation, for although Petrie's results were negative and converted him (with his later work, he became the founder of Egyptian archaeology), pyramid mysticism flourished again and was freshly sustained by Max Eyth's novel *Der Kampf um die Cheopspyramide* (1902). The search for a new orientation after the end of World War I saw the appearance of a flood of new works, books in which even atomic weight and the length of the pregnancy of mammals were derived from the measurements of the pyramids! For others, the pyramids were a stone calendar, a gigantic observatory for stargazing, or an orientation point for geodetic measurements. The authors of these works always assumed that at the time the pyramids were built, the Egyptians were at a scientific level that was reattained in Europe only in the nineteenth century. Thus, for instance, it was claimed that they were aware of the heliocentric view of the solar system and of the precession of the earth's axis. Peter Tompkins knew how this level of scientific knowledge had been lost: Alexander the Great ordered the destruction of Heliopolis, "the center of Egyptian science," in order to build a capital of his own at Alexandria, and it is known that Heliopolis "was considered the greatest university in the world." Tompkins does not state that Moses and Pythagoras matriculated there, but "there were said to be 13,000 [priests] there in the time of Ramesses III" (p. 214).

This new outbreak of an "epidemic" (so to speak) of pyramid explanations led to Ludwig Borchardt's lecture "Gegen die Zahlenmystik an der grossen Pyramide bei Gise" (Against numerical mysticism in the Great Pyramid of Giza); the lecture was given in 1922, just before the discovery of the treasure of Tutankhamun, which somewhat displaced the pyramids from the public interest. Borchardt pointed out that we must not consider the pyramids in isolation, for they were part of a larger whole that included extensive constructions, such as cult places; this would have been a rather exhorbitant expenditure for nothing more than a Weights and Measurements Office (as a place where standard measurements were kept, which some thought were embodied in Cheops' sarcophagus). Beyond that, any sort of nonsense could be extracted or demonstrated from numbers.

But even Borchardt proved unable to put an end to the speculations that constantly broke out. Once again, we meet with Rosicrucians and theosophists, such as Georges Barbarin, whose *Le Secret de la Grande Pyramide ou la fin du monde adamique* (The secret of the Great Pyramid, or the end of the Adamic world), appeared in 1936 in the Éditions Adyar. In Adam Rutherford's *Pyramidology* (4 vols., 1957–1972), the Great Pyramid and the Bible are revelations of the Creator, the former in stone, the latter in word. Rutherford founded his own Institute of Pyramidology in England, and he defined this topic as "science that deals with the Great Pyramid's scientific demonstration of Biblical truth, true Christianity and the Divine plan respecting humanity on this planet"; the pyramids are thus early evidence of Christianity. Since 1971, similar speculations have been widely circulated by Peter Tompkins' already-mentioned book, *Secrets of the Great Pyramid;* an advertisement for the German-language edition makes the point, "the Great Pyramid was not a royal tomb, but rather the center of all the knowledge of the ancient Egyptians." Moreover, there has been a constant emergence of "initiates" with precise information regarding the secret chambers in the pyramid, who try to persuade archaeologists to discover, at long last, the completely preserved burial of Cheops, with all its mysteries.

Even Luis Alvarez, the important American physicist, partook in the hunt for *Hidden Chambers* in 1968, with the help of proof from cosmic rays. The 1980s saw a boom in this modern treasure hunting, thanks to the accommodation of the Egyptian Antiquities Service; details can be found in Rainer Stadelmann's book on the pyramids. The result was a little drifting sand that had blown in and was found when holes were bored in the pyramid. These efforts were ultimately influenced by Herodotus' ancient account of a channel beneath the Great Pyramid. There has also been no end to the attempts to explain the miracle of the pyramids and their erection by means of supernatural capabilities on the part of the Egyptians.

There have also been quite different, amusing explanations of these royal tombs, such as that by an Austrian engineer for whom these constructions were devices for watering the desert (W. Ennsthaler, *Regenzauber der Pharaonen,* "Rain magic of the pharaohs," 1976), or the fantastic theory of Davidovits, communicated a number of times to congresses, that the pyramids were built of artificial stone! According to another discovery published as recently as 1997 (Manfred Dimde, *Die Heilkraft der Pyramiden,* "The healing power of the pyramids"), the entire plateau of Giza, including the obelisks and the Sphinx, is a sort of "transformer" for cosmic and terrestrial energies, a charging station for bioenergies, and thus of practical help in life. Tompkins had already reported observations made in Italy and Yugoslavia in which milk in pyramid-shaped packaging stayed fresh indefinitely without refrigeration (p. 297), and the

Czechoslovakian Patent Office is supposed to have granted a patent to an engineer for his razor-blade sharpener in the shape of the pyramid of Cheops. Since all of this has been known for decades, it is inconceivable that there is still no pyramid (of whatever material) in every household, making a refrigerator and many other devices unnecessary.

Since 1993, the German Archaeological Institute in Cairo has been cleaning and exploring the "air channels" (better: model corridors for the ascent of the *ba*-soul or the *ka* of the deceased king) in the Cheops pyramid with the help of a robot constructed by the engineer R. Gantenbrink. Because of a blockage in the southern corridor, this work has inspired fresh speculations about hidden treasures. There have also been new theories about the great antiquity of the Sphinx of Giza, whose erosion has been traced back to immense rainfalls and thus to a prehistoric wet phase, which for its part was connected with a certain constellation in the sky around the year 10,500 B.C.E.; all these speculations have enjoyed wide circulation and influence on the public thanks to the media.

Such "discoveries" are not new, for as early as 1911–1912, there was a controversy in the media about the age of the Sphinx and its stellar interpretation; Howard Carter, who discovered the tomb of Tutankhamun, discussed it in one of his letters. More convincing is the poetic explanation of al-Iskandarâni (d. 1135), who viewed the Sphinx of Giza as a chaperone who keeps the amorous Great Pyramids apart.

In recent years a growing flood of literature has portrayed the pyramids as the work of extraterrestrials. Von Däniken has found many imitators in this matter, and even in these circles, Hermes Trismegistus is sometimes evoked. The deities of Egypt have been styled extraterrestrials who guide the destiny of humankind from afar and sometimes even intervene directly. The recent turn of the millennium gave further stimulus to speculations of this sort, including the claim that pyramids and a sphinx had been spotted on Mars.

Rainer Stadelmann (p. 279) gives the following description of what else is going on in the pyramid of Cheops:

> Before and just after sunrise, the faithful of the pyramid mystery sects, along with members of Masonic lodges with mystical leanings, gather in the tomb chamber and the so-called Queen's Chamber and devote themselves to hours of meditation and soft chanting.

He also notes the dangers posed to the ecosystem in the pyramid. There was a major celebration at the pyramids of Giza on the night of December 31, 1999.

Along with the pyramids, Egyptian mummies (Figure 31) exert a great fascination. Travelers to the Nile were bringing mummies home with them as early as the seventeenth century (see chapter 11), and in the nineteenth century, especially in England, it was fashionable to treat their unwrappings as social occasions to which people would invite their friends or even paying guests (Figure 32). In the 1830s, the public demonstrations carried out by the physician Thomas Pettigrew were a great sensation. Pettigrew made these "dehydrated bodies," as Heinrich Schäfer called them, more popular than ever and a topic of literature. In the late eighteenth century, "decorative mummies" were to be found in architecture.

March 19, 1696, had already seen the performance in Paris of *Les Momies de l'Égypte* (The mummies of Egypt), a comedy by Jean-François Regnard (1655–1709). This long-lost play in the style of the *Commedia dell'arte* was brought to light again by Claude Aziza at the colloquium "L'Égyptomanie à l'épreuve de l'archéologie" (Egyptomania tested by archaeology) in Paris; he included the text of the play on pages 561–583 of the published acts of this colloquium. In the play, Osiris is embodied by Scaramouche, Mark Antony by Arlequin, and Cleopatra by Colombine, who also clothes herself as an Egyptian woman; moreover, "several mummies" enter into the action. In scene 5, the set changes into ruins "among which we see Egyptian pyramids and a number of tombs." Osiris makes an appearance, and in scene 8, we see Antony and Cleopatra (= Arlequin and Colombine) in the form of mummies who are reconciled after violent quarreling. The tomb of Mark Antony then turns into a table with mummies waiting on it; the company sets about feasting, while the Sibyl recommends embalming for everyone, so as "to remain alive longer."

Jean Paul used the emotive word "mummies" as the subtitle of his fragment "The Invisible Lodge" (1792), in which we also encounter Count Cagliostro and a mixed being ("an Egyptian deity, an incomplete being with an animal head and a human torso"). Following the intense interest in mummies in the early nineteenth century, Edgar Allan Poe wrote his tale "Some Words with a Mummy" (1845), in which he begins with a typical mummy demonstration in which the mummy is removed from its nested coffins. In an original touch, he has the mummy brought back to

31. One of the royal mummies from Deir el-Bahari, found in 1881 and drawn by G. Schweinfurth. From *Die Gartenlaube* 32 (1884): 629.

The Nobility and Gentry, Visiters and Inhabitants of BATH and its Vicinity, are respectfully informed, that

TWO EGYPTIAN

MUMMIES,

A MALE AND FEMALE,

In the highest State of Preservation, *with various other Relics,*

BROUGHT TO THIS COUNTRY BY

Mr. BELZONI,

The celebrated Traveller, are now open for Exhibition at

10, New Bond-Street.

The MUMMIES are of the first Class: the Inspection of them it is presumed must be highly satisfactory to every Person, as exhibiting two distinct Specimens; the Bandages of the Male having been entirely removed from the Body, which is perfect, while the mode of applying them is beautifully illustrated in the Envelope of the Female.

The CASES are covered with Hieroglyphics, enriched with Ornaments most elaborately executed; the Interiors containing the Histories of the Lives of their very ancient Occupiers, in Egyptian Characters, as fresh as when inscribed by the Hand of the Artist, after a Lapse of probably

THREE THOUSAND YEARS.

" Perchance that very Hand, now pinioned flat,
" Has hob-a-nob'd with Pharaoh glass to glass,
" Or dropp'd a halfpenny in Homer's hat,
" Or doff'd its own to let Queen Dido pass,
" Or held, by Solomon's own invitation,
" A torch at the great Temple's dedication."

AMONG THE OTHER RELICS WILL BE FOUND

A MUMMY OF THE IBIS,

THE SACRED BIRD OF EGYPT;

An Urn with Intestines from Elci; an Inscription on the far-famed Paper of Egypt (the Papyrus); a massive Fragment of Granite with Hieroglyphics from Memphis; a variety of Idols in Stone, Clay, and Wood, from the Tombs of the Kings in the Valley of Beban-el-Malook, and the Ruins at Carnac; Urns, Vessels of Libation, Bronzes, Coins, &c. &c.

N.B. A few EGYPTIAN and other ANTIQUITIES for SALE.

Admittance, One Shilling each.

☞ PURCHASERS WILL BE ALWAYS RE-ADMISSIBLE.

A DESCRIPTIVE ACCOUNT of this COLLECTION will be published in a few Days.

WOOD and CO. Printers of the Bath and Cheltenham Gazette, UNION-STREET, BATH.

1842

32. Announcement of a public mummy exhibit in Bath, England, 1842.

life with the help of electric shock and carry on a conversation "in very capital Egyptian" with the attendees, with Mr. Gliddon (previously an American consul in Cairo) as translator. Poe regretted that there was no hieroglyphic type in the cases of American printers; otherwise, he would have communicated the conversation to the reader in Egyptian as well. In a delightful *intermezzo*, the freezing mummy is outfitted in coat and tails. He begins his remarks with a declaration of original monotheism, and he proceeds to deride the achievements of modern technology, science, and architecture, for the Egyptians had surpassed them in every respect. In the end, only modern cough drops put the mummy to shame—the ancient Egyptians had not attained this height of pharmaceutical accomplishment!

Our earliest account of a "conversation" with a mummy involves the seventh-century bishop Pisentios from Koptos, who fled from the Persians into the desert, where he hid in a cave filled with mummies. A companion finds him returning in conversation with one of these mummies, which has been resurrected for the purpose of this dialogue, and Pisentios explains that they had all been Greeks and idolaters—in other words, late pagans.

Next, Théophile Gauthier (1810–1872) became famous for his *Roman de la Momie* (The mummy's romance, 1857), which he wrote after he had already published *Le Pied de la momie* (The mummy's foot, 1840), as well as two poems on the obelisk from Luxor in Paris (1851). Gauthier, who was not able to travel to Egypt until 1869, depended heavily on the Old Testament, and Moses and the Exodus were of special interest to him. He had a German imitator in the person of August Niemann (1839–1919), who published *Das Geheimnis der Mumie* (The mummy's secret) in 1885.

Gauthier writes of a Lord Evandale, who is based on Belzoni, who discovers a tomb in the Valley of the Kings with the help of the Egyptologist Rumphius (that is, Lepsius!). The tomb is based on that of Sethos I, though its entrance belongs to that of Ramesses III. In the sarcophagus lies the mummy of Tahoser, along with a papyrus that turns out to be the "Roman de la momie," her own biography. She was loved by Pharaoh, but she herself loved a Hebrew who in turn loved another woman, the Jewish Rachel. Her Jewish lover's demand that she reject the deities of Egypt gives Tahoser an opportunity to expound on original monotheism, a belief held by most learned people in the nineteenth century. At the end, we encounter the flight of the Hebrews from Egypt and the death of Pharaoh. For the archaeological details in his novel, Gauthier relied largely on his friend Ernest Feydeau, the author of *Histoire des usages funèbres* (History of funerary customs, 1856).

Innumerable mummy novels followed. The two most popular themes were the love of a contemporary man for a mummified woman and its opposite, the love of a mummified man for a contemporary woman, with all the resulting complications. In his last important novel, *Ancient Evenings* (1983), Norman Mailer treated the mummy theme somewhat differently; his Egyptian hero (thanks to reincarnation, the novel takes place at various points in time during the Ramesside Period) graphically describes his own mummification. There is the delightful motif that despite his aversion to doing so, Osiris is obliged to listen to the endless "justifications" of deceased persons at the Judgment of the Dead. We know these justifications from spell 125 of the Book of the Dead, an obligatory confession before the ruler of the netherworld that was assigned reading for every deceased individual.

From 1833 on, there were many musical pieces—operettas, pantomimes, and one ballet—with the word "mummy" or "mummies" in their title. In the case of operas, their titles have often included the name of "Cleopatra" or that of "Sesostris," who was quite popular in the nineteenth century.

Mummies became a theme of horror stories in the work of the Irishman Bram Stoker, the author of the ever-popular novel *Dracula* (1897). In 1903, he published *The Jewel of Seven Stars*, which deals with the resurrection of the mummy of a Queen Tera, which an Egyptologist had brought home to England. Stoker had read up on ancient Egypt, and he credited the ancients not only with special magical powers but also with the use of radioactive materials, which everyone at the time was talking about because of the discoveries of Henri Becquerel and Pierre and Marie Curie. Long before the discovery of the tomb of Tutankhamun, people already believed that such things were possible in the distant past.

The new medium of film quickly made this rewarding theme its own. Stoker's novel was twice adapted to the screen, and then there was the notorious *The Mummy* (1932), Karl Freund's movie starring Boris Karloff. Another example was *The Cat Creature* by Curtis Harrington. But poetry also paid tribute to the mummy, as in the case of Robert Boehringer's

"Mumie" (Mummy), which was brought to my attention by Karl Schefold: "So wonderfully preserved after death: lifeless flesh on a bony frame."

The discovery of Tutankhamun's tomb, along with his mummy and his treasure, gave fresh impetus to this fascination, prompting some to rediscover the ancient practice of mummification and put it to use. The first prominent victim was Lenin, who died on January 21, 1924, at a time when Tutankhamun was on everyone's lips; in March of that year, it was decided that he would be permanently embalmed after the masses had paid their overwhelming adulation to his mortal shell. His "mummy" did not come close to the original style, but it enabled him to be on permanent display in his mausoleum. The same experiment was later repeated on Stalin and Mao Tse-Tung.

In 1994, Bob Brier and Ronald S. Wade conducted the first attempt to mummify a human body using an ancient Egyptian technique. They spent thirty-five days, only half the "ideal" duration of the mummification process, and they used a total of 600 pounds of natron, which posed the problem of how the Egyptians would have disposed of such a huge quantity of this substance. Brier described the moving feeling of standing before a "fresh" mummy for the first time at the end of the process, rather than the darkened, shriveled examples in our museums.

Turning back to the pyramids, notwithstanding the repeated attempts by esoteric circles to ascribe some other purpose to them, this architectural form has remained the prototype of a funerary monument to this day and is still to be encountered in present-day cemeteries, for it is a striking embodiment of the overcoming of death. Already in classical antiquity, Romans used it for this purpose (the pyramid of Cestius), and it was again connected with tombs in the Renaissance, beginning with Raphael's tombstone for Agostino Chigi in 1520. In the centuries that followed, it enjoyed even greater popularity. In Rome in particular, there are many pyramid-shaped tombs from the seventeenth and eighteenth centuries.

Many of these pyramids are fictitious, mirroring an aspired ideal, such as when John Milton promoted a pyramid for Shakespeare in his poem *On Shakespeare* (1630), or when a French architect designed a tombstone for Isaac Newton in the form of a pyramid in 1799. A pyramid was even considered for the grave of Frederick the Great, for "a monument worthy of his stature must be new, must be unique, must endure for millennia, like his name, and the sight of it must arouse reverence and awe," as stated in the proposal. In 1824, Thomas Wilkinson exceeded all dimensions with his design for a pyramid topped by an obelisk "for five million dead."

Actual pyramids were erected for Frederick's brother Prince Heinrich (d. 1802) in Rheinsberg, for Marshal Moritz of Saxony in the church of St. Thomas in Strasbourg (1777), and for Margrave Carl Wilhelm (1823), as well as for certain heroes of the French Revolution, such as Marat. But the monument for General Desaix, who conquered Upper Egypt for Napoleon, on St. Bernhard, did not have the form of a pyramid, as is sometimes maintained. A temporary pyramid of wood was erected for the funeral service of the victims of the siege of the Tuileries in Paris on August 10, 1792.

The earliest design for a monument to Hermann the Cheruscan in the Teutoberger Wald (1788) provided for a pyramid. Antonio Canova (1757–1822) is especially noted for his many pyramid sketches, among others for Titian (uncompleted); his pupils gave his own burial place in Venice the form of a pyramid in 1827. Even in recent times, tomb art has made use of this form—thus, the singer Beniamino Gigli (d. 1957), who participated in many productions of *Aida*, has a pyramid in Recanati. Nonreligious use of the pyramid form is richly attested from the eighteenth century on—at first as cold rooms and nowadays as a hotel (Las Vegas), a sports stadium (Memphis, Tennessee), and at the entrance to the Louvre (Paris).

Obelisks have served not only as war and battle monuments, as well as fountain decorations, but also as burial monuments of individual persons. Beethoven has a monument in the form of an obelisk in the Ehrenfriedhof in Vienna, as does Gluck, and there is an obelisk at the grave of C. F. Meyer in Kilchberg. An obelisk was set up in the Maria Saal church in Klagenfurt for Johann Baptist Türk, the "Andreas Hofer of Carinthia." In Canada, on the Queen Charlotte Islands, which lie directly across from Alaska, I once came upon an obelisk that had been erected as the tombstone of a Native American chief in 1894 (Figure 33).

The overcoming of death, as embodied by ancient Egyptian architectural forms, has provided still other stimuli to art in European and American cemeteries (Figures 34 and 35). Their entrances often take the form of an Egyptian monumental gateway (pylon), and we find Egyptian forms in

33. Headstone of the Haida Chief Albert E. Edensaw near Masset, Queen Charlotte Islands, Canada, 1894. Photo by Elisabith Staehelin.

34. "Egyptian temple" in Kannenfeldpark, Basel; it was the tomb of the classical philologist Johann Jakob Merian (1826–1892). Photo by Elisabeth Staehelin.

35. "Egyptian temple" in Lazienki Park, Warsaw, Poland. Built around 1820 by Jacob Kubicki. Photo by H. Poddebski.

many churchyards, of which Highgate Cemetery in London (with an "Egyptian Avenue" from 1838) and Père Lachaise in Paris are but two examples.

We have already mentioned that the sphinx has become the trademark of everything esoteric and, as Ludwig Volkmann has put it, a "European house pet." For Herder, *the* Sphinx is an "image of hidden wisdom," and there have been many attempts to indicate the mysteries of nature by means of sphinxes, sometimes with many breasts. Sphinxes have been popular in gardens since about 1560, and in particular, they populated the gardens of the eighteenth century. With the beginning of that same century, sphinxes became increasingly common as the bases of clocks, and according to Clemens Brentano (1812), they were "now the order of the day on every fashionable clock." They also served as decoration on furniture of all sorts in classicism, and they experienced a spiritual renaissance among theosophists and symbolists. The German theosophical journal that began to appear in 1886 bore the title *Sphynx*, and it has not been the only periodical to bear that name.

EIGHTEEN

EGYPT À LA MODE

Modern Egyptosophy and Afrocentrism

The tarot, which can be traced back to the fourteenth century and has been a popular method of fortune telling among Gypsies, is one component of modern Hermetism. The first claim that it had its origin in ancient Egypt was probably that made in 1781 by Antoine Court de Gebelin (1725–1784), a noted Freemason (see chapter 14); he postulated a "Book of Thoth" as its source and attributed the invention of the cards to Thoth himself, who had cloaked his wisdom in the garb of a game.

This notion, which has been believed ever since, was picked up by the already-mentioned Aleister Crowley (1875–1947), who was active in various esoteric movements, such as the Hermetic Order of the Golden Dawn, founded in 1886, for which he drew up a pseudo-Egyptian ritual; Papus, who will be mentioned below, was also a member of this order. An angel dictated the *Book of the Law* to Aleister (that is, Edward Alexander) Crowley during a lengthy stay in Cairo in April 1904. The book is full of distorted Egyptian names and phenomena; after an adoration of the sky goddess Nut, the "Queen of Space" announces, among other things "The Khabs is in the Khu, not the Khu in the Khabs."

Later, Crowley published the "Book of Thoth" as a guide to the Tarot, whose twenty-two symbolic cards correspond to the letters of the Hebrew alphabet, along with their Egyptian counterparts. Crowley also headed a Church of Satan, which has members to this day in Switzerland and other countries. Along with Theodor Reuss, he played a leading role in the Oriental Templar Order (O.T.O.), which was founded in 1901.

A "Thoth Book" also made its appearance in Woldemar von Uxkull's *Eine Einweihung im Alten Ägypten nach dem Buch Thoth* (An initiation in ancient Egypt according to the Thoth Book, 1922), in which he portrays the initiation of a youth into the ancient Egyptian mysteries and boldly asserts, "The Thoth Book itself is a historical fact." In the book, we encounter a number of leitmotifs from modern esoterica: the origin of the Egyptians in Atlantis, trial by the elements, a sphinx with the body of a bull and the wings of an eagle, reincarnation, and a great deal of pyramid mysticism. The book's twenty-two illustrations were inspired by the Tarot. Its fantasy-ridden initiation has been much employed and cited in esoteric circles.

In the decades just before and after 1900, Paris witnessed a boom in all sorts of theosophical and Egyptosophical movements, culminating in the International Congress of Spiritualists held in that city in 1900. At the same time, the occult exercised a growing influence on symbolist and abstract painting. A cult book in use at that time was Édouard Schuré's *The Great Initiates: A Study of the Secret History of Religions*, which appeared in 1889 and was reprinted a hundred times down to 1927. Schuré (1841–1929) devotes a chapter to Hermes Trismegistus and describes Egyptian initiation rituals. The theosophist Gerald Massey also exerted a great deal of influence in esoteric circles with his book *Ancient Egypt: The Light of the World* (1907).

We also need to mention Gérard Encausse (1865–1916), who called himself Papus and was a member of the Hermetic Brotherhood of Luxor, the Golden Dawn, and the Martinist Order; the latter even granted the title of Doctor of Hermetic Sciences. Papus became head of the Theosophical Society in Germany in 1888, but he resigned from the society just two years later because of tensions with Helena Blavatsky. At the beginning of his ever useful and often reprinted *Traité élémentaire de science occulte* (Fundamentals of occult science, 1888), he writes, "history informs us that most of the ancient thinkers who gave birth to our West derived their doctrines from the Egyptian mysteries," and elsewhere, he speaks of the "wonderland of Egypt" (p. 255). He himself stood entirely in the tradition of the Hermetic correspondence of the macrocosm and the microcosm: "All is analogous . . . everything is in all" (p. 64); thus for him, the *Tabula Smaragdina* (see above, chapter 6) was a "wondrous synopsis of the occult sciences" (p. 83). Among other works, Papus also published a book on the

Tarot, and he had an influence on Russian occultism, because his works were translated into Russian. He even had some influence in the Czar's court, where Rasputin quickly became his opponent.

An important esoteric was René Adolphe Schwaller de Lubicz (1887–1961), who, along with his wife, Isha, and his stepdaughter, Lucy Lamy, was a devotee of everything occult. In Paris as a youth, and later in his villa in Grasse in the south of France, he devoted himself to the great alchemic opus and possessed many alchemic manuscripts, which were put up for sale not long ago. He spent fifteen years in Egypt, beginning in 1937, and he devoted himself above all to the study of the temple of Luxor, eventually publishing *The Temple in Man: Sacred Architecture and the Perfect Man*, which appeared in three volumes in 1957; in this work, man appears as the measure of all architecture, as had already been the case in the work of Vitruvius and later in the Renaissance. Schwaller equated the various parts of the temple with the human body, which he inserted into a plan of the temple in a drawing (Figure 36). The object of much hostility from Egyptologists and largely ignored by them, Schwaller nevertheless performed the service of having published the most basic study to date on the Luxor temple; anyone concerned with this temple cannot ignore his photographs. With his opinion of the advanced astronomical capabilities of the Egyptians, who already knew the precession of the earth's axis and the metric system of measurements, he came close to pyramid mysticism; furthermore, he sought to connect the zodiac with the layout of temples. By means of the precession of the vernal equinox, which shifted by one constellation every 2200 years, he was of course able to point to Amun for the Age of the Ram, and to Apis for the preceding Age of Taurus, and he wished to connect the preceding Gemini with the dualistic thought of the Egyptians, which had its origin in prehistory.

We shall take only passing notice of the phenomenon of "Egyptian" reincarnations. The best-known cases are Rosemary and Omm Seti (Dorothy Louise Eady, 1904–1981), a "British eccentric" (as she is called in *Who Was Who in Egyptology*), who came to Egypt in 1933, believed that she was a reincarnated lover of Sethos I, and "kept watch over" his temple at Abydos for decades, at first under the aegis of the Egyptian Antiquities Service. We have extensive records regarding the medium Rosemary (Ivy Carter Beaumont, 1883–1961) and her Egyptian xenoglossy; in 1931, she made the claim that she had been a temple dancer named Vola in the reign

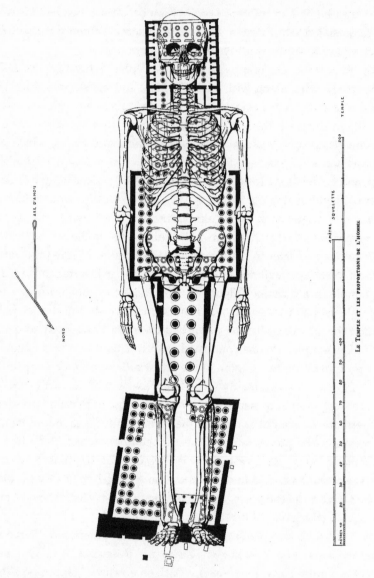

36. Proportions of Man and of the temple of Luxor. From R. A. Schwaller de Lubicz, *Le Temple de l'Homme*, vol. 2 (Paris, 1957), pl 15.

of Amenophis III and that she spoke for a Babylonian princess at the Egyptian royal court. A record was made of the nearly 5000 sentences of the statements she made in trances over a period of six years. She supposedly spoke fluent Egyptian, but her vocabulary was evidently derived from Budge's *An Egyptian Hieroglyphic Dictionary* (1920), and her syntax was clearly deficient. We must therefore give up any hope of reconstructing the vowels of the ancient Egyptian language, which remain unknown, with the help of this medium.

Belief in reincarnation, which has an old tradition in India, is quite widespread today, for it restores belief in eternal life to modern man and thus has become a new tiding of salvation. Characteristically, most of these alleged earlier lifetimes have been located in pharaonic Egypt, with a preference for Egyptian princesses or high priests who "remember" their earlier lifetime. Ancient Egypt is immensely important in this form of the esoteric, which has come to replace the apparitions and visions of the Middle Ages.

The Mormons, that is, the Church of Jesus Christ of the Latter-Day Saints, is an example of a modern religious community that seeks to connect itself with ancient Egypt. Its first prophet, Joseph Smith (1805–1844), who founded the church in July 1830 in Fayette, New York (it later moved to Ohio), acquired some mummies and papyri, and also a headboard, stemming from Thebes, in 1835, and in the same year, he "deciphered" the papyri as books by Abraham and Joseph, which they had written in Egypt. His "translation" of Abraham's book was first published in 1842 under the title *The Pearl of Great Price*. It was an account of creation and the priesthood of Abraham. Like Smith's interpretation of the vignettes and the headboard, his translation is entirely influenced by the Old Testament, and sometimes in verbatim agreement with it, which is reminiscent of Gustavus Seyffarth's "translation" of the Book of the Dead. Actual ancient Egyptian was foreign to Smith, and even Re, Osiris, and Isis were unknown to him. In reality, one of the papyri is an entirely normal "Book of Breathing," while another is a late Book of the Dead prepared for a woman named Ta-sherit-Min.

The angel Moroni, son of Mormon, had already told Joseph Smith of the gold plates containing the Book of Mormon in September 1823, and in 1830, at the time he founded the church, Smith published the book, which today stands at the center of the religious community. Written entirely in the style of English translations of the Old Testament (though some of the names sound rather like King Arthur's round table), it portrays a continuation of the Bible on American soil, proceeding from the assumptions that the Bible is not the final word of God, but rather that it can be continued, and that God also intended his revelation for Native Americans. The narrative begins with the timely emigration of a group of Jews prior to the destruction of Jerusalem in 586 B.C.E. and ends around 421 C.E. Here, Smith already makes mention of the Egyptian writing system, and in chapter 9 of "Book of Mormon," there is a reference to the use of "reformed Egyptian" characters—whatever that might mean.

Joseph Smith exhibited his Egyptian treasures to visitors for a fee of twenty-five cents (he had, after all, invested a considerable sum on their purchase), and he displayed one of the mummies as "pharaoh Necho," though scholars of his day were not yet acquainted with any genuine royal mummies. Toward the end of his life, he had plans to compose a grammar of the Egyptian language. News of Jean-François Champollion and his decipherment had not yet reached the American west, and indeed, the decipherment remained the subject of debate in Europe for a long time after Champollion's death.

After Joseph Smith's assassination in June 1844, Brigham Young led the "great trek" into the west in 1846–1847 and founded Salt Lake City in Utah, which has remained the seat of the church down to this day. The fate of the Egyptian antiquities left behind by Smith is unclear, though some of them were supposedly destroyed by the Great Fire in Chicago in 1871. In 1967, the Metropolitan Museum of Art in New York City returned eleven papyrus fragments to the Mormon church, which thereupon invited certain American Egyptologists, including John A. Wilson and Klaus Baer, to state their opinion regarding the texts. Bitter controversies ensued, with representatives of the church pointing out that since the Egyptologists were of different opinions they were therefore unreliable. They could thus feel confident in returning to the divine inspiration of Joseph Smith as the single true interpretation, as had happened once before in 1912 after criticism from Bishop Spaulding, who had relied on the authority of James Henry Breasted.

The gurus who have made their appearance in recent decades have drawn on Asian schools of thought, not on Egypt. Tibet and the Himalayas, in particular, have offered their services as new spiritual centers.

Even Jesus Christ must have been schooled by Indian or Tibetan wise men: according to N. A. Notovitch (*The Unknown Life of Jesus Christ*, 1894), he spent several years in Tibet, where he was initiated into Buddhist doctrine. Others have tried to prove that his tomb was in Srinagar, and such speculations have continued down to this day. The great, mysterious masters invoked by the founders of the Theosophical Society were also located in Tibet.

Meanwhile, though, things have progressed considerably. Instead of mysterious masters in Tibet or the Himalayas, extraterrestrials now guide what happens in the world. "Do we owe the achievements of our culture to cosmic teachers?"—this is the new question, which is ever more zealously answered in the affirmative, and there is a constantly growing branch of esoteric literature concerned with otherworldly creatures. In books with titles like *God Came from the Stars*, literature of this sort attempts to base itself on statements in the Bible. But Egypt preserves its importance even in the age of extraterrestrials, if only as the place where their messengers preferred to land; it is often pointed out that Egyptian deities traveled in celestial ships, thus illustrating "space travel."

Like everything else, the "extraterrestrial" component of esoteric literature goes back to antiquity. We find it already in ancient Egyptian texts regarding the afterlife, which often mention "entering" the sun; in *Coffin Texts*, vol. 7, p. 56 m, "those on the moon" announce the deceased's arrival in the sky. In the second century C.E., Lucian described the first journey to the moon and the stars in the unbridled fantasy of his *True History*, in which he describes a battle between the inhabitants of the moon and the sun:

> The expeditionary force numbered a hundred thousand, exclusive of transport, engineers, infantry, and foreign auxiliaries, eight thousand being mounted on vultures, and the other twenty on saladfowls. Salad-fowls, incidentally, are like very large birds, except that they are fledged with vegetables instead of feathers and have wings composed of enormous lettuce-leaves.
>
> The main force was supported by a battery of Peashooters and a corps of Garlic-gassers, and also by a large contingent of allies from the Great Bear, consisting of thirty thousand Flea-shooters. . . . Flea-shooters are archers mounted on fleas—hence their name—the fleas in question being approximately twelve times the size of elephants.

The Pythagoreans, as well as Lucretius and Plutarch, seriously believed that other heavenly bodies are inhabited. The discovery of the telescope in the seventeenth century provided further stimulus to such thoughts, though Athanasius Kircher and others denied the existence of extraterrestrials on theological grounds. In 1686, Bernard Le Bovier de Fontenelle published his *Dialogues on the Multiplicity of Worlds*, in which he populated the other planets with humanoids, with Mars already at the center of interest. At the same time, Christian Huygens also propounded the thesis that the planets were inhabitable. This concept became common in the eighteenth century, and we find it in the writings of Swedenborg (who stressed the differences between the inhabitants of the various planets), Kant, Herder, Klopstock, and Voltaire. Albrecht von Haller hypothesized, "The stars are perhaps the seat of transfigured spirits. / Just as vice reigns here, so virtue is master there." For the theosophists, all the planets are inhabited by human beings. After Schiaparelli discovered the "canals" of Mars in 1877, there was a new boom in "men from Mars." A high point occurred in October 1938, when Orson Wells broadcast his radio adaptation of Herbert George Wells' 1897 novel *The War of the Worlds*; Wells' depiction of the conquest of New York by beings from Mars was so realistic that it led to mass panic. Interstellar warfare has played a role in the popular media ever since.

Flooded as it is with tourists, Egypt no longer furnishes some remote spot that we can populate with an imaginary school where esoteric wisdom is taught. Yet for just this reason, the Hermetic philosophy and worldview has become all the more relevant; Hermetism is no longer at home in the expanses of central Asia, but rather here, among us, even in the modern natural sciences. When Carl Friedrich von Weizsäcker speaks of the "unity of nature," he is invoking an age-old Hermetic theme. The physicist Wolfgang Pauli (1900–1958) gave serious consideration to the view of nature as a unity and the old Hermetic analogy of macrocosm and microcosm; in 1993, a conference on the irrational in the natural sciences, held on the Monte Verità, was dedicated to him. In dialogue with C. G. Jung and in the name of alchemy, Pauli concerned himself with the unknown and with the interaction of spirit and matter, in which we must see complementary aspects of a unity that must be ever again achieved. Thus the reversion to alchemy and to the standpoint of Robert Fludd, who proclaimed, in opposition to Kepler and his trinitarian view, the "dignity of the quaternarium," which includes, along with the quantifiable outside world, a world of feelings, dreams, and symbols, and thus "a completeness of experience that is not possible within the perspective of the natural sciences" (Pauli).

In a book on *Das Plocher Energie-System* (The Plocher energy system, 1993), Ernstfried Prade, with whom qualified physicists and professors had collaborated, thus lending him an aura of respectability, writes,

> From the highest *logos* of the All, down to the densest matter, everything is in oscillation. Even contemporary physics is aware of this. But thousands of years ago, ancient Egyptian teachers were proclaiming this principle. The more material a substance, the more slowly it oscillates. (p. 140)

For the author, it is a matter of "regaining consciousness of earlier cosmic laws, the so-called 'Hermetic principles,' into which only selected circles were once initiated through oral tradition" (p. 136), and he explains these "principles" as

> going back to the legendary figure of Hermes Trismegistus . . . the "master of all masters" . . . , who is supposed to have lived in the third millennium B.C.E. in Egypt, where he was also called Thoth . . . , and we must assume that Hermetic doctrine had a basic influence on all major philosophies and religions in both the West and the East. Hermes Trismegistus handed down seven Hermetic principles, with which we wish to compare Plocher's system of energy. (p. 148)

And as we have seen, a number of natural scientists have romped about in pyramid mysticism without troubling themselves about the historical order in which these monuments were constructed.

Hermetic societies that draw on ancient Egypt continue to spring up like daisies. Many employ Egyptian wisdom and mastery of magic only for practical advice, but some are formal religious communities that include Egyptian deities in their cults and develop new rituals for their worship. All this is often mixed with the Far Eastern practice of yoga, such as the equation of the erection of the *djed*-pillar with the ascent of the *kundalini* serpent. Even the cabala is included in these syncretisms, and there is also the *Akasha Chronicle,* a recollection of the cosmos that was brought to light by the theosophists. In these circles, people often write of *neter,* using the Egyptian word for "deity"; in doing so, they draw on Schwaller de Lubicz and his wife, who viewed the *neter* as ideas that are immanent in nature and in cosmic functions; for them, Osiris was the "*neter* of nature."

As an example of these countless societies, let us consider the "Sacred Hermetic Order of Asar-Ra" in London, an order that offers practical exercises and shows people how to found an "Egyptian" lodge and practice Egyptian magic. The order is organized into lodges on the Masonic model, and it imparts seven stages of initiation, which are even available via a correspondence course. Moreover, this Hermetic order, as its arch-priest Peter Paddon proclaims in *The Book of the Veil* (1985), supplies direct access to the deities of Egypt, in whom he himself believes. He thus invites us to take a "guided tour of the universe according to the Priesthood of Khem" and bids the reader to "have fun, and open your eyes to the beauty of this world." He gives practical advice on how to meditate so as to encounter various deities, and at the end of a meditation or ritual, he recommends a "hot drink," for the priests of ancient Egypt usually drank a "hot chocolate" after their spiritual work was done (p. 31 and often elsewhere). The sources of this knowledge are essentially Budge and Plutarch, with a little cabala mixed in; he draws on Christian Jacq for Asar-Ra, who was known only to the high priests. Original, though, is the "practical magic" he teaches, for instance, the mending of a broken bone, for which the goddess Sakhmet is responsible; in this day and age, the prerequisite cultic purity can be achieved through showering, and in the ritual, fragrant oils are also used. It is important to have an *image* of the deity on every occasion, and amulets and sacred signs are also employed. If we are to believe Paddon, there is a modern religion of Isis in more than sixty nations (p. 43).

In book stores and on the Internet, there is no lack of practical advice on how to contact the deities of ancient Egypt or on how to put "Egyptian" magic to practical use. Alchemy has been resurrected, along with amulets, in particular the popular *ankh,* the Egyptian hieroglyph meaning "life," which the theosophists have made into a respected symbol.

During the 1980s, the Kuoni Travel Agency often invited the public to take an "esoteric journey to the Egyptian places of initiation." Yet its itinerary was basically a normal tour of Egypt; on the fourth day, a "visit to the pyramids of Giza and the Sphinx" was combined with an "opportunity to shop in the bazaar." Such tours are otherwise quite popular. The publishing house Goldmann puts out a series entitled "Magischreisen" (magical tours) that includes a volume by B. A. Mertz entitled *Ägypten. Land von Isis und Osiris* (Egypt: Land of Isis and Osiris, 1991). In it, we read:

> Ancient Egypt, the earliest comprehensible high culture in the world, reveals connections with Creation, the Divine, and original Knowledge in an abundance that is not to be found elsewhere. Anyone wishing to understand our modern world, its problems, origin, development, and ultimate end, must experience Egypt. (p. 7)

By publishing religious texts, Egyptology has made fresh sources available to esoteric movements. Helena Blavatsky seized on the Egyptian Book of the Dead as an initiation text, and it remains popular in esoteric circles to this day. Albert Schulz, who wrote under the pseudonym Peryt Shou, published a *Geheimlehre des ägyptischen "Totenbuchs"* (The secret teachings of the Egyptian "Book of the Dead," 3d ed., 1931), S. Mayassis often portrayed it as an initiation text, and since 1954, G. Kolpaktchy has exerted a great deal of influence with his theosopically inspired "translation," which is essentially a free rendering. But the Book of the Dead has also been understood as an initiation text by Egyptologists in Vienna; according to Wilhelm Czermak, it is one of "the Hermetic books that were in fact accessible only to initiates," while for Gertrud Thausing, it is a "Book of the Living employed in initiations on earth."

Many poets of the twentieth century have been inspired by E. A. Wallis Budge's edition of the Book of the Dead. It played a role in Ezra Pound's work, beginning with his first book of poetry, which appeared in 1908, and in James Joyce's *Finnegans Wake*, published in 1939; Lawrence Durrell, who authored the Alexandria Quartet, also planned to write a *Book of the Dead*.

The Pyramid Texts, a much older collection of spells from around 2350 B.C.E., have still to attract the attention of esoteric writers, notwithstanding the fact that they are humankind's most ancient "initiation texts" and have been known since 1881. There has evidently been as yet no Budge to introduce these difficult texts to a wider public.

The Books of the Netherworld from the New Kingdom, which had already fascinated Champollion when he visited the Valley of the Kings, was the next corpus of texts to inspire modern writers. Franz Werfel, who portrayed a "passage through the Egyptian realm of the dead" in chapter 13 of his novel *Hearken unto the Voice* (1937), speaks not only of the Book of the Dead, but also of the Amduat and the Book of Gates, and he mentions regions in the netherworld such as Rosetau and Wernes, as well as Apopis, the enemy of the sun, and the concept of dying a second time. In the novel *Passage de Milan* (1954), Michel Butor describes the nightly journey through the netherworld from the Book of Gates (which has yet to be translated into French!) as it takes place in an apartment building in Paris; the twelve chapters follow the twelve hours of the night, and one of the tenants dreams about the barque of the sun and his journey as a mummy.

The Books of the Netherworld have only quite recently entered into actual esoteric literature, though as long ago as 1971, Gertrud Thausing, basing herself on my own edition of 1963, called the Amduat an "initiation book" on page 147 of her *Sein und Werden: Versuch einer Ganzheitschau der Religion des Pharaonenreichs* (Being and becoming: toward a holistic view of pharaonic religion), after explaining the Book of the Dead as an initiation text and connecting it with the practice of yoga. She has no hesitation about arbitrarily mangling a text and the meaning of its words, turning the simple word *aut* "food offering" into *akhu* "blessed dead," which she then renders "initiate." In the same vein, in spell 79 of the Book of the Dead, she makes the phrase "elder of the divine tribunal" into a "great one of the Covenant" to support her claim that there was a "covenant of initiates" in ancient Egypt (p. 55), a belief that had also been held by Czermak. For her, the passage through a royal tomb of the New Kingdom was an initiation path (p. 74).

Even Jan Assmann, who is otherwise not inclined toward esoteric interpretations, sees "secret Hermetic wisdom" and a "sort of cabala" in the Books of the Netherworld from the royal tombs. K. Dietzfelbinger, in *Mysterienschulen* (Schools of the mysteries, 1997) calls the Amduat a detailed description of the celebration of a mystery and a "representation of a mystery path"; he is convinced that "the mystery lore of the West . . . had its beginning in Egypt" (p. 34), which brings us back to our starting point. It remains for us to take a brief glance at recent attempts to derive all the wisdom of the west from Africa.

The Afrocentric Movement

With his *Black Athena: The Afroasiatic Roots of Classical Civilization* (2 vols., 1987–1991), Martin Bernal, a grandson of the noted Egyptologist Sir Alan Gardiner, has familiarized both Europe and the east with the Afrocentric movement. In the United States of America, this tradition can be traced as far back as 1854, and it also includes the French Count Volney (pseudonym of Constantin-François Chassebeuf), whose travelogue of 1787 was the only book about Egypt that Napoleon took with him on his expedition. When the "pan-Negro patriot" Edward Willmot Blyden visited Egypt in 1866, he experienced the spontaneous feeling that the pyramids had been built by his forebears, and he expressed this view in his book *Christianity, Islam and the Negro Race* (1887). In the Freemason George G. M. James' *Stolen Legacy* (1954), we encounter an esoteric Egypt colored by Masonry: according to him, the Great Lodge of Luxor had branches everywhere in the world, even among the Maya, the Aztecs, and the Inca, and thus in ancient America.

Prior to Bernal, the best-known exponent of this Afrocentric viewpoint was Sheikh Anta Diop (1923–1986) from Senegal; from 1946 on, he studied (including Egyptology) at the Sorbonne, where he twice failed to obtain a doctorate, for his thesis that ancient Egypt was the earliest black African high culture was rejected. In 1960, he succeeded in his third attempt to obtain a degree, and after that, in his homeland, Diop struggled for cultural independence from the former colonial powers, strongly opposing Senghor, its first president. His vision was that African humanity should build on its ancient Egyptian heritage, just as westerners built on Graeco-Roman antiquity. On his monument in Dakar, which is decorated with hieroglyphs, it is stressed that he rehabilitated "Negro civilizations." But there was more; in his last work, *Civilization or Barbarism* (1981), he goes so far as to question the Graeco-Roman heritage of the West, for classical antiquity had already been influenced by ancient Egyptian, and thus black African, wisdom. His successors, who revere him as "pharaoh of knowledge," have continued to stress this viewpoint, propagating it in particular among African-Americans, stressing age-old close relations between ancient Egypt and ancient America and spreading fantastic accounts of "Egyptian" finds on American soil.

The content of this message, which is already being officially taught on many American campuses, is that all the wisdom of antiquity stemmed from Africa and specifically from Egypt. "Hardly a week goes by when an article does not appear by an Afrocentrist writer observing that the discoveries attributed to the Greeks rightly belong to the ancient Egyptians," writes Mary Lefkowitz (1996, p. 5). We know that Solon, Pythagoras, and Plato were in Egypt, but even Aristotle is supposed to have been in Alexandria with his pupil Alexander the Great, helping himself to the treasures of the Library and thus "stealing" from Egypt the whole of his philosophy, on which all later western philosophy has been based. (In the meantime, we have learned that Donald Duck's nephews have discovered this library intact, as we read in the comic book "The Guardians of the Lost Library," by the Disney cartoonist Don Rosa). Legends about the Library of Alexandria were already being spun at an early date, and they were handed down in particular by medieval Arab historians. The best known is the Caliph Omar's dictum, which was handed down in fullest form by Ibn al-Qiftî (d. 1248): when the contents of the writings in the Library agree with the Koran, they are superfluous, and when they differ, they are certainly unnecessary and should be destroyed. With such a justification, Omar is supposed to have ordered the destruction of the books, which Muslims had captured in Persia (so Ibn Khaldûn). Supposedly, the public baths of Alexandria were heated for six months by the contents of the Library. In reality, it seems that the Library already no longer existed in the time of the historian Orosius, who was in Alexandria in 415, for Christian zealots had already made it a tabula rasa.

A fine wrinkle in Afrocentric doctrine is the claim that Stonehenge was built by Africans (so Crawford), and that Pliny described the ancient Britons in such a way that they can only have been Africans. England as an African colony—a fitting revenge for European colonialism! As early as 1740, William Stukeley connected Stonehenge with the wisdom of Egyptian priests who emigrated to England after the Persian conquest, and he believed that further traces of the Egyptians were to be found on English soil.

Mary Lefkowitz depicts (*Not Out of Africa*, p. 2) a scene at a college in Massachusetts in February 1993, where a Dr. Yosef ben-Jochannan, who was introduced as "a distinguished Egyptologist" (though he is entirely unknown to the field of Egyptology), lectured on modern Afrocentric doctrine. When she objected that the Library of Alexandria could only have

been constructed after the death of Alexander and Aristotle, Lefkowitz
was branded a "racist."

But racism is an integral part of the new doctrine, according to which
there are only blacks in Africa, with the result that anyone born there is
necessarily black. Obviously, then, Nefertiti was black (along with Teye
and Ahmose-Nofretari, of whom we in fact have black representations),
and also Osiris, god of the dead, as well as Hannibal, Cleopatra, and St.
Augustine. Even Socrates might at least have had blacks among his forebears, for Alcibiades commented that he looked like a Silenus. . . .

In any event: everything created by the ancient Egyptians was the fruit
of a "black" culture, from which European culture derived its basic principles. Curiously, this view, which denies the Greeks all their originality, relies overwhelmingly on the testimony of ancient Greek writers, on a picture of Egypt that was "made in Greece." Even Johann Gottfried von
Herder wrote, in his *Reflections on the Philosophy of the History of Mankind*,
"Egypt would not easily have attained the high reputation it enjoys for
wisdom, but for . . . the ruins of its antiquities, and above all the tales of
the Greeks."

These points have already been made by Mary Lefkowitz, one of the
leading opponents of this point of view. But aside from the fact that she
excludes western Asia from her considerations, we encounter several er-
rors, as when the decipherment of the hieroglyphs is dated to the year
1836 (after the death of Champollion), or when she calls Neith "a relatively minor goddess" (*Not Out of Africa*, p. 65). And when she writes,
"Ancient Egyptian Civilization deserves to be remembered (and respected) *for what it was*, and not for what Europeans, ancient and modern,
have imagined it to be" (p. 126, emphasis added), that all sounds well and
good, but it touches on an awkward point. For us, there is no ancient
Egyptian culture *in and of itself*, but only what we make of it. In what way
was Adolf Erman's view of Egypt more correct than that of Sheikh Anta
Diop? To be sure, both these figures belong to the past, but even contemporary Egyptology's view of Egypt (to the extent it can be called a unity)
is nothing more than a stage along the way, and there will probably never
be a definitive picture.

Afrocentrists rely on the notion that there are "different ethnic truths,"
that like the ancient Greeks and modern Europeans, black Africans should
develop their own view of Egypt. Clinton Crawford states clearly, "It is

also imperative that ancient Egypt be understood as a Black civilization if it is to be a source of self-esteem for African-Americans" (p. 25). But when this viewpoint is built on demonstrably false and often abstruse "facts" and condemns any critical objection, then it hardens into dogma. Crawford, for instance, cites Champollion, who demonstrated Egyptian monotheism with the help of Papyrus Ebers, notwithstanding the fact that Champollion died long before Papyrus Ebers was discovered. And these writers (who zealously copy from one another) intend that such "facts" will soon be the basis of public school education in the United States of America. Just as science advances to new understandings on the basis of new data, such ethnic understandings must be open to new facts, or they will become objects of ridicule.

But behind these sometimes abstruse claims, there stands an earnest concern to create a new Black African identity, one that Christianity and Islam, in their noble competition for the salvation of the souls of African-Americans, can no longer supply: thus the turning back to a respected high culture that irrefutably originated and developed on African soil. I can refer to a personal recollection of an Ewe from Ghana who visited me in Basel and sang to me by rote the traditions of his tribe, according to which his people believed that they had originated in Palestine and made their way to west Africa via Egypt. In such traditions, there are divine names that are quite Egyptian; in the case of the Hausa and the Yoruba in southwestern Nigeria, Dierk Lange has pointed to close connections with Canaan and the Hebrews (and even further, with Ugarit and the Babylonian New Year's festival), which rest not only on the similarity of names, but also on structural equivalences of myths and rituals. There seem to be festivals that preserve many pre-Islamic traditions, though they are threatened today by forced Islamization. Egypt belongs to Africa, and its culture indubitably deeply influenced that continent; but we are lacking in reliable sources and evidence to follow this cultural transmission in its details or to prove direct dependence. Millennia separate the ancient high culture and its distant echoes in contemporary Africa.

OUTLOOK

Egypt as Hope and Alternative

In a text written on March 6, 1930, but which has only just been published (Figure 37), Thomas Mann wrote in the guest book of the Winter Palace hotel in Luxor, "where we feel quite at home":

> In fairy tales, those born under a lucky star visit enchanted meadows at the bottom of deep well shafts. The human past is such a well shaft, and this land is such an enchanted meadow: here, swept back through the millennia, we find ourselves in a different light, deep in the past, wandering among the sacred monuments of the beginning of human culture.

Let us also note what was written by someone from an entirely different world, Evliya Celebi, a Turkish traveler of the late seventeenth century who arrived in Egypt in 1671:

> In Egypt, there are wondrous and strange things by the hundreds of thousands. We have seen hundreds of them with our own eyes. Before each of them, we have been entirely beside ourselves with astonishment.

Egypt has always been a land of wonder, a land that according to Herder in his *Älteste Urkunde des Menschengeschlechts* (Most ancient records of humankind, 1774) has "the magical power to set the best of people to dreaming." The image of Egypt has always already included the

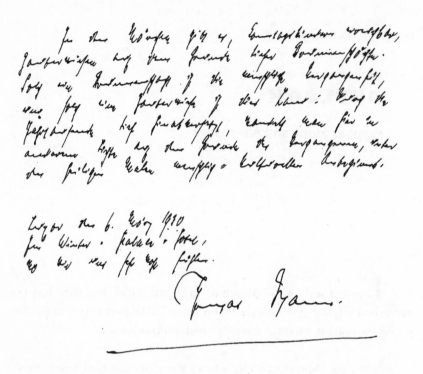

37. Thomas Mann's entry in the guest book of the Winter Palace Hotel, Luxor, March 6, 1930. Photo by André Wiese.

mysterious nimbus of age-old wisdom and magical arts. Herodotus already saw Egypt as the exact opposite of his own land, and after traveling throughout the known world, he declared that Egypt contained "more wonderful things and astonishing works than all other lands" (II 35).

With Herodotus, the "father of history," there began the construction of a concept of Egypt that has taken on a life and a fascination of its own; it has become ever more unlike pharaonic Egypt, its model, and it has been a part of every esoteric movement down to this day. The legend was perfected by Hecataeus, who supplied ideological underpinnings for the newly-founded Ptolemaic kingdom, and it was included by Diodorus in his description of the land. We have seen how generations of ancient writers then contributed to the elaboration of this legend of Egypt, enrolling ever more of the great thinkers of Greece in the schools of Egypt and even transforming Homer into an Egyptian and the son of Hermes Trismegistus. The Romans were the first to turn Egypt into a fashion trend, opening the floodgates to a stream of tourists that has never ceased, though it has sometimes slowed down to a trickle.

In the meantime, every period of history has had an Egypt of its own, onto which it has projected its fears and its hopes, down to the black Egyptians of contemporary African-Americans. The learned writers of classical antiquity founded an *Egyptosophy* that flourishes to this day and cannot be ignored by our discipline. From ancient Egyptian roots, a whole tree of explanations of Egypt has blossomed, and Egyptology is but one of its relatively new branches. The ancient Greeks were entirely aware that their spiritual and cultural roots reached back to the ancient Near East and to Egypt—a knowledge that was still generally present in the eighteenth century and was lost only in the course of the nineteenth and the twentieth. In the view of classical antiquity, Egypt—an ideal, imaginary Egypt—became for the first time an alternative to contemporary culture. That was a phenomenon that would often be repeated: dissatisfied with the world around them, people would cast their gaze back on the source from which a purer wisdom flowed.

Diodorus' esteem of Osiris had its effect on the Middle Ages and the Renaissance, when Isis and Osiris were regarded as the figures who imparted culture to humankind. Osiris was also connected with alchemy, which had claimed an origin in Egypt since antiquity, and which in fact displayed astonishing parallels to the myth of Osiris.

The new Platonic Academy of fifteenth century Florence was strongly oriented toward Egypt, but it was a late, Hermetic Egypt that had little to do with the pharaonic era. The wisdom embodied in Hermes Trismegistus, this god who was at the same time the founder of a religion, opened a new and even older revelation, above and beyond the Bible, that served to legitimate the new humanism that was then emerging. It thus created a freedom, beyond the doctrines of the official Church, like that which had been supplied in a different way by the Old Testament Song of Songs.

The founder of this Hermetic religion, whom even Christianity and Islam venerated as a predecessor of their own prophets, became an integrating figure during the early modern period, a bearer of hope and patron of a body of knowledge independent of the Bible and the Quran. Even Copernicus could appeal to him in founding his new system. Hermes and his religion were also a way of escaping the generally obligatory Aristotelian-scholastic philosophy.

Hieroglyphs, it was thought at the time, bore witness to a primeval language invented by Hermes Trismegistus, a universal language that predated the Tower of Babel and was in principle comprehensible to all periods and people, if only it could be deciphered. But although the obelisks of Rome, with their original hieroglyphs, had been rediscovered, Renaissance concern with hieroglyphs was not directed toward genuine Egyptian art and writing but rather toward classical writers, who had in fact not illustrated their works. Thus originated the fantastic hieroglyphs of the Renaissance, which were anything but Egyptian, and after that, a new fashion in devising emblems. By much the same token, as late as the eighteenth century, representations of pyramids were modeled on the steep pyramid of Cestius in Rome, and not on original Egyptian pyramids. Even Montfaucon's magnum opus of the early eighteenth century clings to the Baroque style of his day and to the Hellenistic world of forms.

This Egypt, so foreign and false to our contemporary sensibilities, had an astonishing influence on the intellectual life of Europe. As theological debates and bloody religious wars intensified in the wake of the Reformation and Counterreformation, there was an intensified longing for the tolerance and reconciliation embodied by Hermes as a god of moderation. For Giordano Bruno, original divine wisdom was not mirrored by the corrupted Christianity of his own day but rather by the religion of the "all-knowing Egyptian Mercury," that is, Hermes Trismegistus. A short time later, on the eve of the Thirty Years' War, Rosicrucians anticipated a general renewal of the world by the spirit of Egyptian wisdom.

Ancient Egypt was also significant to the eighteenth century as a political alternative, a model of peace, material well-being, just and wise laws, and cultural flowering. Since there were as yet no new sources, writers continued to rely on the accounts from classical antiquity; depending on their respective viewpoints, they viewed Egypt positively as a model of a strong, enlightened monarchy or negatively as an example of oppression and priestly rule. The notion of the Egyptian priesthood as a sort of Catholic clergy began in this period and was long held, though at the same time, Ignaz von Born took the priests of Egypt to be the ideal, original Freemasons. Notwithstanding many negative voices, the feeling prevailed that if there were ever a Golden Age, it had been in ancient Egypt.

The French expedition of 1798 was not the cause, but already the result, of the turn toward Egypt. In the end, it transcended the picture of Egypt derived from classical writers and brought scholars to the broader front of original evidence from the pharaonic period. Like so many others, Bonaparte set out to lift the veil of Isis. He and his 40,000 soldiers suffered a military defeat, but at the same time, the more than 100 artists and scholars who accompanied him achieved an enduring cultural victory whose fruits continue to this very day. A greater number of original Egyptian works of art became known in Europe, making it possible to free the image of Egypt from its classical chains.

Though there was soon thereafter a paradigm shift in favor of classical antiquity and a growing criticism of the adoption of ancient Egyptian forms, the leading theosophists of the nineteenth century, along with contemporary Rosicrucians, continued to evoke Egypt as the home of an original knowledge that had been lost or that lived on only among a few. Ancient Egypt was an alternative and a source of hope for them as well, and they have been followed in this opinion by most of the esoteric movements of our own day—although, as we have seen, there are important gurus who have for the time being exchanged the age-old mystery schools of Egypt for monasteries in Tibet and, more recently, have wandered into extraterrestrial spaces. Even extraterrestrials, however, seem to display a special affinity with and preference for Egypt.

It is no wonder that there have always been searchers along the way— individuals, entire groups, and whole torrents. Romantic poets sent many of their heroes to the east to drink from the fount of wisdom and to gaze upon the veiled image at Sais whose inscription—"I am all that is and was and will be, and no mortal has lifted my veil"—was for no less a figure than Immanuel Kant the loftiest sentiment ever voiced.

Hermann Hesse lent expression to this steady stream of pilgrims in his story *The Journey to the East* (1932), whose protagonist states, "but in reality . . . this expedition to the East was not only mine and now; this procession of believers and disciples had always and incessantly been moving towards the East, towards the Home of Light . . . towards light and wonder." Regarding their destination, he writes, "our goal was not only the East, or rather the East was not only a country and something geographical, but it was the home and youth of the soul, it was everywhere and nowhere, it was the union of all times." Hesse's pilgrims travel in the direction of a coming rule of the spirit, a realm of the "magical," to which even poetry belongs. They are initiates of an anonymous "League" with an age-old history whose membership includes Zoroaster, Lao Tse, Plato, Pythagoras, Albertus Magnus, and Novalis. Hermes is missing, and Hesse did not have ancient Egypt in mind, though "Africa" occurs a number of times as a leitmotiv. Only one of his poems invokes "statues of eternal existence," referring to the Egyptian collection in the Turin Museum. His gaze was directed further eastward; India and China somehow seemed more familiar to him, and he had little knowledge of Egypt.

Another great poet of the twentieth century undertook a quite different, individual journey to the east: Rainer Maria Rilke, who journeyed up the Nile as far as the First Cataract in 1911. He traveled with Cooks on the comfortable steamer "Ramses the Great," so his entire trip can be exactly reconstructed. It seemed at first to be an utter failure, for he ended up in a sickbed in Helwan and in financial straits. But like the military failure of Napoleon's expedition, Rilke's journey to the east endowed him with something lasting, and he himself spoke of it as a "watershed" in his life. All his late poetry is imbued with Egypt, with his experience of the "greatness" of that world, as he saw it in front of the Sphinx at night and then in the "inscrutable temple world of Karnak," before the "relentless great things of Egypt." He was filled with astonishment "that such endurance belonged to the existence in which we died," and in the seventh Duino Elegy, there is also a pride "that we could accomplish such things," reason for the praise that Orpheus receives in his poem, for

This *stood* among men
  at one time
    stood in the midst of fate
of destructive fate
  stood in the midst of not
    knowing where to go
as if it existed
  and bent the stars
    down toward it
from the established heavens.

In the tenth elegy, this picture of the stars is intensified into a bold vision of the Great Sphinx of Giza,

that has silently
  and forever
    set the human face
to be weighed
  on the scale
    of the stars.

Rilke felt he had achieved his goal—"there is no remaining, / no place to stay," as he says in the first elegy—yet there it was, and he wished to send his son there, if he had one: "there it is . . . go through the pylon, stand and behold." At the end of the second elegy, there stands his wish to discover a

    pure, contained
  human, narrow
    strip of land
      between river and rock,

as he had experienced it in Egypt. For Rilke, the deities of Egypt were still valid—and this at a time when Egyptology was quite unsympathetic toward them. But he states:

None of the gods perishes. We need them all and each one,
each one avails us, each fashioned image.

The ancient high culture on the Nile has ever been a source of religious inspiration; as early as the second millennium B.C.E., symbols like the winged sun disk and the *ankh* sign, along with forms such as the scarab and the sphinx, were borrowed by western Asia. Later, it was the Phoenicians who spread Egyptian deities and religious concepts throughout the Mediterranean world; in the first millennium B.C.E., the Egyptian god Bes was omnipresent all around the Mediterranean. Later, Greeks and Romans encountered the religiosity of "the most pious of peoples," as Herodotus called the Egyptians, and then there was the triumphal procession of Hermes Trismegistus, with Sarapis, Osiris, Anubis, and other Egyptian deities in his train. In the Hermetic tractate *Asclepius*, Egypt was the "temple of the entire world." The cult of Isis was one of the last bastions of ancient pagan religion, even in Rome and Italy; notwithstanding its victory, Christianity could not fully rid itself of its remnants. It enjoyed another heyday during the French Revolution, for which Egypt represented the land where religion, and human culture more generally, originated. In opposition to the Christianity that reigned, temples were erected to Isis as goddess of nature and reason, and a calendar based on that of ancient Egypt was introduced. In all periods, there have also been mystery cults based on what Apuleius had to say about the Isis mysteries.

Egypt as a humane counterculture to modern barbarism, as hope for a new humanity beyond the horrors of modern history—no one has pictured this image more impressively than Thomas Mann in his great novel *Joseph and His Brothers*, which appeared during the darkest period of modern barbarism. His work began at the end of 1926, between his first and second trips to Egypt. Part I appeared in 1933, and Part II in 1934; Part III, "Joseph in Egypt," was already a work of exile, particularly in Zurich, and it could no longer appear in Germany. The work concluded with Part IV, which was written in California and was not completed until after America entered World War II. There was no blessing on Europe at that time, God knows, and Mann countered the situation by invoking a culture and a humanity that shared in a double blessing: from heaven above and from the depths that lay below.

At the very beginning of the novel, Mann stresses that he is concerned with *human essence*, "that riddling essence of which our own . . . existences form a part." As he wrote to Stefan Zweig on November 8, 1933, it was supposed to be "simply a book of readings, a primer of human history." In search of someone who could typify the essence of the human condition, he found him in Egypt of the Amarna Period, in the figure of a Hebrew in an Egyptian environment. His novel drew on the great enthusiasm for Egypt and for Akhenaten that followed upon the discovery of the tomb of Tutankhamun in the 1920s. Ever since, Egypt has been associated in the public imagination with the mask of "King Tut," which is ubiquitous on posters and book covers. Publishers evidently feel obliged to provide every other book about ancient Egypt with a dust jacket portraying this mask.

The protagonists of Thomas Mann's novel travel down predictable paths, repeating the ever-valid patterns of myth. Joseph is the incarnation of Hermes, his effect is moonlike and directed toward balance. Unlike

Rilke, for Thomas Mann, Egypt was only an episode in his life and creative effort, and immediately afterward, he penetrated entirely different areas with his work on "Doctor Faustus." Yet he stressed that his sympathy and predilection for ancient Egypt and its culture stemmed from his childhood. He was already on the trail of Egypt in his *The Magic Mountain*, but there, it was a "Hermetic history," the Hellenistic Egypt of Hermes Trismegistus, before whom Settembrini "bent his knee." In his lecture on Schiller shortly before his death in 1955, Mann was still moved by concern for contemporary humanity, which had "drunk of stultification" and was reeling from constant hubbubs over the setting of new records.

Thomas Mann overcame the Goethean conflict for which Egypt contrasted "gravely, even horrifically" with the "purest cheerfulness" of classical civilization. For Hölderlin ("Death of Empedocles"), "the brothers in Egypt" were "the more serious." Yet what Goethe had in mind was not pharaonic Egypt and the cheerfulness of its tomb decoration (of which nothing was known in his day) and its so-often-humorous literature but rather a Hermetic-Hellenistic Egypt that otherwise seemed quite serious, though it was cheerfully transfigured in Mozart's music for "The Magic Flute." Goethe and Herder had no presentiment of the immense richness of pharaonic culture. Thomas Mann, however, discovered and drew on a multitude of sources that had in the meanwhile been reconstructed by Egyptology and other disciplines, including even dry archaeological reports.

The rediscovery of ancient Egypt and the ancient Near East is one of the great and enduring achievements of modern scholarship. Just as Columbus and other explorers blazed trails in space and discovered new continents, Champollion and those who followed him paved the way to new continents in time; they expanded the boundaries of the known, investigating backwards in time through millennia and freeing themselves from the straitjacket of biblical chronology. Egypt became a window that afforded a glimpse into a much older high culture.

Characteristically, there was then a focus on commonalities, a search for contemporary forms in the depths of the past and a belief they had been found: "the ancient Egyptians already . . ." Pyramid mysticism has credited the ancient Egyptians with knowledge of all the important constants of the natural sciences, including even atomic weight and the distance from the earth to the sun. Akhenaten, of course, has been a welcome figure to those holding such a point of view, for he was the first "modern" man, a precursor of Jesus Christ (displacing Hermes Trismegistus from this role) and the preacher of a monotheism.

During the twentieth century, Egypt became more and more interesting in regard to its alterity, as a counterculture and an alternative, as Mann and Rilke experienced it. Egypt was especially viewed as a counterculture in its attitude toward death, which was connected with the idea of regeneration and with the nightly journey of the sun and the soul, in its being filled with gods (so Rilke), its closeness to myth, and in its thoroughly pragmatic ethics, which rested on the concept of *maat*. A role was also played by the notion that painful experiences have freed us from the fascinating idea of continual progress, teaching us that every step forward onto a new level can entail a step backward. More urgent than before was the question of origin, of beginning—and Egypt was a beginning in the history of humanity. The first half of this history, from 3000 B.C.E. to 500 C.E., was stamped almost entirely by Egypt and Mesopotamia, and only after that did other cultures step into the foreground of political and intellectual developments.

The curricula of our schools and universities blithely ignore this fact, concentrating almost exclusively on the second half of history, a fact that is connected with other, relatively recent developments. The philosophy of history has not succeeded in integrating these early cultures, with their uniqueness and their independent achievements, into its systems. In the work of Karl Jaspers and Arnold Toynbee, lack of familiarity with the sources and a superabundance of clichés led to grotesque misinterpretations. Thus, Jaspers claims (*On the Origin and Goal of History*), "hence the account of the history of these millennia is eventful in the extreme, and yet its events do not bear the character of historical decisions vital to humanity," while Toynbee (*A Study of History*) concluded that the material resources of those early cultures, which could have been turned to gaining mastery over the forces of nature, had instead been diverted to idolatry. Only Eric Vogelin did a better job of respecting the Egyptian sources in the monumental system of his *Order and History*, though he, too, had difficulty with them.

We may doubt how much sense such systems would make even if they more adequately took account of early high cultures. History cannot be squeezed into a corset. Paradigm shifts in scientific and intellectual history are yet another consideration. From antiquity down to the end of the eighteenth century, there was a dominant, ideal picture of a Hermetic-Hellenistic Egypt that had its influence on nearly all educated people; the Renaissance, with its strong Egyptian component, was a rebirth of late antiquity, not of the classical period. It would be a rewarding task to study the paradigm shift around 1800 that shaped the nineteenth century and much of the twentieth; there is a great deal of such material in Martin Bernal's *Black Athena*, though because of its misplaced focus (all wisdom stems from Africa), it must be used with care and considered with critical acumen.

With the rediscovery of the "classical" and the Greek struggle for independence from the east, the center of interest shifted to classical antiquity. The founding of many new universities at that time, along with the growing tendency toward specialization (previously, an Athanasius Kircher could be a professor of ethics, mathematics, and oriental languages!) lent support to this new predominance of Classics in academia, while Egypt drifted off into the exotic; following the law of inertia, the situation has remained the same to this day, and the great discoveries that followed Champollion's decipherment of the hieroglyphs have changed little or nothing. Meanwhile, Egyptology has remained the only discipline that concerns itself with the entirety of an ancient high culture and not just with selected portions.

In the consciousness of the general public, however, the twentieth century saw a paradigm shift from the classical world back to the East. Even a poet like Hofmannsthal, who was so deeply rooted in the classics, wrote in a late essay on K. E. Neumann's rendering of Buddhist texts (1921): "We shall endure only if we create a new antiquity for ourselves: and a new antiquity will emerge for us as we view Greek antiquity, on which our spiritual existence rests, from the perspective of the Orient." Above all, Egypt belongs to this "Orient," which for Hofmannsthal also included India. This is no longer the Hermetic-Hellenistic Egypt, however, but the pharaonic one, though some bits of the former picture might still adhere to it.

Astounding, yet interesting, is the strange mixture of Hellenistic and pharaonic Egypt that occurs in modern esoteric literature and in the popular mix of Budge and Plutarch as sources of knowledge. Developments in anthroposophy, as well as Rosicrucian thought and Freemasonry, exemplify how there has been a trend toward pharaonic Egypt as understood by modern Egyptology. Psychoanalytic theory, along with the natural sciences, have also shed some of their dependence on Hellenistic Egypt and adopted insights from the modern discipline of Egyptology.

The holistic thought of the ancient Egyptians seems closely akin to that of modern science, to the world of quarks and bosons, which, in a rather Hermetic manner, is intensely concerned with the unity of nature—a unity we so desperately need as a counterweight in times of increasing fragmentation and in view of our environmental problems. We meet with related structures that suggest fruitful comparison of quantum mechanics with Egyptian religious thought. Here, too, there is hope for further interesting and significant developments that will counter the growing fragmentation of academic disciplines.

Perhaps we are today witnessing a phenomenon that also occurred in the late Middle Ages, when industrious monks, with their collecting and copying of classical authors (and we must not forget the great importance of Arabic translators in the contemporary intellectual flowering of Islam!) were laying the foundations of the Renaissance that followed. Today, a constant succession of discoveries in Egypt and the Near East has been coming to light and attracting a growing interest on the part of the general public. Are we heading for a new Renaissance in which Egypt, though in a very different form, will again play a role? This is at least a possible scenario for a post-postmodernism in which, for a time, all will be possible and nothing will be obligatory. Such reveries and speculations will lend some inspiration to our labors and prevent us from barricading ourselves all too securely behind the walls of our narrow disciplines. Egyptology itself maintains constant contact with the general public. That music, theater, and art have been inspired by their encounter with ancient Egypt is already encouraging, and major exhibitions of Egyptian art have also been influential. Ancient Egypt has undeniably become a component of our contemporary culture.

The impending turn of the millennium nourished hopes of new spiritual light for humankind in the aspirations of many. Egypt will surely play a role in such developments in both its forms: pharaonic Egypt and the esoteric-Hermetic Egypt. There has been increasing talk of the relevance of the Hermetic Weltanschauung as a point of view that can contribute to making sense of our modern world by seeking a direct connection with the original wisdom of the oldest cultures and with the core idea of all esoteric thought, according to which the ancient wisdom continues to be valid even in a world that has been transformed.

All Hermetism is by its very nature tolerant. Hermes Trismegistus is a god of harmony, of reconciliation and transformation, and he preaches no rigid dogma. He is thus an antidote to the fundamentalism that must be overcome if we desire to live in peace.

CHRONOLOGY

Archaic Period (c. 3000–2705 B.C.E.)

Dynasties 1 and 2

Old Kingdom (c. 2705–2180)

Dynasty 3 (Djoser, Imhotep)	*2705–2640*
Dynasty 4 (Snofru, Cheops, Chephren)	*2640–2520*
Dynasty 5 (Wenis, Pyramid Texts)	*2520–2360*
Dynasty 6 (Pepi II)	*2360–2195*

First Intermediate Period (2180–1987)

Dynasties 9/10 (Herakleopolis)

Dynasty 11 (Thebes)

Middle Kingdom (1987–1640)

Dynasty 11 (Mentuhotpe)	*1987–1938*
Dynasty 12 (Amenemhet, Senwosret)	*1938–1759*
Dynasties 13/14	*1759–1640*

Second Intermediate Period (1640–1530)

Dynasties 15/16 (Hyksos)

Dynasty 17 (Thebes)

New Kingdom (1540–1075)

Dynasty 18	*1540–1292*
Hatshepsut	1479–1458
Tuthmosis III	1479–1426
Amenophis III	1390–1353
Amenophis IV/Akhenaten	1353–1336
Tutankhamun	1332–1323

Ramessides:

Dynasty 19	*1292–1190*
Sethos I	1291–1279
Ramesses II	1279–1213
Merenptah	1213–1203
Dynasty 20	*1190–1075*
Ramesses III	1188–1157
Ramesses IV	1157–1150

Third Intermediate Period (1075–664)

Dynasty 21 ("Theocracy of Amun")	*1075–945*
Dynasties 22/24 (Libyans)	*945–712*
Dynasty 25 (Kushites)	*740–664*

Late Period (664–332)

Dynasty 26 (Saites)	*664–525*
Apries	589–570
Amasis	570–526
Dynasty 27 (Persians)	*525–404*

Dynasties 28/29   *404–380*

Dynasty 30 (Nectanebo I and Nectanebo II)   *380–343*

Macedonians (332–305)

Ptolemies (305–30)

Romans and Byzantines (30 B.C.E.–642 C.E.)

GLOSSARY

Amarna Period.   The reigns of King Akhenaten (c. 1353–1336 B.C.E.) and his immediate successors; so called after Tell el-Amarna, Akhenaten's new capital
city.

Amduat.   The oldest Egyptian description of the netherworld and the nocturnal
journey of the sun through it; composed around 1500 B.C.E. and recorded in
the tombs in the Valley of the Kings.

Archons.   In Gnosticism, the rulers over the eons who dwell between the tran-
scendent and the earthly realms and enslave humankind.

Ba.   The mobile, active "soul" of an ancient Egyptian; it had material needs and
repeatedly returned to the corpse after death.

Book of the Dead.   A later collection of illustrated spells for use in the afterlife,
written on papyri from the New Kingdom on.

Book of Gates.   After the *Amduat*, the second great Book of the Netherworld, in
which the nocturnal journey of the sun is described.

Book of the Two Ways.   Composition that forms part of the Coffin Texts; the
first attempt to describe the netherworldly realm in texts, vignettes, and maps.

Coffin Texts.   Collection of texts that continue the Pyramid Texts; written on the
coffins of officials of the Middle Kingdom.

Demiurge.   The creator of this world; in Gnosticism, he is an evil principle who
is subordinate to the actual, goodly creator of the cosmos.

Demotic.   Late form of cursive script attested from the seventh century B.C.E.
on; it was used in place of the older hieratic for letters, legal documents, and
literary works.

Djed.   Originally perhaps a stake to which ears of grain were bound in layers;
later, the hieroglyph for "endurance" and also an image of Osiris, and in widespread use as an amulet to assure salvation.

Eye of Horus. See *Udjat*.

Horapollo. Fifth century C.E. philosopher in Alexandria who wrote a widely-used book on the hieroglyphs.

Imhotep. Official of King Djoser (c. 2650 B.C.E.) who was later revered as a sage and a healing god and equated with the Greek Asclepius.

Ka. Potent, life-bestowing principle in deities and humans, connected with provisioning and life force.

Maat. The rightful, balanced order of things, the "Right" in every respect, including "truth" and "righteousness."

Menes. The legendary first king of Egypt, revered from the New Kingdom on as the founder of the state.

Ogdoad. System of four pairs of primeval deities from whom the child sun god emerged at the time of creation.

Ouroboros. Serpent depicted biting its own tail; the Greek designation of the serpent imaged with its body running back into itself, called "Tail-in-mouth" by the Egyptians; symbol of cyclical new beginnings.

Phoenix. Greek form of *benu*, the ancient Egyptian name for the primeval bird that repeatedly rises renewed from its ashes.

Pyramid Texts. The oldest collection of religious spells, serving to enable survival after death; recorded in the pyramids of the Old Kingdom, beginning with that of King Wenis (c. 2350 B.C.E.).

Sarapis (Serapis). Chief god of Alexandria and of the Ptolemaic kingdom, also venerated in many provinces of the Roman empire; he combined traits of the gods Osiris, Amun, and Zeus, and Egyptians and Greeks were united in his worship.

Sistrum. Egyptian rattle used in the cults of goddesses.

Sothis. The star Sirius, manifestation of the goddess Isis and harbinger of the Nile inundation.

Thoth. Egyptian god of wisdom and writing, as well as moon god and divine messenger; equated by the Greeks with Hermes.

Udjat. The "hale" eye that was wounded and later healed, often connected with the god Horus, whose eye was wounded in combat with Seth; extremely popular as an amulet.

BIBLIOGRAPHY

A complete bibliography for all areas of "esoteric Egypt" would fill several volumes. Here, I can offer only a limited selection of sources for each of them. The sources should afford readers a preliminary orientation to these schools of thought, as well as the means of penetrating more deeply into individual questions, for the works cited provide a wealth of references to further literature.

Introduction

On the general topic of the western encounter with Egypt, see S. Morenz, *Die Begegnung Europas mit Ägypten* (Zurich, 1969); J. S. Curl, *The Egyptian Revival* (London, 1982) [reissued under the title *Egyptomania: The Egyptian Revival* (Manchester, 1994)]; J. Baltrušaitis, *La Quête d'Isis: Essai sur la légende d'un mythe* (Paris, 1985); J. M. Humbert et al., *Kataloge der Ausstellung Egyptomania/Ägyptomanie* (Paris and Vienna, 1994); and E. Staehelin and B. Jaeger (eds.), *Ägypten-Bilder*, Orbis Biblicus et Orientalis 150 (Freiburg and Göttingen, 1997). I wish to thank Elisabeth Staehelin for her criticisms and references and Marla Stukenberg for carefully checking my manuscript.

1. The Ancient Roots of the "Other" Egypt

The citation at the beginning of the chapter is from *Urkunden des ägyptischen Altertums* (Leipzig, 1903 ff.), Part IV, 1820; for Pharaoh as "Thoth in every respect," see ibid., 1074, line 4. On the Book of Two Ways, see E. Hermsen, *Die zwei Wege des Jenseits*, Orbis Biblicus et Orientalis 112 (Freiburg and Göttingen, 1991). There is a general discussion of Thoth by P. Boylan, *Thoth: The Hermes of Egypt* (London, 1922); on Thoth in the pharaonic period, see H. Spiess, "Untersuchungen zum Gott Thoth bis zum Beginn des Neuen Reiches," Ph.D. dissertation, Hamburg University, 1991. On the development of the person of Trismegistus, see J. Quaegebeur, "Thot-Hermès, le dieu le plus grand!", in *Hommages à F. Daumas* (Montpellier, 1986), 525–544.

The Pyramid Texts are cited after the edition of K. Sethe, *Die altägyptischen Pyrami-*

dentexte (Leipzig, 1908; reprint ed., Darmstadt, 1960), and the Coffin Texts after A. de Buck, *The Egyptian Coffin Texts,* 7 vols. (Chicago, 1935–1961). See also the translations by R. O. Falkner, *The Ancient Egyptian Pyramid Texts,* 2 vols. (Oxford, 1969) and *The Ancient Egyptian Coffin Texts,* 3 vols. (Warminster, 1973–1978; reprint ed., 1994). On the Book of the Dead, see the translations of E. Hornung, *Das Totenbuch der Ägypter* (Zurich, 1979), and of R. O. Faulkner in *The Egyptian Book of the Dead: The Book of Going Forth by Day,* ed. E. von Dassow (San Francisco, 1994). Haremhab's hymn has been translated by J. Assmann, *Ägyptische Hymnen und Gebete* (Zürich, 1975), no. 222.

The writing system in the temple of Esna has been treated by S. Sauneron, *L'Écriture figurative dans les textes d'Esna,* Esna 8 (Cairo, 1982). Horapollo's work has been translated from the Latin version by H. Weingärtner, *Horapollo: Zwei Bücher über die Hieroglyphen* (Erlangen, 1997); see also H.-J. Thissen, *Vom Bild zum Buchstaben–vom Buchstaben zum Bild: Von der Arbeit an Horapollons Hieroglyphika,* Akademie der Wissenschaften und der Literatur in Mainz, Abhandlungen der Geistes- und Sozialwissenschaftlichen Klasse 1998, no. 3 (Mainz, 1998). On the interpretation of the vulture, see E. and U. Winter, in *Viribus Unitis* (Festschrift B. Stillfried, Bern, 1996), 523–537. The symbol of the *ouroboros* has been treated by B. H. Stricker, *De grote Zeeslang* (Leiden, 1953).

On the problem of the mysteries and initiation, see E. Hornung, "Altägyptische Wurzeln der Isismysterien," in *Hommages à J. Leclant* (Cairo, 1994), 3, 287–293, and L. Kákosy, *Tempel und Mysterien,* Hildesheimer Ägyptologische Beiträge 37 (Hildesheim, 1994), pp. 165–173. For Apuleius, see J. G. Griffiths, *Apuleius of Madauros: The Isis-Book* (Leiden, 1975).

On the nightly journey through the netherworld, see E. Hornung, *Die Nachtfahrt der Sonne* (Zurich, 1991); idem, *Ägyptische Unterweltsbücher* (Zurich, 1972); and idem, *The Ancient Egyptian Books of the Afterlife* (Ithaca, 1999). Humankind's "Fall" is treated in E. Hornung, *Der ägyptische Mythos von der Himmelskuh: Eine Ätiologie des Unvollkommenen,* Orbis Biblicus et Orientalis 46 (Freiburg and Göttingen 1982; 3d ed., 1997). Ramesside and Hermetic religious beliefs have been treated by J. Assmann in *Egyptian Solar Religion in the New Kingdom* (New York, 1995) and *Moses the Egyptian: The Memory of Egypt in Western Monotheism* (Cambridge, Mass., 1997).

2. Foreign Wonderland on the Nile: The Greek Writers

See the general treatments by T. Hopfner, *Orient und griechische Philosophie* (Leipzig, 1925); C. Froidefond, *Le Mirage égyptien dans la littérature grecque d'Homère à Aristote* (Paris, 1971); and J. Assmann, *Weisheit und Mysterium: Das Bild der Griechen von Ägypten* (Munich, 2000). On the etymology of the name Atlantis, see W. Schenkel, *Göttinger Miszellen* 36 (1979): 57–60, and J. G. Griffiths, *Atlantis and Egypt* (Cardiff, 1991), 3–30.

For Diodorus, see A. Burton, *Diodorus Siculus, Book I: Commentary* (Leiden, 1972). For Plutarch, see J. G. Griffiths, *Plutarch: De Iside et Osiride* (Cardiff, 1970). For the ancient traditions regarding Homer, see A. Leroy-Molinghen, *Chronique d'Égypte* 60 (1985): 131–137; Plato, see B. Mathieu, "Le Voyage de Platon en Égypte," *Annales du Service des Antiquités de l'Égypte* 71 (1987): 153–167; and Eudoxus of Cnidus, see G. Goyon, *Bulletin de l'Institut Français d'Archéologie Orientale* 74 (1974): 135–147. For Strabo's discussion of Egypt, see J. Yoyotte and P. Charvet, *Strabon: Le Voyage en Égypte, Un regard romain* (Paris, 1997) and H. L. Jones, *The Geography of Egypt,* vol. VIII (London, 1982).

3. Power and Influence of the Stars

On ancient Egyptian astronomy, see O. Neugebauer and R. A. Parker, *Egyptian Astronomical Texts*, vol. 3, Brown Egyptological Studies 5 (London, 1969); L. Kákosy, "Decans in Late-Egyptian Religion," *Oikumene* 3 (1982): 163–191; idem, *Egyptomi és antik csillaghit* (Egyptian and classical beliefs regarding the stars, Budapest, 1978), and cf. W. Brunsch, *Göttinger Miszellen* 54 (1982): 83; B. Bohleke, *Studien zur Altägyptischen Kultur* 23 (1996): 11–46. On R. Merkelbach, *Abrasax*, see the bibliography to chapter 7 below. I. E. S. Edwards, *Oracular Amuletic Decrees of the Late New Kingdom*, Hieratic Papyri in the British Museum, 4th Series (London, 1960), text L 1. On the earliest attested astronomical concepts, see R. Krauss, *Astronomische Konzepte und Jenseitsvorstellungen in den Pyramidentexten* (Wiesbaden, 1997).

For the armbands of Hornakhte, see P. Montet, *La Nécropole royale de Tanis*, 1 (Paris, 1947), 68, fig. 22.; for the naos of the decans, see C. Leitz, *Altägyptische Sternuhren* (Leuven, 1995). On the statue of Harchebis, see P. Derchain, *Chronique d'Égypte* 64 (1989): 74–89, and M. Clagett, *Ancient Egytian Science*, 2 (Philadelphia, 1995), 489–496. Further sources are J. F. Quack, "Dekane und Gliedervergottung," *Jahrbuch für Antike und Christentum* 38 (1995): 97–122; R. Krauss, *Göttinger Miszellen* 42 (1981): 49–60 (King Nechepso); C. Desroches–Noblecourt, *Amours et fureurs de La Lointaine* (Paris, 1995), 201–242 (the Egyptian zodiac); and S. Cauville, *Le Zodiaque d'Osiris* (Louvain, 1997).

4. Alchemy: The Art of Transformation

On Zosimus of Panopolis, see M. Mertens (ed.), *Zosime de Panopolis: Mémoires authentiques*, Les Alchimistes Grecs, vol. 4/1 (Paris, 1995). On alchemy, see C. G. Jung, *Psychology and Alchemy*, Bollingen Series 20/12 (Princeton, 1953); J. Lindsay, *The Origins of Alchemy in Graeco-Roman Egypt* (London, 1970); F. Daumas, "L'Alchimie a-t-elle une origine égyptienne?", in *Das römisch-byzantinische Ägypten: Akten des internationalen Symposions 26.–30. September 1978 in Trier*, Aegyptiaca Treverensia 2 (Mainz, 1983), 109–118; P. Derchain, "L'Atelier des Orfèvres à Dendera et les origines de l'Alchimie," *Chronique d'Égypte* 65 (1990): 219–242; S. Cauville, *Bulletin de la Société Française d'Égyptologie* 112 (1988): 23–36 (also on Dendara); S. Aufrère, *L'Univers minéral dans la pensée égyptienne* (Cairo, 1991); B. D. Haage, *Alchemie im Mittlelalter* (Zurich, 1996); and C. Priesner and K. Figala (eds.), *Alchemie: Lexikon einer hermetischen Wissenschaft* (Munich, 1998).

On the inscription of Harwerre, see D. Kurth, *Göttinger Miszellen* 154 (1996): 57–63. On *Urkunden*, vol. 4, see the bibliography to chapter 1 above. For Ramesses II as "geologist," see T. de Putter, *Zeitschrift für ägyptische Sprache und Altertumskunde* 124 (1997): 131–141. For the formula from Edfu, see D. Kurth, *Treffpunkt der Götter* (Zurich, 1994), text no. 13.

The Arab tradition has been studied by Ingolf Vereno, *Studien zum ältesten alchemistischen Schrifttum* (Berlin, 1992). For the four elements, see B. H. Stricker, *De geboorte van Horus*, vol. 2 (Leiden, 1968). For the Eranos lectures, see the bibliography to chapter 16 below. On the "Place of Annihilation," see E. Hornung, "Schwarze Löcher von innen betrachtet: Die altägyptische Hölle," in T. Schabert and E. Hornung (eds.), *Strukturen des Chaos*, Eranos, n.s. 2 (Munich, 1994), 227–262. I thank Theodor Abt and Thomas Hofmeier for references.

5. Gnosis: Creation as Flaw

For treatments of gnosticism, see H. Jonas, *Gnosis und spätantiker Geist* (Göttingen, 1934; 4th ed., 1989); W. Foerster and A. Böhlig (eds.), *Die Gnosis*, 3 vols. (Zurich, 1969–1980); J. M. Robinson, *The Nag Hammadi Library in English* (Leiden, 1988); L. Kákosy, "Gnosis und ägyptische Religion," in *Le Origine dello Gnosticismo*, Supplements to *Numen* 12 (Leiden, 1967), 238–247 (along with other contributions in this volume); D. M. Parrott, "Gnosticism and Egyptian Religion," *Novum Testamentum* 29 (1987): 73–93; and P. Sloterdijk and T. H. Macho, *Weltrevolution der Seele: Ein Lese- und Arbeitsbuch der Gnosis* (Zurich, 1993).

6. Hermetism: Thoth as Hermes Trismegistus

Important sources are: J. Ruska, *Tabula Smaragdina: Ein Beitrag zur Geschichte der hermetischen Literatur* (Heidelberg, 1926); A. J. Festugière, *La Révélation d'Hermès Trismégiste*, 4 vols. (Paris, 1950–1954); B. H. Stricker, *De Brief van Aristeas* (Amsterdam, 1956); P. Derchain, "L'Authenticité de l'inspiration égyptienne dans le Corpus Hermeticum," *Revue de l'Histoire des Religions* 161 (1962): 175–198; J.-P. Mahé, *Hermès en Haute-Égypte: Les Textes hermétiques de Nag Hammadi et leurs parallèles grecs et latins*, 2 vols., Bibliothèque copte de Nag Hammadi, Section "Textes" 3 (Quebec, 1978–1982); E. Iversen, *Egyptian and Hermetic Doctrine*, Opuscula Graecolatina 27 (Copenhagen, 1984), especially on cosmology; G. Fowden, *The Egyptian Hermes: A Historical Approach to the Late Pagan Mind* (Princeton, 1993); B. P. Copenhaver, *Hermetica* (Cambridge, 1992); A. Faivre, *The Eternal Hermes: From Greek God to Alchemical Magus* (Grand Rapids, Mich., 1995); R. Liedtke, *Die Hermetik: Traditionelle Philosophie der Differenz* (Paderborn, 1996); C. Colpe and J. Holzhausen, *Das Corpus Hermeticum: Deutsche Übersetzung, Darstellung und Kommentierung in drei Teilen* (Stuttgart, 1997).

On the Demotic "Book of Thoth," see J.-P. Mahé, *Vigiliae Christianae* 50 (1996): 353–363; R. Jasnow and K.-T. Zauzich, "A Book of Thoth?" in C. J. Eyre (ed.), *Proceedings of the 7th International Congress of Egyptologists* (Leuven, 1998), 607–618. For Asclepius = Imhotep, see D. Wildung, *Imhotep und Amenhotep: Gottwerdung im Alten Ägypten*, Münchner Ägyptologische Studien 36 (Munich, 1977). On Isis and the Kore Kosmou, see H. Jackson, *Chronique d'Égypte* 61 (1986): 116–135.

For surveys of Arab Hermetism, see F. Sezgin, *Geschichte des arabischen Schriftums*, 4 (Leiden, 1971), 1–300; M. Ullmann, *Die Natur- und Geheimwissenschaften im Islam* (Leiden, 1972); idem, *Das Schlangenbuch des Hermes Trismegistos* (Wiesbaden, 1994); I thank Ursula Sezgin for many valuable references. On Newton's commentary on the Tabula Smaragdina, see B. J. T. Dobbs, in I. Merkel and A. G. Debus (eds.), *Hermeticism and the Renaissance* (Washington, 1988), 182–191; eadem, *The Janus Faces of Genius: The Role of Alchemy in Newton's Thought* (New York, 1991).

7. Egypt of the Magical Arts

The monographs on this topic are innumerable. See especially L. Kákosy, *Zauberei im alten Ägypten* (Leipzig, 1989); the Christ-Horus amulet is dealt with ibid., pp. 161–162 and pl. 16; G. Pinch, *Magic in Ancient Egypt* (London, 1994); and A. Roccati and A. Silotti (eds.), *La Magia in Egitto ai tempi dei Faraoni* (Milan, 1987). A selection of texts is to be found in J. F. Borghouts, *Ancient Egyptian Magical Texts* (Leiden, 1978); the First and Second Stories of Setne have been translated by M. Lichtheim, *Ancient Egyptian*

Literature: A Book of Readings, vol. 3: *The Late Period* (Berkeley, 1980), 125–151. The Greek magical texts from Egypt are published by K. Preisendanz, *Papyri Graecae Magicae: Die griechischen Zauberpapyri* (Leipzig, 1928–1931; 2d ed., Stuttgart, 1973); see also H. D. Betz, *The Greek Magical Papyri in Translation* (Chicago, 1986), and R. Merkelbach, *Abrasax: Ausgewählte Papyri religiösen und magischen Inhalts*, 4 vols. (Opladen, 1990–1997). Coptic texts have been published by A. M. Kropp, *Ausgewählte koptische Zaubertexte*, 3 vols. (Brussels, 1930–1931); see 2: 9–11, for the text from the Faiyum first published by A. Erman, *Zeitschrift für altägyptische Sprache und Altertumskunde* 33 (1895): 43–51, and see also M. Meyer (ed.), *Ancient Christian Magic: Coptic Texts of Ritual Power* (San Francisco, 1994). The letter to Usersatet (*Urkunden* IV, 1343–1344) has been studied by W. Helck, *Journal of Near Eastern Studies* 14 (1955): 22–31. For the invocation of Amun of No in the cabala, see M. Idel, in G. Benedetti and E. Hornung (eds.), *Die Wahrheit der Träume*, Eranos, n.s. 6 (Munich, 1997): 100–102.

8. The Spread of Egyptian Cults: Isis and Osiris

An extensive survey of this topic is afforded by G. Hölbl in *Lexikon der Ägyptologie*, vol. 6 (Wiesbaden, 1986) s.v. "Verehrung ägyptischer Götter." On Rome, see especially A. Roullet, *The Egyptian and Egyptianizing Monuments of Imperial Rome* (Leiden, 1972); E. Buchner, *Die Sonnenuhr des Augustus* (Mainz, 1982); and K. Lembke, *Das Iseum Campense in Rom* (Heidelberg, 1994). See also R. E. Witt, *Isis in the Ancient World* (Baltimore, 1997; 1st ed., Ithaca, 1971); J.-C. Grenier, *Anubis alexandrin et romain* (Leiden, 1977); and R. Merkelbach, *Isis regina–Zeus Sarapis* (Stuttgart, 1995).

For the Horus stela on the Esquiline, see F. de Salvia, *Studia Aegyptiaca* 14 (1992): 509–517. On the Isis sanctuaries, see H. W. Müller, *Der Isiskult im antiken Benevent*, Münchner Ägyptologische Studien 16 (1969) and the exhibit catalogue *Iside: Il mito il mistero la magia* (Milan, 1997). On Antinous, see G. Grimm, "Antinous renatus et felix?" in M. Minas and J. Zeidler (eds.), *Aspekte spätägyptischer Kultur* (Festschrift E. Winter, Mainz, 1994), 103–112, and E. Winter in E. Staehelin and B. Jaeger (eds.), *Ägypten-Bilder*, Orbis Biblicus et Orientalis 150 (Freiburg and Göttingen, 1997): 97–102. On the Egyptianization of Greek myths in Pompeii, see R. Merkelbach, ibid., 81–96.

9. Medieval Traditions

See the treatments by J. Doresse, *Des hiéroglyphes à la croix: Ce que le passé pharaonique a légué au christianisme* (Istanbul, 1960); M. Smith, *Jesus the Magician* (San Francisco, 1978); F. Zimmermann, *Die ägyptische Religion nach der Darstellung der Kirchenschriftsteller und die ägyptischen Denkmäler* (Paderborn, 1912); A. Weis, *Die Madonna Platytera* (Königstein/Ts, 1985); S. Runciman, *The Medieval Manichee* (Cambridge, 1947). On the importance of Egypt and its imagery for the Christian Credo, see M. Görg, *Mythos, Glaube und Geschichte* (Düsseldorf, 1992). For the citation from Shenute, see J. Leipoldt, *Schenute von Atripe* (Leipzig, 1903). On the Holy Family in Egypt, see E. Landolt, "Legenden um die Flucht nach Ägypten," *Sandoz Bulletin* 36 (1974): 23–44, and on the Coptic traditions, see O. F. A. Meinardus, *Auf den Spuren der Heiligen Familie von Bethlehem nach Oberägypten* (Koblenz, 1978). For Adelard, see U. Sezgin, *Zeitschrift für Geschichte der arabisch-islamischen Wissenschaften* 9 (1994): 268–269, notes 141 and 146.

On the cabala, see G. Scholem, *Die jüdische Mystik in ihren Hauptströmungen* (Frankfurt a.M., 1957); E. Benz, *Die christliche Kabbala* (Zurich, 1958); J. Maier, *Die Kabbalah:*

Einführung, Klassische Texte, Erläuterungen (Munich, 1995); and G. Mussies, "The Interpretatio Judaica of Thot-Hermes," in *Studies in Egyptian Religion Dedicated to Professor Jan Zandee* (Leiden, 1982), 89–120. For Hermes (alias Henoch) in the Jewish writers of the Middle Ages and the Renaissance, see M. Idel, "Hermeticism and Judaism," in I. Merkel and A. G. Debus (eds.), *Hermeticism and the Renaissance* (Washington, 1988), 11–34. For a treatment of Princess Thermutis as a Christian saint, see A. Hermann, "Das Kind und seine Hüterin," *Mitteilungen des Deutschen Instituts für ägyptische Altertumskunde in Kairo* 8 (1939): 171–176.

10. The Renaissance of Hermetism and Hieroglyphs

See the treatments by L. Volkmann, *Bilderschriften der Renaissance* (Leipzig, 1923; reprint ed., 1962); E. Iversen, *The Myth of Egypt and Its Hieroglyphs in European Tradition* (Copenhagen, 1961); F. A. Yates, *Giordano Bruno and the Hermetic Tradition* (London, 1964); E. Wind, *Pagan Mysteries in the Renaissance* (London, 1958; 2d ed., 1968); L. Dieckmann, *Hieroglyphics: The History of a Literary Symbol* (St. Louis, 1970); and I. Merkel and A. G. Debus (eds.), *Hermeticism and the Renaissance* (Washington, 1988).

On the renewed concern with the obelisks of Rome, see E. Iversen, *Obelisks in Exile*, vol. 1: *The Obelisks of Rome* (Copenhagen, 1968). On the Mensa Isiaca, which was originally published by Lorenzo Pignorius in 1605, see E. Leospo, *La Mensa Isiaca di Torino* (Leiden, 1978). On the Palazzo Tè, see B. Jaeger, "L'Egitto alla corte dei Gonzaga," in C. M. Govi, S. Curto, and S. Pernigotti (eds.), *L'Egitto fuori dell'Egitto: Dalla riscoperta all'egittologia* (Bologna, 1991), 233–253.

For the continuation of the Renaissance understanding of Horapollo down into the Romantic period, I am grateful to Johanna Schmitz for allowing me to look into an unpublished work. Still useful is a bibliography of works on the hieroglyphs before their decipherment compiled by H. Gauthier, *Bulletin de l'Institut Français d'Archéologie Orientale* 5 (1906): 80–86. For the citation regarding Dürer, see Volkmann, op. cit., p. 95. For *multimammia* and Isis as goddess of nature, see E. Staehelin, "Alma Mater Isis," in E. Staehelin and B. Jaeger (eds.), *Ägypten-Bilder*, Orbis Biblicus et Orientalis 150 (Freiburg and Göttingen, 1997), 103–141.

11. Travels to Egypt: Wonder upon Wonder

For a general treatment, see J. Guérin dalle Mese, *Égypte—La Mémoire et le rêve: Itinéraires d'un voyage, 1320–1601* (Florence, 1991), with a discussion of Hermes Trismegistus on pp. 551–559. A bibliography of travelogues down to 1918 is supplied by M. R. Kalfatovic, *Nile Notes of a Howadji* (London, 1992).

On early accounts (Egeria, etc.), see H. Donner, *Pilgerfahrt ins Heilige Land: Die ältesten Berichte christlicher Palästinapilger (4.–7. Jahrh.)* (Stuttgart, 1979). On the pictures of Moses and Aaron that Egeria supposedly saw in the City of Ramesses, see O. Keel, in *Peregrina Curiositas: Eine Reise durch den Orbis antiquus, zu Ehren von Dirk van Damme*, Novum Testamentum et Orbis antiquum 27 (Freiburg and Göttingen, 1994), 155–166. European preconceptions are treated by O. Keel in E. Staehelin and B. Jaeger (eds.), *Ägypten-Bilder*, Orbis Biblicus et Orientalis 150 (Freiburg and Göttingen, 1997), 55–57: Champollion thought that the Asiatics depicted at Beni Hasan were Greeks, while Wilkinson and others took them to be Hebrews. On the trade in mummies, see R. Germer, *Mumien: Zeugen des Pharaonenreiches* (Zurich, 1991), 15–26.

For a reverse case of an early Egyptian traveler to Europe, we may consider Yusuf ibn Abu Dhaqn, called "Barbatus," a Copt from Cairo who was sent by Patriarch Gabriel VIII to the pope in 1595 and who also traveled extensively in France, England, and central Europe, coming into contact with Casaubon, Scaliger, and Kepler; see A. Hamilton, "An Egyptian Traveller in the Republic of Letters," *Journal of the Warburg and Courtauld Institutes* 57 (1994): 123–150.

12. Triumphs of Erudition: Kircher, Spencer, and Cudworth

On Kircher, see J. Godwin, *Athanasius Kircher: A Renaissance Man and the Quest for Lost Knowledge* (London, 1979) and J. Fletcher (ed.), *Athanasius Kircher und seine Beziehungen zum gelehrten Europa seiner Zeit* (Wiesbaden, 1988). Since 1996, there has been a monograph series entitled Studia Kircheriana, edited by O. Hein and R. Mader. Spencer, Cudworth, and Warburton's treatments of Egypt have been studied by J. Assmann, *Moses the Egyptian* (Cambridge, Mass., 1997).

I am grateful to F. Ebeling for information regarding H. Conring; see further M. Stolleis (ed.), *Hermann Conring (1606–1681): Beiträge zu Leben und Werk* (Berlin, 1983). On the Nile mosaic, see P. G. P. Mayboom, *The Nile Mosaic of Palestrina: Early Evidence of Egyptian Religion in Italy*, Religions in the Graeco-Roman World 121 (Leiden, 1995). For the Apis altar, see now D. Syndram, *Die Ägyptenrezeption unter August dem Starken: Der "Apis-Altar" Johann Melchior Dinglingers* (Mainz, 1999).

13. "Reformation of the Whole Wide World": The Rosicrucians

See F. A. Yates, *The Rosicrucian Enlightenment* (London, 1972), with stress on influence from England; G. Wehr, *Die Bruderschaft der Rosenkreuzer* (Munich, 1984; 5th ed., 1995); R. Edighoffer, *Die Rosenkreuzer* (Munich, 1995); C. Gilly, *Adam Haslmayr: Der erste Verkünder der Manifeste der Rosenkreuzer* (Amsterdam, 1994); C. Gilly (ed.), *Cimelia Rhodostaurotica: Die Rosenkreuzer im Spiegel der zwischen 1610 und 1660 entstandenen Handschriften und Drucke*, catalog of the exhibition in Wolfenbüttel and Amsterdam, 1995 (Amsterdam, 1995); R. Edighoffer, *Les Rose-Croix et la crise de la conscience européenne au XVIIe siècle* (Paris, 1998).

The citations regarding the modern Rosicrucians stem from literature published by the Lectorium Rosicrucianum and in part from information obtained through correspondence. I am grateful to Birgit Schlick-Nolte for references.

14. The Ideal of a Fraternity: The Freemasons

A fundamental source is E. Lennhoff and O. Posner, *Internationales Freimaurerlexikon* (Vienna, 1932; reprint eds. 1965 and 1973). See also S. Morenz, *Die Zauberflöte: Eine Studie zum Lebenszusammenhang Ägypten–Antike–Abendland*, Münstersche Forschungen 5 (Münster, 1952); K. R. H. Frick, *Die Erleuchteten: Gnostisch-theosophische und alchemistisch-rosenkreuzerische Geheimgesellschaften bis zum Ende des 18. Jahrhunderts—Ein Beitrag zur Geistesgeschichte der Neuzeit* (Graz, 1973); idem, *Licht und Finsternis: Gnostisch-theosophische und freimaurerisch-okkulte Geheimgesellschaften bis an die Wende zum 20. Jahrhundert*, 2 vols. (Graz, 1975–1978); H. Reinalter (ed.), *Freimaurer und Geheimbünde im 18. Jahrhundert in Mitteleuropa* (Frankfurt a.M., 1983); G. Steiner, *Freimaurer und Rosenkreuzer: Georg Forsters Weg durch Geheimbünde* (2d ed., Berlin, 1987); G. Galtier, *Maçonnerie égyptienne, Rose-Croix et Néo-Chevalerie: Les Fils de Cagliostro*

(Monaco, 1989); E. Staehelin, "Zum Motiv der Pyramiden als Prüfungs- und Einweihungsstätten," in S. Israelit-Groll (ed.), *Studies in Egyptology Presented to Miriam Lichtheim* (Jerusalem, 1990), 2, 889–932; J. S. Curl, *The Art and Architecture of Freemasonry* (London, 1991); L. Nefontaine, *Symboles et symbolisme dans la Franc-Maçonnerie* (Brussels, 1994), with bibliography.

On the cycle of frescos in the Villa Cornaro, see D. Lewis in I. Merkel and A. G. Debus (eds.), *Hermeticism and the Renaissance* (Washington, 1988), 366–399. The original title of Anderson's Constitutions was "The Constitutions of the Free-Masons containing the History, Charges, Regulations, etc., of that most Ancient and Right Worshipful Fraternity." For the lodge seal from Naples, see R. di Castiglione, *Alle sorgenti della massoneria* (Rome, 1988), pl. 8 (I owe this reference to B. Jaeger). For Cagliostro, see K. H. Kiefer (ed.), *Cagliostro: Dokumente zu Aufklärung und Okkultismus* (Munich, 1991); the citation from Bode in the text is taken from p. 191 of this volume. See also A. Lenoir, *La Franche-Maçonnerie rendue à sa véritable origine, ou l'antiquité de la Franche-Maçonnerie prouvée par l'explication des mystères anciens et modernes* (Paris, 1814) (the illustrations stem from J. M. Moreau the younger). On Forster to J. Müller, see G. Steiner, op. cit., p. 157. On Masonic temples in ancient Egyptian style, see C. E. Gernandt, *Der Gottesbegriff der alten Aegypter (mit Beilage "Die dynastische Freimaurerei der alten Aegypter")* (Stockholm, 1905).

I thank Elisabeth Staehelin for preparing the essential materials for this chapter and Jürgen Horn for additional information regarding the "Africanische Bauherren."

15. Goethe and Romanticism: "Thinking Hieroglyphically"

On the eighteenth century, see D. Syndram, *Ägypten-Faszinationen: Untersuchungen zum Ägyptenbild im europäischen Klassizismus bis 1800* (Frankfurt a.M., 1990). On Goethe and Egypt, see R. C. Zimmermann, *Das Weltbild des jungen Goethe: Studien zur hermetischen Tradition des deutschen 18. Jahrhundert*, 2 vols. (Munich, 1969–1979); L. Volkmann, "Goethe und Ägypten," *Zeitschrift für ägyptische Sprache und Altertumskunde* 72 (1936): 1–12; and S. Hummel, "Goethes ägyptische Sammlung," *Goethe Jahrbuch* 97 (1980): 212–223.

On the comparison of the Chinese and Egyptian writing systems, which goes back to Giovanni Pietro Maffei (1588), see R. Müller-Wollermann, in L. Gestermann and H. Sternberg El Hotabi (eds.), *Per aspera ad astra* (Festschrift Wolfgang Schenkel, Kassel, 1995), 91–105. An Egyptian conquest of India and China was claimed by Pierre-Daniel Huet, *Histoire de commerce et de la navigation des anciens peuples* (Paris, 1716); see also Charles Joseph de Guignes, *Mémoire dans lequel on prouve, que des chinois sont une colonie égyptienne* (Paris, 1759); and Friedrich S. Schmidt, *Dissertation sur une colonie égyptienne établie aux Indes* (Bern, 1758).

On Herder's assessment, see S. Morenz, *Die Begegnung Europas mit Ägypten* (Zurich, 1969), 132–133. On the inscription from Sais, see G. Steindorff, *Zeitschrift für ägyptische Sprache und Altertumskunde* 69 (1933), 71 (K. Reinhold is his source); E. Graefe, *Göttinger Miszellen* 2 (1972): 19–21; C. Harrouer, "Ich bin was da ist . . . ," in *Sphairos*, *Wiener Studien* 107/108 (1994/1995): 337–355; and J. Assmann, *Das verschleierte Bild zu Sais* (Stuttgart, 1999). I am grateful to J. Schmitz for the reference to Hamann; the citation stems from 1762. On Desprez, see Syndram, op. cit., 181–182. On De Quincey, see A. Assmann, in E. Staehelin and B. Jaeger (eds.), *Ägypten-Bilder*, Orbis Biblicus et Orientalis 150 (Freiburg and Göttingen, 1997), 182–186. On the exotic view of Egypt, see M. Kaiser, *Zeitschrift für ägyptische Sprache und Altertumskunde* 97 (1971): 78–94. On "Orientalism," see E. W. Said, *Orientalism* (New York, 1978).

16. Theosophy and Anthroposophy

Theosophy: see K. R. H. Frick, *Licht und Finsternis: Gnostisch-theosophische und freimauererisch-okkulte Geheimgesellschaften bis an die Wende zum 20. Jahrhundert*, 2 vols. (Graz, 1975–1978); P. Washington, *Madame Blavatsky's Baboon* (New York, 1993); and V. Gunturu, *Krishnamurti: Leben und Werk* (Munich, 1997). There were already works bearing the title *Theosophia* in antiquity; see H. Erbse, *Fragmente griechischer Theosophen* (Hamburg, 1941). We have cited Blavatsky's *Isis Unveiled: A Master-Key to the Mysteries of Ancient and Modern Science and Theology* from the sixth edition (New York, 1891). On Monte Verità (Ascona), see the exhibit catalogue *Monte Verità: Berg der Wahrheit* (Munich, 1980). Since 1993, the Eranos lectures have been regularly published on an annual basis in the *Eranos* (n.s.) series edited by E. Hornung and T. Schabert; the citation from E. Neumann is from *Eranos Jahrbuch* 44 (1975): 5.

Anthroposophy: see R. Steiner, *Ägyptische Mythen und Mysterien* (Berlin, 1911; 4th ed., Dornach, 1978); idem, "Hermes," in *Antworten der Geisteswissenschaft auf die grossen Fragen des Daseins* (Dornach, 1987); see also his many lectures and his book *Mein Lebensgang* (Dornach, 1953). Further sources are C. Lindenberg, *Rudolf Steiner* (Reinbek, 1992); idem, *Rudolf Steiner: Eine Biographie* (Stuttgart, 1997); E. Uehli, *Kultur und Kunst Ägyptens: Ein Isisgeheimnis* (Dornach, 1955); E. Horstmann, *Beiträge zur Bewusstseinsgeschichte des alten Ägypten* (2d ed., Stuttgart, 1997); F. Teichmann, *Die Kultur der Empfindungsseele* (Stuttgart, 1990). I am grateful to Mrs. Irene Sury for obtaining relevant literature and to Frank Teichmann for obtaining the photo of a set from the play.

17. Pyramids, Sphinx, Mummies: A Curse on the Pharaohs

See in particular E. Graefe, "Das Pyramidenkapitel in Al-Makrizi's 'Hitat,'" Ph.D. dissertation (Leipzig, 1911); R. Borchardt, *Gegen die Zahlenmystik an der grossen Pyramide bei Gise* (Berlin, 1922); J. P. Lauer, *Le Mystère des pyramides* (Paris, 1974), 191–258; and R. Stadelmann, *Die ägyptischen Pyramiden*, Kulturgeschichte der antiken Welt 30, 3d ed. (Mainz, 1997), 264–284. On the Islamic tradition, see U. Haarmann, "Das pharaonische Ägypten bei islamischen Autoren des Mittelalters," in E. Hornung (ed.), *Zum Bild Ägyptens im Mittelalter und in der Renaissance*, Orbis Biblicus et Orientalis 95 (Freiburg and Göttingen, 1990): 29–57.

On the employment of Egyptian architectural forms, see F. Werner, *Ägyptenrezeption in der europäischen Architektur des 19. Jahrhunderts* (Weimar, 1994). L. Kákosy discusses the connection of the pyramid of Cheops with alchemic practices in *Antik Tanulmányok* 16 (1969): 195–198 (Hungarian). B. Brier and R. S. Wade report on their modern experiment in mummification in *Zeitschrift für ägyptische Sprache und Altertumskunde* 124 (1997): 89–100. The changes in the figure of the Sphinx are treated by H. Demisch, *Die Sphinx: Geschichte ihrer Darstellung von den Anfängen bis zur Gegenwart* (Stuttgart, 1977).

18. Egypt à la Mode: Modern Egyptosophy and Afrocentrism

For a general treatment, see K. R. H. Frick, *Licht und Finsternis: Gnostisch-theosophische und freimaurerisch-okkulte Geheimgesellschaften bis an die Wende zum 20. Jahrhundert*, 2 vols. (Graz, 1975–1978). There is rich material on the influence of the occult, and especially of theosophy, on painting in the exhibit catalog *The Spiritual in Art: Abrstract Painting 1890–1985* (Los Angeles, 1986).

Schwaller de Lubicz has been defended against "orthodox scholars" by J. A. West, *Serpent in the Sky: The High Wisdom of Ancient Egypt* (New York, 1979); in this book, all Egyptian wisdom is traced back to immigrants from Atlantis, and it is claimed that there was no further development in Egypt itself. On Schwaller, see also A. van den Broeck, *Al-Kemi: Hermetic, Occult, Political, and Private Aspects of R. A. Schwaller de Lubicz* (Great Barrington, Mass., 1987). I wish to thank H. T. Hakl for referring me to G. Massey, as well to material on Crowley, Evola, and other figures.

The "case of Rosemary" is treated by J. G. Griffiths, "Some Claims of Xenoglossy in the Ancient Languages," *Numen* 33 (1986): 141–169. M. Hulin has supplied an excellent analysis of modern beliefs in reincarnation in "Die Seelenwanderung: Indogriechischer Mythos oder Herausforderung an das zeitgenössiche Denken?" in F. Graf and E. Hornung (eds.), *Wanderungen*, Eranos n.s. 3 (1995): 135–165.

The Mormon church is treated as an example of a modern religion of revelation by E. Meyer, *Ursprung und Geschichte der Mormonen* (Halle, 1912). See also F. S. Spaulding, *Joseph Smith, Jr., as a Translator* (Salt Lake City, 1912); J. A. Wilson, *Thousands of Years* (New York, 1972), 173–177; and J. A. Larson in *For His Ka: Essays Offered in Memoery of Klaus Baer* (Chicago, 1994), 159–178.

Jesus' connection with India and Tibet is the topic of R. Heiligenthal, *Der verfälschte Jesus* (Darmstadt, 1997), which includes a treatment of the forged Benan letter that connects him again with Egypt and more specifically with the school of wisdom in Heliopolis.

On the extraterrestrial tradition, see E. Benz, "Der Kopernikanische Schock," *Eranos Jahrbuch* 44 (1975): 15–60, and K. S. Guthke, *Der Mythos der Neuzeit: Das Thema der Mehrheit der Welten in der Literatur- und Geistesgeschichte von der kopernikanischen Wende bis zur Science Fiction* (Bern, 1983).

On W. Pauli, see the collaborative volume by H. Atmanspacher, H. Primas, and E. Wertenschlag-Birkhäuser (eds.), *Der Pauli-Jung Dialog und seine Bedeutung für die moderne Wissenschaft* (Berlin, 1995).

There have been many with an orientation similar to that of P. Paddon, though they have not gone so far as to found an order. Rather, they offer practical counseling, such as the advice to be found in J. Houston, *The Passion of Isis and Osiris* (New York, 1995), which supplies instructions on how to connect with the world of the *neters*, along with a typical mixture of reincarnation, Kundalini Yoga, and the Akasha Chronicle (which is supposed to have been transmitted by the Egyptian goddess Seshat).

I thank G. Schmidt for a number of references regarding Ezra Pound. On James Joyce, see M. L. Troy, *Mummeries of Resurrection: The Cycle of Osiris in* Finnegans Wake, Acta Universitatis Upsaliensis, Studia Anglistica Upsaliensia 26 (Uppsala, 1976).

On esoteric literature regarding the Book of the Dead, see W. Czermak, *Zeitschrift für ägyptische Sprache und Altertumskunde* 76 (1940): 9–11; S. Mayassis, *Le Livre des Morts de l'Égypte ancienne est un livre d'initiation* (Athens, 1955); and G. Thausing and T. Kerszt-Kratschmann, *Das grosse ägyptische Totenbuch* (Cairo, 1969). The citations from J. Assmann are to be found in A. Assmann (ed.), *Weisheit*, Archäologie der literarischen Kommunikation 3 (Munich, 1991), 246, 248, n. 13; see also ibid., p. 247: "Magic is an exact science." In May 1997, T. Hofmeier referred me to 7,617 World Wide Web pages demonstrating contemporary interest in Egypt and esoterica.

For the topic of Afrocentrism, see especially M. Bernal, *Black Athena: The Afroasiatic Roots of Classical Civilization*, 2 vols. (London, 1987–1991); M. Lefkowitz, *Not Out of Africa: How Afrocentrism Became an Excuse to Teach Myth as History*, 2d ed. (New York, 1997); M. R. Lefkowitz and G. MacLean Rogers (eds.), *Black Athena Revisited* (Chapel

Hill, 1996), which contains contributions by Egyptologists; C. Crawford, *Recasting Ancient Egypt in the African Context* (Trenton, 1996). There was an art exhibit on "Egypt in Africa" in Indianapolis in 1996. On the Hausa, see D. Lange, *Saeculum* 46 (1995): 161–203, and on the Yoruba, idem, *Zeitschrift der Deutschen Morgenländischen Gesellschaft* 147 (1997): 77–136.

As examples of speculations regarding ancient cultural contacts with America, we cite only I. van Sertima, *They Came before Columbus: The African Presence in Ancient America* (New York, 1976) and C. Pellech, *Die ersten Entdecker Amerikas* (Frankfurt a.M., 1997); in the latter volume, there are examples of the application of pyramid mysticism to Mexican pyramids (p. 511), along with a bizarre tradition to the effect that the Templars discovered the Ark of the Covenant in the ruins of Jerusalem, and that it contained the age-old secret lore that had been transmitted to Moses; this information later made it possible for Columbus to discover America, and it is now evidently being stored in the archives of the Vatican.

19. Outlook: Egypt as Hope and Alternative

On Thomas Mann's text, see A. B. Wiese in A. Brodbeck (ed.), *Ein ägyptisches Glasperlenspiel* (Berlin, 1998): 254–256. For Evliya Celebi, see U. Haarmann, "Evliya Celebis Bericht über die Altertümer von Gize," *Turcica* 8 (1976): 157–230.

For a treatment of Rilke and Egypt, see A. Hermann, "Rilkes ägyptische Gesichte," *Symposion* 4 (1955): 367–461 (separately reprinted Darmstadt, 1966); E. Hornung, *Eranos Jahrbuch* 53 (1984): 371–373; and A. Grimm, *Rilke und Ägypten* (Munich, 1997).

On Thomas Mann, see A. Grimm, *Joseph und Echnaton: Thomas Mann und Ägypten* (Mainz, 1992), along with various contributions in *Thomas Mann Jahrbuch* 6 (1993). Mann also expressed himself regarding Egypt in a poetry reading in Vienna on November 5, 1928 (GW XI 626–629) and in a lecture entitled "Joseph und seine Brüder" given in Washington, D.C., on November 17, 1942 (GW XI 654–669).

INDEX

Numbers in italics refer to illustrations.